WITHDRAWN FROM
KENT STATE UNIVERSITY LIBRARIES

HANDBOOK OF LIBRARY COOPERATION

Handbook of Library Cooperation

Edited by
Alan F. MacDougall
and
Ray Prytherch

Gower

© Alan F. MacDougall, Ray Prytherch 1991

All rights reserved. No part of this publication may be reproduced, stored in a retrieval system, or transmitted in any form or by any means, electronic, mechanical, photocopying, recording, or otherwise without the prior permission of Gower Publishing Company Limited.

Published by
Gower Publishing Company Limited
Gower House
Croft Road
Aldershot
Hants GU11 3HR
England

Gower Publishing Company
Old Post Road
Brookfield
Vermont 05036
USA

Typeset by P Stubley, Sheffield

British Library Cataloguing in Publication Data

Handbook of library cooperation.
   1. Great Britain. Libraries. Cooperation
I. MacDougall, Alan II. Prytherch, Ray
021.640941

ISBN 0-566-03627-4

Printed in Great Britain by
Billing & Sons Ltd, Worcester

Contents

List of contributors		vii
Preface		viii
Introduction: an examination of cooperative initiatives and developments		1
ROYSTON BROWN		
1	Cooperation : a conceptual framework for librarians	9
	ALAN MACDOUGALL	
2	International cooperation – pain or gain?	15
	STELLA KEENAN	
3	The European Communities as a focus for library cooperation	42
	MICHAEL HOPKINS	
4	The Government role in cooperation	67
	PETER BEAUCHAMP	
5	The role of the British Library in cooperation	98
	ANDY STEPHENS AND STUART EDE	
6	The role of professional associations in cooperation	118
	JACK MEADOWS	
7	Public library cooperation	131
	STUART BREWER	
8	Academic library cooperation	158
	JOHN FLETCHER	
9	Subject cooperation	174
	Law	175
	BARBARA TEARLE	
	Medicine & health-care	186
	SHANE GODBOLT	

		Audiovisual materials HELEN P HARRISON	197
		Sport and recreation CAROLYNN RANKIN	206
10		Functional cooperation: an exercise in bridge building DIANA EDMONDS	214
11		Bibliographic cooperation: an overview PETER STUBLEY	225
12		Regional library cooperation:	245
		LASER JEAN PLAISTER	245
		Regional roller coaster: the accelerating progress of the Regional Library Systems DIANA EDMONDS	251
13		Who wins? Some issues concerning 'compound' library cooperatives at the local level PETER STUBLEY	264
14		Conclusion NORMAN HIGHAM	282

Appendix A: Select list of organisations — 297

Index — 303

List of contributors

Peter Beauchamp is Library Adviser, Office of Arts and Libraries
Stuart Brewer is City Librarian and Arts Officer, City of Newcastle upon Tyne
Royston Brown is Chairman, Library and Information Services Council (England) (LISC)
Stuart Ede is Director, National Bibliographic Service, British Library
Diana Edmonds is a Library and Information Consultant and Director of Instant Library
John Fletcher is Polytechnic Librarian, Coventry Polytechnic
Shane Godbolt is Librarian, Charing Cross and Westminster Medical School
Helen Harrison is Media Librarian, Open University
Norman Higham is Chairman, Library and Information Cooperation Council (LINC)
Michael Hopkins is Deputy Librarian, Pilkington Library, Loughborough University
Stella Keenan is a Library and Information Consultant (*formerly* Secretary-General, International Federation for Documentation (FID))
Alan MacDougall is Director, Library and Information Statistics Unit, (LISU), Loughborough University
Jack Meadows is Professor, Department of Library and Information Studies, Loughborough University
Jean Plaister is Director, London and South Eastern Library Region (LASER)
Ray Prytherch is an Information Consultant
Carolynn Rankin is Information Officer, National Coaching Foundation and Chair of the Sport and Recreation Information Group (SPRIG)
Andy Stephens is Personal Assistant to the Chief Executive, British Library

Handbook of Library Cooperation

Peter Stubley is Sub-Librarian (Engineering), University of Sheffield
Barbara Tearle is Librarian, Bodleian Law Library, University of Oxford

Preface

A new volume on Library Cooperation is long overdue; there has been an enormous growth in interest in cooperation in recent years, and the Library and Information Plans initiative supported by Government bodies in the UK has put the spotlight onto the opportunities that may be possible. Cooperation may comprise activity between libraries, or between libraries and other organisations, public or private, or may occur outside any institutional framework. There has been no full-scale treatment of the topic as it now stands, and earlier attempts do not in any way reflect the scale and complexity of current provision and ideas.

In compiling this overview of the major components of cooperation in the UK, we have based our work on a combination of personal and professional knowledge, supported by an examination of recent literature, and we have invited contributors whom we were confident could provide a sound summary of activity based on their status within the profession or key organisations, their personal experience of cooperation, and their publication record in this field. Our only intentional omission is that we have not sought to explore communications technology; we have concentrated on policy behind cooperation, types of cooperation, and trends in progress, but although networking and other technological features are part and parcel of cooperation, they are dealt with here only as relevant and necessary. Fuller treatments are available elsewhere, and we would recommend for example *Mechanics of Library Cooperation: Getting our Act Together* (Proceedings of the 13th Annual Seminar of the MARC Users' Group) edited by Verina Horsnell (Gower Publishing Group, 1989) as a good summary of recent activity and further reference.

We have drawn together the common threads that appear in these chapters; themes and areas to be covered were discussed with contributors, who have obviously based their papers on their personal experience and expertise within the overall guidelines.

Handbook of Library Cooperation

We should like to thank all contributors for the work that they have put into this volume, and to acknowledge the support of many organisations who have offered advice, allowed the reproduction of documents, and enabled the contributors and ourselves to present the most complete picture that we can assemble. Our particular thanks are due to Peter Stubley for his expertise in desktop publishing, his invaluable advice throughout, and production of camera-ready copy from original texts and discs.

ALAN MACDOUGALL
RAY PRYTHERCH
January 1991

Introduction

An examination of cooperative initiatives and developments

ROYSTON BROWN

'No more complicated field of study in librarianship exists than that of library cooperation. By its nature it implies an appreciation of the purposes and functions of libraries of all kinds, and of the needs of the readers who make use or are encouraged to make use of their services. The permutations possible between 'library' and 'reader' give many opportunities for cooperative activity. At the same time, the historical condition of libraries governs both the type of cooperation that is being practised and the basis from which future cooperation must develop.' (Jefferson, 1977)

It is with this statement that Dr. George Jefferson begins the final Chapter, headed 'The future', of his history of library cooperation during this century. He saw the year 1972 as a turning point as it was the year that marked the arrival of the local Government Act and the British Library Act. The former completely re-structured the public library systems in England and Wales and the latter established the newly created British Library as the apex of the nation's library services. In view of these and other developments, Jefferson saw the decade of the 1980s as having a unique opportunity to re-assess the old and to capitalise on innovations in library techniques and on communications technology in looking to the future.

This book will explore the extent to which that has happened, examining the current state of the art of library cooperation and potential future developments. There is no doubt that since Jefferson's account of the scene in the 1970s significant changes have occurred in the perception of the role of cooperation; the methods by which it is practised; the scale and complexity of its operation; and its future potential. Looking back on its history this century Jefferson commented that 'cooperation, like Topsy, 'just growed', partly to remedy deficiencies inherent in the national library structure and partly to meet the special needs of different types of library as they arose. As a consequence the pattern of cooperation was distinguished by its uncoordinated nature and by duplication at national and local levels'. Writing in 1981, Philip Sewell (1981), in his book *Resource sharing* which he sub-titled *cooperation and coordination in library and information services* said:

> 'Resource sharing may appear to be nothing more than a new term for the familiar concept of library cooperation. True, many of the same activities are included, but there is a significant difference in the approach. The earlier term takes the existence of libraries for granted and describes how they can achieve their objectives better by working together. The new term appears rather to assume a range of physical, intellectual and conceptual resources on the one hand and a body of people with library and information needs on the other hand and covers the activities involved in organising the one into a set of optimum relationships to meet the needs of the other. Resource sharing may be seen as a term for working out inter-institutional relationships for the benefit of users in a profession which is frequently described as changing from a materials-orientation to a client orientation.'

This change of approach to cooperation is also evident in the reports on the future development of libraries and information services. *Working together within a national framework* (Future development..., 1982) sets out the underlying philosophy of the Library and Information Services Council as 'the achievement of cooperation and coordination through an evolutionary approach'. Informal cooperation should be replaced by more deliberately planned relationships and services should move from a 'holdings' strategy to an 'access' strategy. This could only be achieved if more effective techniques of cooperation were developed and something closer to planned interdependence was introduced.

In other words, library cooperation should move from an informal supporting role for individual library services to that of a major strategic instrument in the organisation of the available national resources to

Introduction

meet clients needs. Why was this fundamental change seen as necessary, and what is the current and potential significance of library cooperation? In the 2nd CLSI annual lecture on library automation (Brown, 1986) I summarised the case for more effective forms of library cooperation:

> 'First, there is no shortage of materials – last year's published output in the United Kingdom reached another all time high, and shows no signs of declining. The growing sophistication of other forms of media and their proliferation means that we are all suffering from information overload through a bewildering multiplicity of media.
> Secondly, there is no shortage of demand. Supply seems to generate more demand and there is a rising generation emerging from our schools and colleges to whom the computer will be as familiar as the telephone is to us, and who will increasingly expect information to be packaged and presented to meet their needs.
> Thirdly, there is no shortage of technology which is growing ever more sophisticated and which offers exciting possibilities for identifying and locating required material, for its transfer over long distances and for local storage and manipulation.
> Fourthly, there is continuing pressure on existing financial resources and a growing requirement to ensure the best use of current funding arrangements, the generation of new forms of income and the creation of new markets both at home and abroad to sustain the level of investment and the supply of goods and services that the economy needs. Our problems are therefore organisational. The key question is how can we organise and mobilise the total national resources in the best interest of our present and future clients?'

The positive adoption of library cooperation as a major strategic instrument is also reflected in the British Library's strategic plan for 1989–1994, *Gateway to knowledge*. In a section which sets out some aspirations for the British Library in the year 2000 the plan states:

> 'We foresee that from its two principal sites at St. Pancras and Boston Spa, the Library will offer an integrated pattern of services, based upon a single British Library collection, and a range of cooperative relationships with other libraries in the UK, Europe and abroad.

'The strategy of the 1990s will be to achieve comprehensive access to recorded knowledge, rather than comprehensiveness of collection; our goal will be to guide users swiftly and accurately to the information they need.' (British Library, 1989)

Dr. Brian Enright's report for the British Library *Selection for survival: a review of acquisition and retention policies*, also contains a specific recommendation that 'the Library should promote contacts with other libraries with national responsibilities, both in the UK and abroad, and with academic and professional bodies with subject expertise, in order to develop national strategies for acquisition, retention and disposal' (Enright, 1989).

The scope for cooperative arrangements of this kind is considerable, and the next decade will see substantial developments as the impetus gathers strength. This recognition of the importance of library cooperation as a major strategic instrument is by no means confined to the United Kingdom. In 1979 the White House Conference on Library and Information Services produced a resolution on networking which put the case for resource sharing concisely: 'resource sharing is now mandated by the information explosion, the advance of modern technology, the rapidly escalating costs of needed resources, and the wide disparity between resources available to individuals by reason of geographic location or socio-economic position' (White House, 1979).

The European Commission's *Plan of Action for Libraries in the EC* is another example of a conscious attempt to promote international cooperation between the member states in the provision of library and information services, and to improve networking and resource sharing both within and between the European nations. In addition to the change in attitude towards the strategic role of library cooperation there are significant forces at work in the Community which are increasingly influencing its nature and scope. Principal amongst these are the actions of both central and local government. Major features of government policy, such as privatisation, contracting out, sponsorship, and income generation, are contributing to the redefining of the traditional roles and relationships of the public and private sectors. The joint Libraries and Information Services Council/British Library Research and Development Department report *Joint enterprise* (1987) examined the changing nature of this relationship in the provision of library and information services. The report noted that the public and private sectors, 'far from being

Introduction

separate and independent, are in reality inter-dependent. Their traditional relationships have developed in recent years into genuine interactive cooperation in many areas of activity, and could develop further, given favourable conditions and the right climate of opinion' (Joint enterprise..., 1987).

The report went on to illustrate a range of joint ventures through case studies and submissions, and explored issues of policy and practice, providing guidelines and encouraging further developments in public/private sector cooperation. The Minister for the Arts is currently using his Public Library Development Incentive Scheme to stimulate experimentation and innovation in this field of cooperative partnership.

Largely as a response to central government policies, there has been a significant change in the role and functioning of local government over the last decade which will continue to influence its behaviour in the future. The local authority associations in England commissioned a review by the Institute of Local Government Studies at Birmingham University which identified an important future role for local authorities. Whereas local government had always combined the roles of provider and facilitator the report identified a major shift in the balance between these roles. This move from direct provision of services to facilitating service provision through a variety of arrangements with other agencies has become known as 'the enabling council'. It is a role which involves harnessing and integrating current or potential resources outside the direct control of local authorities. A catalytic style drawing together, aiding and stimulating the efforts of different public agencies, voluntary organisations, private enterprise and communal care is required. This climate within a local authority also affects the public library services for which it is responsible and is another strong influence in favour of cooperation with outside agencies. All of these initiatives and influences are helping to move cooperation away from library to library links into a new area of cross sectional cooperation with public, private and voluntary agencies.

One of the most significant recent influences on library cooperation was the publication of the LISC report on the future development of libraries and information services: *Progress through planning and partnership* (Future development..., 1986).

This report proposed a new planning process which would bring together all the agencies involved in library and information services within a geographical area and suggested the production of Library and

Information Plans (LIPs) which would enable planned cooperation to take place within a recognised framework. The advent of this new initiative was timely and appropriate, given the environmental factors outlined earlier in this introduction, and the concept has been taken up and applied in a number of different areas and is being developed by experimentation, and experience. At the present time over 20% of England is covered by authorities producing LIPs. Plans have also been produced for the whole of Northern Ireland and are underway in some Scottish regions and for the whole of Wales. Within the planning framework of the LIP initiative a whole new field of cooperative activity is developing. This includes local, regional and national cooperation, and represents quite remarkable progress in only four years. The LISC initiative is backed by the Minister for the Arts through his Public Library Development Incentive Scheme, and will be overseen by the Library and Information Cooperation Council (LINC) a newly formed body created from the previous National Committee on Regional Library Cooperation at the suggestion of LISC. LINC has the potential for developing and supporting this new range of cooperative activity in addition to maintaining the best traditions of current practice; the current Chair of LINC contributes the final Chapter of this volume.

Any introduction to a study of library cooperation in the final decades of this century would have to register the significance of the impact of new technology. There has been a revolution in the ways in which information is produced, transmitted, stored and used due to the remarkable advances in electronics and telecommunications. Individual library and information systems have adopted new technology developments at different speeds and in different ways, but in doing so have transformed internal housekeeping routines and services to their clients . These technological developments have frequently been market-led and have sometimes resulted in the installation of systems which are piecemeal and incompatible with other systems within the same organisation and more frequently beyond it.

In the next decade, concentration will be focused on the convergence of elements of communication systems which are currently disparate, and on compatibility. Open Systems Interconnection (OSI) as it develops will enable different computer systems to communicate with each other, and will open up the potential for local, regional, national, and international cooperation on a scale not envisaged hitherto. Work currently in hand to establish technological standards and protocols is

Introduction

essential to these developments. Professional and managerial thinking and planning should be anticipating this future potential, and devising cooperative strategies to take advantage of the technological capability as it becomes available.

The tone of this introduction to the subject of library cooperation has thus far been positive in pointing to the environment in which it is taking place and the continuing developments in policy and practice. It is also fair to note, however, that there are pressures working against cooperation which present challenges to its adoption and development. Many libraries are under severe financial pressure through a combination of central and local government policy decisions and rising operational costs. In these circumstances it is all too easy for cooperative activity to be relegated to a lower position in the list of priorities when survival appears to be of paramount importance. Library cooperation, rather than being seen as an instrument for management to use in producing strategies for service maintenance and development, can be seen as a threat to the prime responsibility of a service to its clientele. A further conflict is seen between the political drive for competition, value added services, and income generation, on the one hand and the spirit of partnership and cooperation on the other. Are these two mutually exclusive? The best cooperative schemes, such as the LIPs, provide a framework within which such pressures and conflicts can be reconciled, and satisfactory solutions negotiated between the partners. It is a sign of the growing strengths of such cooperative agreements that they are able to cope with the painful realities of life.

The message of this introduction is that library cooperation has been assuming a new significance, a new direction, and a new impetus during the last decade. All the signs are that this process will continue during the next decade. The following Chapters explore the current state of the art in more detail at international, European, and UK levels, and point the way ahead.

REFERENCES

British Library (1989), *Gateway to knowledge; the British Library strategic plan 1989–1994*. British Library.

Brown, R. (1986), Library cooperation at a local level. *CLSI annual lectures on library automation, no. 2*. CLSI.

Enright, B. J. (1989), *Selection for survival: a review of acquisition and retention policies.* British Library.

The future development of libraries and information services: 1 the organisational and policy framework; 2 working together within a national framework. (1982). (Office of Arts and Libraries, Library and Information Series No. 12). HMSO.

The future development of libraries and information services: progress through planning and partnership. Report by the Library and Information Services Council. (1986). (Office of Arts and Libraries, Library and Information Series No. 14). HMSO.

Jefferson, G. (1977), *Library cooperation, 2nd rev. ed.* Deutsch.

Joint enterprise: roles and relationships of the public and private sectors in the provision of library and information services. Report by the Library and Information Services Council and British Library Research and Development Department Working Party (1987). (Office of Arts and Libraries, Library and Information Series No. 16). HMSO.

Sewell, P. H. (1981), *Resource sharing: cooperation and coordination in library and information services.* Deutsch.

White House (1979), *Conference on library and information services, 1979. The final report; summary.* Washington D.C. National Commission on Libraries and Information Science.

1

Cooperation : a conceptual framework for librarians

ALAN MACDOUGALL

Cooperation for some participants has been elevated to the status of a deity; its power for good remains unquestioned. The disciples may preach about it from their different denominational viewpoints (for example, resource sharing, partnership, joint venture, collaboration, networking and coordination) but essentially the activity of cooperation can be defined as 'the reciprocally beneficial sharing of resources, developed or pre-existing, by two or more bodies' (Edmonds, 1986). As Brewer later states in the Chapter on public libraries 'library cooperation is an umbrella term for a wide spectrum of cooperative processes and mechanisms'. The primary mechanism for the transmission of the gospel is by means of the good books (for example, The future development of libraries..., 1982, The future development of libraries..., 1986, Joint Enterprise..., 1987). The word is then received and more librarians are encouraged by good practice or through financial support. One of the fundamental tenets of cooperation 'maximising the resource base' is not only believed to be advantageous but positively attainable. Concepts of brotherly and sisterly love, or at least partnership abound. Cooperation then, in the library and information world is seen as an obvious and guaranteed path to an excellent library service. Or is it? At the other end of the spectrum the unconverted or unbeliever claim to see the false god who deceives. The supposed gift bestowed by cooperation can only be seen, at best, as illusory, or at worst, a counter-productive sham.

Both perceptions may be regarded as exaggerations. There are no absolute truths, common to all, to be derived from a study of cooperation, although there will be some indications which can be interpreted within the context of individual circumstances. Careful assessment of the advantages and possibilities compared with the disadvantages and drawbacks requires assessment within a framework of cooperation. Recent research (Edmonds, 1986) suggests that although the definition of cooperation given above is readily understood, the term 'cooperation' within the context of library and information services 'varied enormously from librarian to librarian and from authority to authority'. Indeed Edmonds in Chapter 12 on Regional Library Systems, comments further that 'for many librarians, the practical face of interlibrary cooperation in this country is the Regional Library System'.

This Chapter therefore provides a conceptual framework within which to study the multi-faceted approaches to the study of the subject of cooperation, and thereby, the opportunity to assess both its potential and its viability.

CATEGORIES

The categorisation outlined below was used by Wilson and Marsterson (1974) and subsequently utilised by Edmonds (1986). This approach offers the opportunity for cooperation to be viewed through three major forms of activity: firstly in terms of 'exchange'; secondly by 'coalition' (working together); and thirdly 'entrepreneurial and one-way marketing'. The last category has been disputed by those who claim it is not a true cooperative activity, but in recent times it has begun to gain more credibility as a concept. Traditionally these three major forms have been discussed in the context of interlibrary cooperation, but now emphasis is being placed on cooperation with other information providers in the business, commercial and voluntary sectors. Furthermore, these boundaries are no longer parochial in character and have been expanded to embrace cooperation at various levels, including local and regional, national, European and international dimensions through informal as well as formal mechanisms.

Since each individual Chapter considers various instances of, approaches to and strategies for cooperation, specific library based examples are avoided here – the following framework is proposed as a basis for a more systematic analysis from which the reader can extrapolate as necessary.

Exchange

Cooperation can be viewed first as a form of exchange. This can be subdivided and may be considered under such headings as:

- exchange of materials of all kinds
- information (for staff)
- information (for reader enquiries)
- users
- bibliographical
- staff

These headings cover a multitude of activities: some are initiated for reasons of altruism; at the other end of the spectrum the motivation is pure self interest. Some examples includes exchange of catalogues, catalogue information, serial title holdings lists, accessions lists, development of access policies, exchange of minutes of staff meetings and working parties. In the last example, this can be effected with the minimum of effort and expense but perhaps produce valuable cross fertilisation of ideas to assist in the process of decision making.

Coalition

The second form of cooperation may be termed coalition. This can be defined as 'working together' in the broadest sense although Brewer, in his Chapter in this book, alludes to the campaigning nature of the activity. The concept of coalition has been gaining ground over recent years, encouraged and promoted partly by government initiatives, and characterised by the phrases 'partnership' and 'joint venture'. Beauchamp makes this clear in his Chapter later in this book.

There are many ways of working together, both within the library sector and with other information agencies. Some of the main sub-headings within the broad heading of coalition would include:

- development of service tools
- development of resources
- research
- training
- publishing

Under the heading of development resources one could consider software developments, networking or general development and understanding of IT, organisation of events, acquisition (and/or disposal) of material. This might include Conspectus (discussed in this book), joint appointment of staff, and allocation of financial matters, building or use of shared accommodation, or dual use of transport and equipment. Under the heading of research, organisations might consider cooperative research for their common good, or to take it one step further, it could even be extended to the level of cooperative research about cooperation (MacDougall, 1988), and sponsorship of research.

The heading of training includes the various ways of providing an effective, viable and systematic range of training organised from a cooperative view point. The cooperative publishing heading offers the opportunity of information providers to consider the production of catalogues of library holdings and joint publication of books and journals.

Entrepreneurial and one-way marketing

Although cooperation is normally perceived as exchange and coalition, it has recently been extended to include entrepreneurial and one-way marketing in its own right. The activity under this heading could however also be included under coalition. A service undertaken by one party for another and for payment includes services such as British Library Document Supply Centre and Regional Library Systems, where it might be argued that unless there is close cooperation between parties, both are liable to lose. Equally, entrepreneurial and one-way marketing can be applied to those information organisations offering services for direct monetary gain.

The categorisation above is somewhat arbitrary and it recognised that the headings are not mutually exclusive – for example BLCMP could be considered under all three headings. Nonetheless, a brief outline of types of activities is described which to some organisations will be self evident, yet to others will seem beyond any consideration of intended cooperative activity. The categories have only been described, and deliberately not illustrated, since the text of this book concentrates on activities of particular importance.

ENVIRONMENT

It is appropriate at the same time to draw attention to the environment in which cooperation is likely to function. The first, and probably the most important, is the organisational climate and those responsible for policy innovation. This is not to say that individuals have to be totally convinced of the value of cooperation but rather that there should be an open mind in assessing the viability of any intended cooperation within the objectives of the particular organisation. These objectives might have a bias towards economic or political considerations which might colour the final outcome of the cooperative activity. This underlines the statement made earlier that there is no absolute truth about the degree to which cooperation should be undertaken. Local circumstances will play an important role in the eventual outcome, as will perceived and actual benefits to be derived, and their cost.

The second context in which cooperation functions is that of apparent contradiction. At present there is a philosophy of competitiveness in our society which is deemed necessary for survival. Yet paradoxically the government is encouraging library and information services to cooperate. At what point does a successful institution, marketing excellent resources such as library and information services, allow a competitor of inferior sources to make use of these facilities? This, to some, is the real nub of cooperation: why should we cooperate when we appear to be giving more than we receive in return? In such circumstances, unless there is an overriding political dimension, continued cooperation can only be viewed in altruistic terms because it will involve additional expenditure of resources without appropriate benefits in return. In these competitive times organisations may think such altruistic treatment has ceased to exist and that enlightened self-interest governs such decision making.

The evidence, on occasions, suggests otherwise. The lending of books to other requesting libraries (with or without the payment of a British Library Document Supply Centre (BLDSC) form) when it is available at BLDSC, can mean that the supplier is subsidising the receiver – few libraries have costed this operation.

This brings us to the third context: cost effectiveness, cost efficiency and cost benefit. The amount of literature about cooperation, and especially its implicit value, is large. Most of it suggests that cooperation is 'a good thing' yet the literature on the economics is extremely scant. In the past the case for cooperation has been mainly an act of faith which has not always been backed up by hard fact; it is hard to believe that unsubstantiated statements will continue to go unchallenged in the present climate.

Thus the library and information community is now coming to the crossroads – it remains to be seen whether the long overdue evaluation process will explode the myth of cooperation or vindicate it. Time will tell, one suspects sooner rather than later.

REFERENCES

Edmonds, D. J. (1986), *Current library cooperation and coordination: an investigation*. (Office of Arts and Libraries, Library and Information Series No. 15). HMSO.

The Future development of libraries and information services: 1. the organisational and policy framework 2. working together within a national framework (1982). (Office of Arts and Libraries, Library and Information Series No. 12). HMSO.

The future development of libraries and information services: progress through planning and partnership. Report by the Library and Information Service Council (1986). (Office of Arts and Libraries, Library and Information Series No. 14). HMSO.

Joint enterprise : roles and relationship of the public and private sectors in the provision of library and information services. Report by the Library and Information Services Council and British Library Research and Development Department Working Party (1987). (Office and Arts and Libraries, Library and Information Series No. 16). HMSO.

MacDougall, A. F., Wheelhouse, H. and Wilson, J. M. (1988), *A study of various aspects of cooperation between the East Midlands University and Polytechnic Libraries*. British Library Research and Development Department Report No. 5989.

Wilson, T. D. and Marsterson, W. A. J. (1974), *Local library cooperation : final report on a project funded by the Department of Education and Science*. (Occasional Publication Series No. 4). University of Sheffield School of Librarianship and Information Science.

2

International cooperation – pain or gain?

STELLA KEENAN

International cooperation should be based on need – the need to improve services, share resources, and ultimately the need to serve the user. This obvious statement has to be balanced in practical terms against cost. International cooperation is expensive, both in real money terms and in terms of human time and effort. In order to justify the outlay of large sums of money, there has to be apparent benefit to the cooperating parties.

As international cooperation is almost always based on institutions rather than individuals there has to be some discussion of organisations that are involved in cooperative activities. These include the governmental organisations such as Unesco and the professional non-governmental ones – the International Federation of Library Associations and Institutions (IFLA) and the Fédération Internationale d'Information et de Documentation (FID). Often these organisations provide the programme framework and only occasionally some support funding to enable their constituent members – the British Library, Library of Congress and similar institutions to work together to achieve a perceived goal.

Organisations cooperate in order to do something that has a positive value in fostering cooperation at the international level. Activities selected for inclusion in this contribution are the development of international bibliographic networks and the models that have evolved within the international programmes and the document delivery scheme known as ADONIS. These are seen as complementary activities as the one provides information on item location and the other transmits the item to the user. While resource sharing is at the heart of most cooperative programmes, two particular aspects are included. These are the system set up for the 'grey literature' and the international centre that deals with translations. This concentration on activities means that only minimal details of some of the major institutions have been included to bring a sense of historical perspective to the subject under discussion.

Concentration is placed on programmes and current developments that deal with procedures and resources. The aspects selected for inclusion are bibliographic networks – which identify and locate material, and the provision and availability of material that is in high demand or difficult to obtain. This selection brings together various groupings of cooperating institutions as consideration of bibliographic networks is based on IFLA programmes that have been developed with Unesco support. Document delivery systems such as ADONIS are based on cooperation between national services and commercial publishers, while the provision of translations and grey literature have cooperative agreements at their heart.

In spite of the concentration on activities rather than institutions, a section has been included on regional associations as these could be significant in making cooperative progress in the future and they are less well known within the profession.

INFRASTRUCTURE FOR COOPERATION

S. R. Ranganathan (1951) said that 'library service, bibliographic organisation and library classification recognise no national or political boundaries. They are international. The library profession is international. Bibliographers and documentalists are international'. This means that international cooperation could be seen as the ultimate objective of professional activity and development. H. Coblans (1974) wrote a seminal work on library cooperation where he developed an international perspective for library and documentation work. He takes a well informed and farsighted view and discusses the concept of international librarianship and identifies 'methods of cataloguing ..., classification and indexing and bibliographic presentation' as important factors in developing cooperative activities. The requirements that he highlighted for cooperation are 'standardisation, an attitude of positive neutrality as between national systems, a search for a common denominator, especially in all communication and exchange'.

In the same year, in his M.L.S. thesis, Russell Bowden (1974) examined international cooperation from the regional point of view. Like Coblans, he stressed the fact that cooperation is closely tied to the level of infrastructure development. He comments that the library services of individual countries have to reach 'minimal infrastructure' levels before they are in a position to participate successfully in larger cooperative programmes.

Infrastructure development starts with the formation of social groups, the development of legislation, education and resulting literacy levels, and other stages in national development. While the national infrastructure is founded on these basic ideas, the building blocks of the library infrastructure are the publishing and legal deposit procedures, bibliographic services, union lists, standardisation, arrangements for interlibrary loan, and other resource sharing services.

Coming to the infrastructure of the 1990s, other factors come into play. The recent convergence of the computer, databases and databanks in machine-readable format, and communication links available today and being planned for tomorrow mean that any discussion of cooperation and the infrastructure background must take these into account.

PURPOSES OF INTERNATIONAL COOPERATION

Bowden (1974) said that formalised cooperative schemes need five elements to be successful:

i) an appreciation of the necessity to cooperate
ii) an acceptance of the responsibilities involved in cooperation
iii) the tools with which to cooperate
iv) the formal organisation within which to cooperate
v) the basis or national structure or infrastructure – depending on the level of library development achieved – on which to cooperate

In 1990, in a paper given at a seminar on information services and regional cooperation, Bowden gives a clear answer to the question 'what are the objectives of planning, cooperation and coordination?' His 'plain man's guide' states that the objectives are:

- to improve services to the user
- to maximise resources
- to overcome the isolation of libraries

These are all highsounding and altruistic reasons for cooperation – but in reality a realistic and hardheaded approach to the topic may be more appropriate. Commercial multinational information activities are not covered in this contribution but they should not be forgotten in reviewing the range of international cooperative systems ... and they exist to generate income for the parent companies. The leading online service vendors such as DIALOG and the European Space Agency grew out of government information programmes set up initially to support space research programmes and are today expected to be commercially viable.

There is a somewhat cynical definition of cooperation as a situation where one party is doing the cooing while the other party is doing the operating. Cynical though this may be, it does point out one truth about cooperative activities, and that is the need for at least one party to benefit. Without gain, usually economic, to some partners in the cooperative process cooperation will not take place – or, if it does, it will fail or prove ineffective.

This view is echoed in the introduction to the 10th Anniversary Essen Symposium when international cooperation was selected as the theme. Editors A. H. Helal and J. W. Weiss (1987) comment that:

> 'the complexities and rapid development will encourage librarians to cope with [the] high-tech situation. The driving force in technological change is the real market which we have to follow and observe to keep the standard of our service. Policies and standardisation in the field of telecommunication is progressing and continuous rethinking is still needed.
>
> In addition, the severe international cooperation in hardware, software, and telecommunication developments forces firms to come up with cheaper and much (more) powerful equipment and services in a very rapid time and (at) cheaper prices.'

International cooperative programmes that work should benefit both the participants and the users, with the latter often being the second group to be considered. Falling library budgets, increased publication and the shrinking world to the level of the global village have caused significant developments in the handling of resource material.

In today's infrastructure, technological developments have an important role to play. The impact of online information services caused by the linking of the computer, the telephone, and the database was a significant step in breaking the barriers of information access; probably no single development has pushed the wall of the individual library down quite so sharply. However, the online services were possible because of the existence of large files of bibliographic and factual material available in machine-readable form as databases and databanks. These were built up by cooperative agreements between the major producers of abstracting and indexing services to prepare input into the databases. Chemical Abstracts Service – now issuing over 500,000 abstracts per year – made bi-lateral arrangements starting back in the 1960s with countries in Europe. These agreements set up sharing arrangements for the input and dissemination processes tied into producing this major scientific quasi-international information service. In the field of nuclear information, the English language service *Nuclear Science Abstracts* has disappeared and merged in the International Nuclear Information Service (INIS). These are just two examples of a pattern which has emerged in some form or other for most of the major abstracting and indexing services (Keenan, 1978). The reasons for these developments can be directly linked to benefits that accrued both to the service producer and to the user.

Moving back in time from Bowden's 'plain man's guide' (1990), Coblans presented a 'moral for documentation' (Coblans, 1964) when he proposed that a criteria for any system should be:

- is it bibliographically desirable?
- is it technically possible?
- is it economically feasible?

and a final question was added by Keenan (1978)

- is it satisfactory to the user?

THE INTERNATIONAL ORGANISATIONS

Fédération Internationale d'Information et de Documentation (FID)

In 1895 two Belgians (Paul Otlet and Henri LaFontaine), both trained in law and sociology, combined their talents to set up an Office International de Bibliographie with the purpose of establishing *Répertoire bibliographique universel* which would list all published material. In concept this was a forerunner of the programmes for Universal Bibliographic Control (UBC) which will be discussed later. A new concept called documentation entered the professional vocabulary at this time which was later described by F. Donker Duyvis (1940), the Secretary General of FID from 1938–1959:

> 'Documentation ... developed as a reaction against old fashioned concepts of librarianship and archivism, which held that practically the only task of librarians and archivists was to conserve and protect books, manuscripts and other documents.'

FID managed to retain its identity during the first world war and in 1924 it changed from an international organisation of individuals to become a federation of countries. After several name changes, FID became the Fédération Internationale d'Information et de Documentation in 1986. A new programme of professional activities based on five programme areas was adopted at this time which covered:

i) improvements in the availability and applicability of information
ii) developing the information marketplace
iii) development of tools for information work
iv) increasing the basic understanding of the properties of information
v) professional development – especially education and training of documentalists

The most recent thrust of FID's programme priorities is industrial information services.

International Federation of Library Associations and Institutions (IFLA)

The professional scene of the 1920s was described by Coblans (1974) as a 'disordered state of national bibliography, the near anarchy in cataloguing rules, the absence of standards on publication and library statistics, etc., there was clearly an urgent need for some form of international cooperation.' IFLA was formed as a result of an international meeting – the International Conference of Library and Booklovers held in Prague in 1926 when a proposal to set up an international committee representing national library associations was accepted. This was implemented at the fiftieth anniversary conference of the (British) Library Association in 1927 which created an International Library and Bibliographic Committee with representatives of library associations from 15 countries. The name was changed to International Federation of Library Associations at the Third Annual Conference held in Stockholm in 1930. IFLA's activities were initially confined to Europe and North America. Unesco provided financial support for IFLA to be able to establish a paid and permanent secretariat in 1963 and the membership expanded to include countries from Eastern Europe, South America, Asia and Africa.

IFLA's main programme thrust is through core programmes which are:

- Universal Bibliographic Control International MARC (UBCIM)
- Preservation and Conservation (PAC)
- Universal Dataflow and Telecommunications (UDT)
- Universal Availability of Publications (UAP)
- Advancement of Librarianship in the Third World (ALP)

Unesco

Unesco's current information activity is based on the General Information Programme (PGI) which was established in the 1970s. It absorbed two major programmes which had great significance for the information profession. UNISIST started in 1966 when the International Council of Scientific Unions (ICSU) and Unesco's Department of Natural Sciences began to develop proposals to study the feasibility of a world scientific information system which by 1971 had evolved into the concept of 'a flexible network based on voluntary cooperation of existing and future information services'. Another important study which contributed to today's PGI was the National Information System (NATIS) which concentrated more on the library aspects of information service development during the 1970s. PGI is currently working on its Medium Term Programme for 1990–1995 which has an emphasis on regional cooperation and stresses common standards, compatible equipment and uniform practices. These have already been identified as essential elements in developing cooperative information programmes.

International information systems – INIS and AGRIS

The International Nuclear Information Service (INIS) was based on the concept that was to become familiar in the Universal Bibliographic Control (UBC) programme. This is that countries should be responsible for recording the literature produced in their geographical boundaries and sending these records to a central processing facility. INIS is an international programme for nuclear information that gained its impetus from the US Atomic Energy Commission that had been responsible for the English language abstracting and indexing service *Nuclear Science Abstracts*. As the INIS system, based on the International Atomic Energy Agency (IAEA) in Vienna developed, it was necessary for participating countries to agree to common standards and formats in order to build the database which formed the basis of the information retrieval system. The printed *Atomindex* replaced the US abstracting and indexing service publication.

When the Food and Agriculture Organisation (FAO) decided to establish an international information system based on the same philosophy of country contributions, the INIS system was chosen as a model. While the Agricultural Information Services (AGRIS) headquarters is at FAO in Rome, the input centre is in Vienna in offices close to the IAEA operation, and the production of the database and the printed products are closely modelled on the INIS system. The same philosophy of decentralised input with countries being responsible for material published nationally was adopted by AGRIS. Again, standard input procedures have to be followed in order to maintain the system. Countries and regions are able to produce specialised subset publications covering their geographical area, or special publications dealing with particular subjects or crops. INIS and AGRIS have served as models for other international information services such as the International Food Information Service (IFIS), DEVSIS, etc. (Keenan, 1978).

BIBLIOGRAPHIC NETWORKS

In the 1970s Unesco provided initial financial support for an IFLA programme which was to have significant impact on the transfer of information. Universal Bibliographic Control (UBC) started with three propositions:

i) UBC is an integrated process starting with the printing of a book, its cataloguing and storage in libraries and ending with its dissemination and use by the relevant body of readers
ii) the bibliographic information about each book should be provided as completely as possible with a minimum of delay and also in machine-readable form
iii) it is the responsibility of national bibliography in the country of origin to do this quickly and accurately and this implies a compatible basis of bibliographic presentation

Coblans (1974) observed that although this plan was 'simple in formulation, the implications and the implementation, especially for developing countries, are complex and far-reaching in terms of organisation and operation'.

The basic aim of UBC is that national bibliographic agencies should improve their coverage of materials and the speed with which national bibliographic records are created and disseminated.

In 1974 the newly formed Conference of Directors of National Libraries agreed that their main focus should be on the provision of bibliographic data worldwide. An international network study was undertaken by A. J. Wells which recommended that an effective national system in cooperating countries using compatible bibliographic codes and practice should form the basis of a network. There should be communication facilities which would allow the interrogation of bibliographic databases internationally. Reviewing progress to date, Hope E. A. Clement (1989) describes the International MARC Network as a 'practical concept that covers the creation, dissemination and use of standard cataloguing records in machine-readable form'.

The spread of the MARC system can be seen from a directory published by IFLA in 1986 (Wolf and Conrad, 1986) which identified 62 national bibliographic agencies producing MARC records with 19 countries issuing magnetic tape services and 12 countries offering online services. An additional 30 countries were at that time planning new or additional services. A new edition of this directory should include files being issued in CD-ROM formats. In order to facilitate the exchange of records, it is necessary to have agreements on the international transfer of bibliographic records. The cost of maintaining the national bibliographic agency and the ease of copying together with the reduced cost of transmission of MARC records meant that agencies have to set terms and conditions for making records available internationally and guidelines were issued in 1987 (Conference of Directors..., 1987). The work of the International MARC Network Committee concentrates on the international distribution of MARC records, including exchange agreements, copyright, third party use, and new distribution methods such as CD-ROM.

The International Network Committee is also involved in the development, maintenance and promotion of the UNIMARC format. This format was developed by IFLA and is intended as the basis for any new national MARC systems and as an exchange format between existing national MARC formats. This part of the network has been slow to develop as the complex conversion programs take time to write. However, interest in the concept of UNIMARC remains high and it is hoped that more widespread availability of these conversion programs will make the international bibliographic network more of a reality (Clement, 1989).

Looking towards the future, the increasing distribution of bibliographic records on CD-ROM will need to be examined in terms of availability and methods of distribution. One concern is that detailed machine-readable MARC formats have led to the development of complex bibliographic standards. Hope E. A. Clement (chair – International Network Committee) is aware that some bibliographic agencies are beginning to ask if the cost of creating records according to these standards is not too high and if a reduction in level is possible. As the computer made Universal Bibliographic Control a possibility, is it 'now being overtaken by increasing volumes and rising costs. Does the solution lie in a whole new concept of bibliographic control, using information technology in a totally different way to take advantage of the power of computers or telecommunications?' (Clement, 1989).

International cooperation

Bibliographic networks identify and describe material and give its location. The next step in the chain is getting the identified material into the hands of the user.

UNIVERSAL AVAILABILITY OF PUBLICATIONS (UAP)

The end objective of UAP is to put the required publication into the hands of the user wherever and whenever it is needed (Wood, 1988). The principal objectives of the UAP programme are therefore to ensure access and availability of documents to users by:

- stimulating improvements in publishing and bookselling practices
- improving acquisition policies and practices at the local and national level
- improving repository policies and practices
- improving national and international lending policies and practices

As an international programme it depends on national systems which form the essential building blocks. UAP is built on the premise that each country adequately records and has available the publications produced nationally so that each country is self-sufficient. In addition, the national system is expected to meet between 70–80% of total needs with only approximately 30% being provided by international interlibrary loan. Repository planning becomes important and is linked to national repository planning and, in considering the international scene, the UAP programme has developed a number of different schemes for national plans that could link effectively into an international system.

David Wood (1988) at the British Library Document Supply Centre has developed several diagrammatic models which demonstrate the various cooperative situations.

Model 1 shows a very simple cooperative arrangement which is costly but can provide an effective international link as it provides only one main node per country. In this model each individual library (L) uses a national central library facility.

Model 2 is similar to the first, with the central library also fulfilling a national service that is available to individual users as well as the libraries

Handbook of Library Cooperation

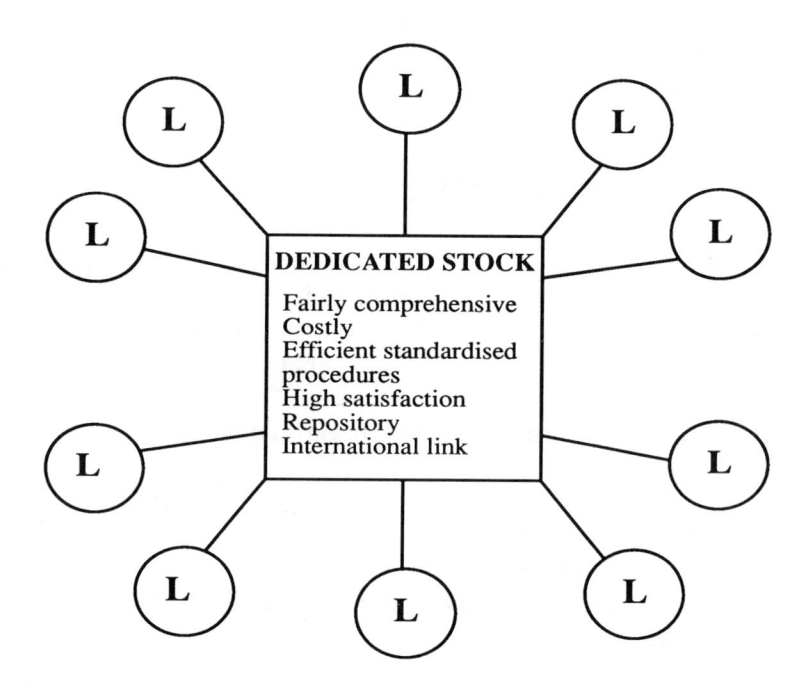

DEDICATED STOCK

Fairly comprehensive
Costly
Efficient standardised procedures
High satisfaction
Repository
International link

Model 1

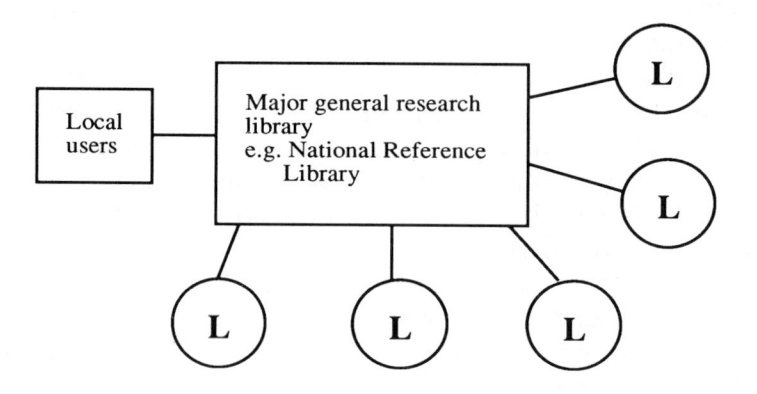

Local users — Major general research library e.g. National Reference Library

Model 2

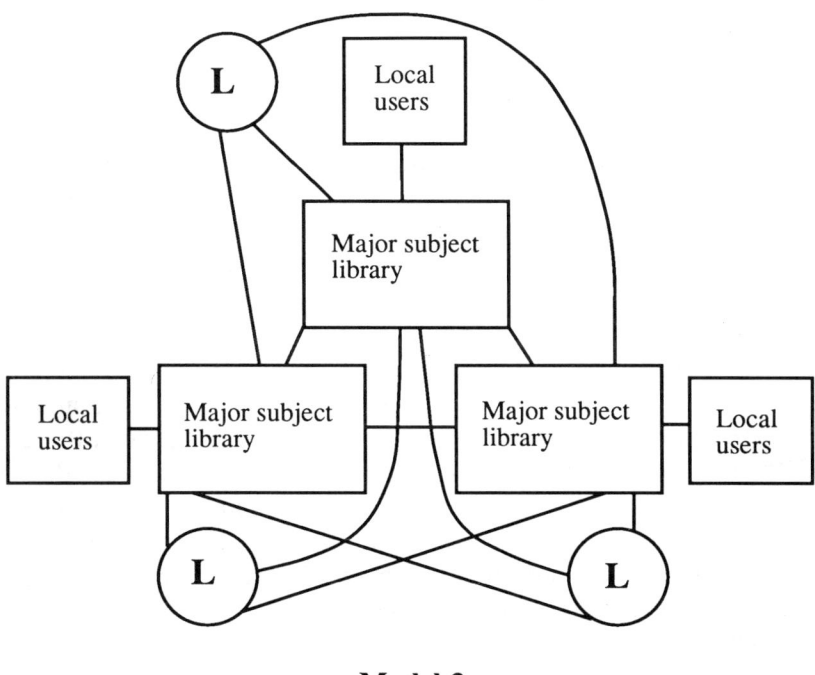

Model 3

in the country. As the central library fulfils another function, it is less expensive. However, there could be a role conflict as the central library has to fulfil more that one function.

A more complex plan – shown in Model 3 – is for several specialist libraries to provide services covering specific subject areas. Role conflict could again be a problem and there would be a need for coordination at the national level before coordination can be achieved internationally.

International cooperation becomes more difficult in Model 4 where more libraries take the responsibility for collecting, conserving and acting as a repository for a relatively narrow subject area. Even more coordination is needed at the national level, users may be unsure about where to send requests and lines of access and communication become increasingly complicated. As a result, international cooperation is less easy to manage efficiently.

Unfortunately, according to Wood (1988) the most frequently occurring arrangement is shown in Model 5. This model shows libraries functioning as individual entities, attempting to maintain discrete collections to serve groups of identified users. It is this unplanned model that is to be found in most countries.

It is based on the false assumptions that the libraries in the country will be able to collect and maintain the majority of the material needed nationally in spite of declining budgets, increased output of literature and shortage of space. It is also assumed that union catalogues will function effectively and that all libraries have efficient internal systems which will allow them to deal with ILL requests quickly. The problem with this system is that standards of service are difficult to agree and more difficult to achieve. Material in heavy or in low demand will frequently not be available and friction can develop between the users and lenders within the network. This is probably the most difficult national model for incorporation into an international network. As there is little or no national coordination, the problem of bringing individual libraries into a functioning national network is difficult. It is virtually impossible at a regional or international level.

Discussions on UAP and the establishment of a workable international cooperative framework have developed a model which combines the national network arrangements of Models 2, 3 and 5.

In this structure (Model 6), countries with a single central library facility (A/B) and the dependant libraries (L) are shown in the left hand segment of the diagram. Countries with several specialised national libraries (C) are shown in the right hand segment, with the more common institutional 'loose' assembly of libraries occupying the bottom segment. This model also shows the communication links from single national libraries and specialist libraries going across national and regional boundaries to each other and to individual libraries in the network.

This model will be slow to develop and will also function slowly. The role conflict will still be present. There will be currency problems in paying for lending and possibly high communication costs. In summarising his discussion of the various possible models at a seminar in the Caribbean Dr. Wood (1988) says that it is likely that no system, even one planned from scratch is likely to emerge in a pure form and the optimum solution will probably lie in a combination of models and may change with time. He suggests that the best way forward for the development of optimum systems is for developing countries to examine

International cooperation

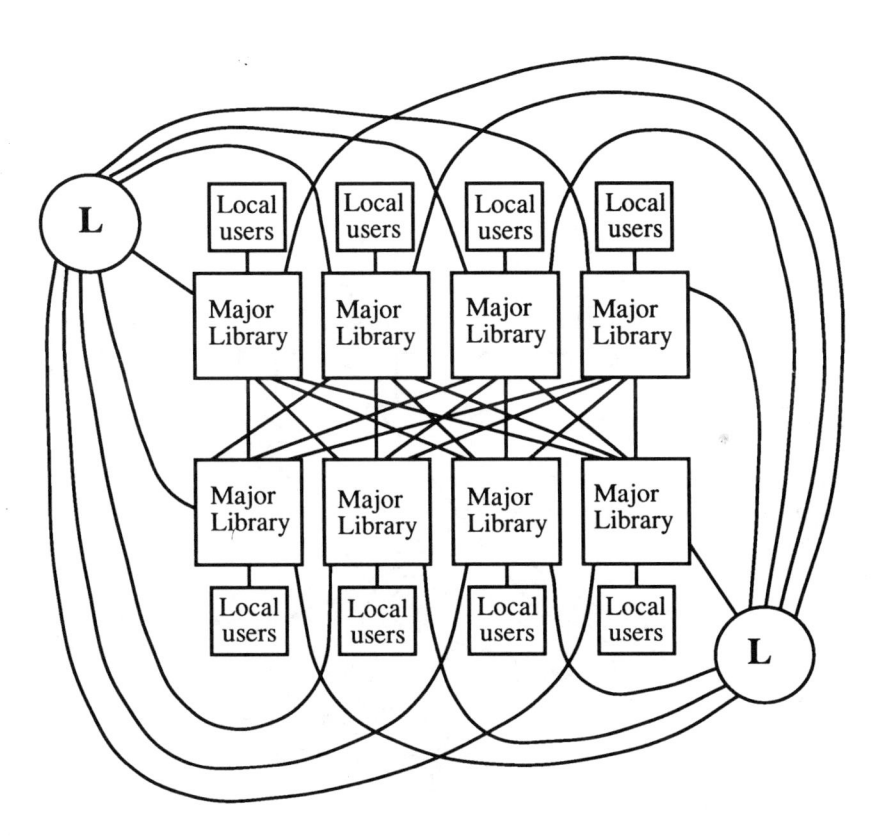

Model 4

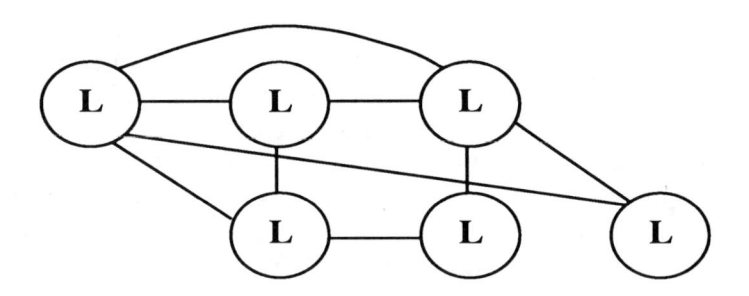

Model 5

Handbook of Library Cooperation

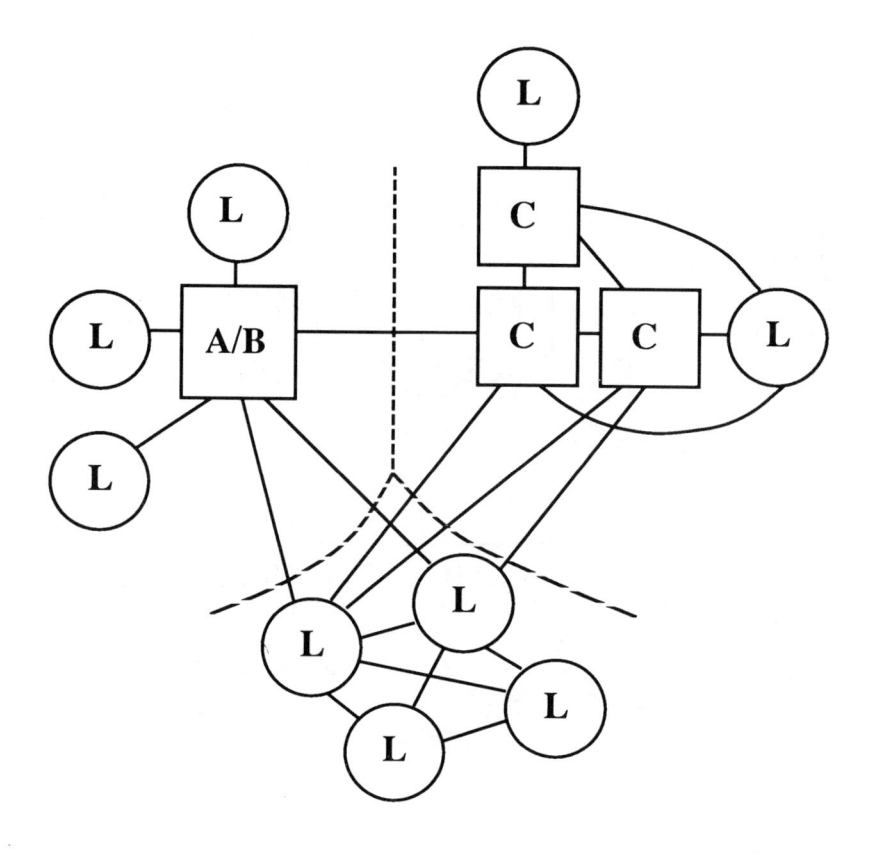

Model 6

their own 'history, politics, adminstration, population distribution, economy, education, research, transport, communication, climate, social factors, existing institutions, buildings, present demand and services, book output distribution, library budgets, existing local cooperation, regional links and international links– and see what sort of hypothetical system would best serve the users in your country – and at the same time make best use of existing resources' (Wood, 1988).

In effect, he is saying examine the basic infrastructure, apply it to the basic objective of serving the user and then see how national and international systems can be established to meet the needs of the users.

30

RESOURCES

Bibliographic networks provide access to information about material and form the arteries of the information system. However, the final link in the information chain is the provision of the actual information to the user. The models discussed above give the bone structure of the connecting network that can support the interlibrary loan system, but the discussion is not complete without considering document delivery systems. The developments in fax services and transmission communication facilities will have significant impact in the future. CD-ROM capability has been at the heart of one of the most significant services that has attracted much investment and study over the past several years. Launched commercially in January 1991, ADONIS is a major cooperative venture that involves not only major information services throughout the world but also leading publishers. It takes advantage of one of the latest available technologies – the CD-ROM – as the document delivery mechanism and has great significance for the future of information provision.

Document delivery systems – ADONIS

The consortium that developed the ADONIS system was formed in 1981 and consisted initially of six publishers – Academic Press, Blackwell Scientific Publications, Elsevier Science Publishers, Pergamon Press, Springer Verlag and John Wiley & Sons. In cooperation with the British Library Document Supply Centre (BLDSC) and the Centre de Documentation Scientifique et Technologie, studies were undertaken to determine the most requested journals. These studies showed that biomedical journals were highly requested and these formed the basis of the pilot project with 219 journals from ten scientific publishers. Articles were indexed and converted to CD-ROM images. The BLDSC was actively involved in the project from the beginning. Seven countries in Europe together with the USA, Mexico, Australia and Japan cooperated in the project. In all thirteen information centres in ten countries cooperated in the two year trial period of the ADONIS system in which over 50,000 documents were printed and supplied.

Journal articles published in 1987 and 1988 formed the basis of the pilot project – a total of 199,440 pages stored on 84 CD-ROM discs. More than 50,000 items were printed out during the pilot phase. The needs of the project – especially the handling of multiple discs – led to several special developments in both hardware and software, notably the so-called 'jukebox' for access to multiple discs and special retrieval management software which was developed by BLDSC. The service started commercially in January 1991 and initially covered over 400 scientific journals (Stern and Compier, 1990).

In summarising the results of the test from the point of view of the British Library, Barden (1990) comments that cooperation on new technology developments across national frontiers is feasible and valuable.

In view of the comment about the over-complexity of bibliographic systems made by Hope Clement in discussing UNIMARC (see above), it is interesting to note that in the evaluation of the trial phase of the ADONIS system in the UK the Universal Standard Bibliographic Code (USBC) was developed at the University of Bradford (Ayers *et al.*, 1990). This code uses a document identifier of 16 characters with one character representing the year, six to represent the author, two for pagination and seven characters for the title. The ISSN is not used and the initial test had a success rate of almost 100% in matching citations from DIALOG with the ADONIS file.

Grey literature – SIGLE

No library or library service can hope to be self-sufficient in terms of serving users and clients by providing all required material. In considering information resources, conventional material can flow through the networks, taking advantage of the new delivery mechanisms such as ADONIS. However, there is one class of literature that falls outside the conventional networks and has recently attracted international attention. This is the so-called 'grey literature' which is defined as literature which cannot readily be acquired through normal bookselling channels and which is therefore difficult to identify and obtain. It includes research reports, discussion and policy documents, working papers, conference papers, theses, some official publications, local authority and local industry papers, etc. (Commission of the European Communities, 1990).

The System for Information on Grey Literature in Europe (SIGLE) has been established to deal with this type of material. An association has been formed in Europe known as the European Association for Grey Literature Exploitation (EAGLE) who have joined with SIGLE to establish a computer searchable bibliographic database which in 1989 held over 150,000 records covering material published since 1980 in pure and applied sciences and technology and, since 1984, also covers economics, social sciences and humanities. Approximately 30,000 records are being added every year.

Translations – ITC

In addition to the bibliographic services that provide records of available material and the interlibrary loan structures that enable material to flow from collection to user, there is another dimension to the problem of material provision. Language can create a barrier to the flow of information and the International Translations Centre (ITC) was formed with the aim of encouraging, improving and facilitating the use of scientific and technical literature published in less accessible languages and to promote international cooperation. Established at Delft University of Technology in the Netherlands in 1961 the ITC has an international board of management and is organised to operate unfettered by political considerations or bias. ITC does not produced translations but acts a referral centre and maintains a network to distribute information on available translations. In effect its work covers 'record creation and data management through to the dissemination of this information to the research community' (Risseeuw, 1990).

ITC currently holds information on over 1,000,000 translations from any source language into Western languages and approximately 30,000 records per year are added to the file. Information is disseminated via the published *World Translation Index* and the machine readable database equivalent contains over 315,000 references to available translations covering conference proceedings, monographs, patents, reports, standards, theses, maps, etc. The 4th edition (1988) *Journals in Translation* contained 1,121 titles. Both these ITC products are produced cooperatively, the former in collaboration with the Institut de l'Information Scientifique et Technique, Centre National de la Recherche Scientifique (INIST-CNRS) and the latter with the BLDSC.

REGIONAL ASSOCIATIONS

In many parts of the world the regional associations are carrying forward cooperative goals. Working with limited resources, too few people are being asked to undertake too many tasks, and there are all the other problems that arise when national considerations have to be coordinated across borders. These practical points were considered by Bowden (1974) when he asked:

> 'what are the problems that have plagued and killed regional cooperative schemes in the developing countries leaving behind tombstones to failures or corpses struggling to remain alive? Some of them are general and therefore typical of most schemes in developing country situations. They usually result from the countries social and economic levels of development or current political situations or the feelings and strengths of nationalism. Some however are peculiar to a specific region or cooperative scheme or are related to the level of library development achieved, although this is not itself always influenced by the general developmental level of the country or countries involved.'

While a discussion of the major regional professional associations may seem like an exercise in alphabet soup, these organisations must have their place in any consideration of national network developments. Looking at some of these organisations, the theme of cooperation is an essential component in their statement of objectives. Even if achievements come slowly and the realities of funding seem insurmountable, their achievements to date and their future potential must be considered in terms of international cooperative activities.

ACURIL

In 1969 the independent Association of Caribbean University, Research and Institutional Libraries (ACURIL) was formed. According to the 1986 constitution its aims are:

- to facilitate development and use of libraries, archives, and information services and the identification, collection and preservation of information services and the identification, collection and preservation of information endeavours throughout the Caribbean areas
- to strengthen the archival, library and information professions in the region

- to unite workers in them
- to promote cooperative activities in pursuit of these objectives

While committees have been established to carry forward these objectives and are recognised as the 'Association's heartbeat' a review of ACURIL achievements (Jordan, 1989) identified that language diversity, poor communications and limited manpower have made it difficult to make progress. However, progress has been identified in areas of cooperative acquisition, bibliography, microfilming and indexing. An identified strength of ACURIL is the diversity of its membership which has representation from the four language groups in the region – Spanish, French, Dutch and English – and spans the 26 countries in the region. ACURIL is seen to have made an indelible impression on interlibrary relations throughout the region and, with clearer priority identification and needs reassessment, will be the organisation to 'chart and steer the best course towards a well coordinated future for this Caribbean arm of the library and information profession as the 21st century approaches'.

ALECSO

Since the First General Conference of ALECSO (Arab League Educational, Cultural and Scientific Organisation) was held in 1970, ALECSO has focused its concern with library and documentation work through its Information Department which believes that communication and information are the basic keywords of our time. The Department programme has set up projects for collecting, storing, and processing, as well as evaluating, analysing and disseminating information and data gathered from the Arab States. One area of particular concern has been the effort to unify terminology, especially in the area of information science (Khafagi, 1989).

COMLA

The Commonwealth Library Association (COMLA) was formed in 1972 and its aims are (Swaby, 1989):

- to support and encourage library associations in the Commonwealth

- to forge, maintain and strengthen professional links between the librarians of the Commonwealth
- to promote the status and education of librarians and the reciprocal recognition of qualifications in librarianship
- to initiate research projects designed to promote library provision and to further technical developments in libraries in Commonwealth countries
- to improve libraries in the Commonwealth

COMLA bases its programme on meetings organised within the region and it works closely with other organisations such as IFLA internationally and other regional groups such as SCECSAL (Standing Conference of East Central & Southern Africa Librarians).

CONSAL

The Congress of Southeast Asian Librarians (CONSAL) was formed in August 1970. It fostered a growing sense of regional Southeast Asian identity which had started with the formation of the Association of South East Asian Nations (ASEAN) in 1967 and the South East Asian Ministers of Education Organisations (SEAMEO). CONSAL's activities are based on the organisation of conferences at least once every three years with the first on the theme of international cooperation held in Singapore in 1970. Overall aims are (Anuar, 1989):

- to establish, maintain and strengthen relations among librarians, library schools, library associations and related organisations in the region
- to promote cooperation in the fields of librarianship, bibliography, documentation and related activities in the region
- to cooperate with other regional or international organisations and institutions in the fields of librarianship, bibliography, documentation and related activities

SCECSAL

The Standing Conference of Eastern, Central and Southern African Libraries (SCECSAL) differs from the other groups discussed above. It is not a formally constituted body as it has a 'floating' secretariat linked to the organisation of a biennial conference held in one of the countries in the region. The secretariat is held by the country that is hosting the current conference. In some ways the informal network is effective in bringing professionals from a number of countries together. But its lack of a central organisational entity makes it difficult for this particular group to work on cooperative projects with other regions.

LIBER

All the above organisations are regional organisations that deal with developing country interests.

There is a professional organisation which is concerned with Europe. The Ligue des Bibliothèques Européennes de Recherche was formed in 1971 as a non-governmental association of European research libraries. Over 170 major libraries from more than 23 countries in Europe belong to LIBER. The members are primarily national and university libraries with some special research libraries. A feasibility study for a register of microform masters was undertaken in 1986. This is an important project in terms of resource preservation as it will record approximately 450,000 masters held in European libraries other than masters held in the UK and the USA where registers already exist. In addition, LIBER is responsible for a directory of library networks and network facilities in European countries (Koch, 1988).

STANDARDISATION

It is not possible to consider the topic of international cooperation without considering standardisation, especially with the stress on bibliographic networks and use of CD-ROMs that have been selected for detailed discussion in this contribution. An essential component in the connected infrastructure that forms the information society is the national standards body for the country. While a standards organisation such as the British Standards Institution (BSI), the Deutsches Institut für Normung e.V. (DIN), and similar bodies cover many areas of industry with library and information applications forming only a small part of their programme, they are necessary components in developing national standards. More importantly for the subject under consideration, they are the necessary links to the International Organisation for Standardisation (ISO). This body works through internationally organised committees which are drawn from the national bodies and from professional organisations.

The problem with the development of standards at the local and the international level is the slow progress that is made as consultation requirements are ponderous and time consuming. This means that many standards are developed on a *de facto* basis. Large systems set up particular procedures to enable them to function effectively and these are copied by other organisations. The style of bibliographic references for scientific abstracting and indexing services was established for many services by the style used by Chemical Abstracts Service. The MARC format was initially established by the Library of Congress and has gone through tortuous negotiations through the American National Standards Institute and ISO to set an international standard for the exchange of bibliographic information on magnetic tape.

A more serious problem arises when industry develops conflicting standards. Those people who bought a beta-max video recorder before the television industry settled for the VHS system will know all too well the penalties that can be imposed on the user. In view of the increased amount of information being made available in CD-ROMs, the same problem is arising. Although there is an international standard for CD-ROMs (ISO 9660 – the 'so-called' High Sierra system) this is not accepted by all the major CD-ROM manufacturers. There are increasing signs that some of the other major manufacturers are going to produce a rival standard that will cause problems for information systems that are trying to take advantage of this form of information delivery.

FUTURE PAIN – OR GAIN?

The crystal ball of the future reveals two concerns. First, new technological developments will have an impact on cooperative programmes in the future. CD-ROMs were relatively unknown in the library and information field five years ago. Today they are increasing in number and in the diversity of the material being made available in this format. The cooperation of major libraries, publishers, and equipment manufacturers has brought this new information product into being. Its future will be governed by user acceptance and the marketplace. It is becoming clear that information supplied on CD-ROM can be more directly comparable to the printed publication than online retrieval services.

The second is a lesson that should be learnt from hindsight, but still needs to be stressed and has the potential for causing much pain, namely the continuing importance of, and necessity for, standardisation. The evolution of new technologies requires agreements on standards and there are unresolved areas where commitment and investment by the industry are still needed. Users need to invest in equipment and can be adversely affected by lack of agreement on standards. The complexity of bibliographic standards could lead in the future to some changes in the level of detail required in order to make some forms of input and use easier.

In the longer term, the potential of Open Systems Interconnection (OSI) and the introduction of the Integrated Services Digital Network (ISDN) will have an important impact on standardisation. The former will establish a set of communication protocols which will have an effect on cataloguing, interlibrary lending, serials management, etc. ISDN could be implemented as part of the programme of developments that may happen as a result of 1992. It could have a substantial impact on document delivery systems.

In discussing international programmes, the benefits for the developing world are often stressed. Many programmes – UBC, AGRIS, etc. – have the potential to bring all countries into cooperative schemes and give them improved information provision. Experiments with CD-ROM and other technologies indicate that information can be distributed in a more appropriate form for use in the third world. However, manpower limitations and the lack of basic technical support can still mean that these services can not be used effectively. Although many of today's developments are encouraging, there is still the potentially widening gap between the information rich and the information poor countries and this must be a continuing professional concern.

The objectives put forward in Bowden's 'plain man's guide' (1990) to cooperation should continue to guide future developments. Cooperation should improve the services to the user; maximise resources; and overcome the isolation of libraries.

REFERENCES.

Anuar, H. (1989), The why and how of CONSAL as a Regional Library Association. *IFLA Journal*, vol. 15, no. 3, pp. 237–242.

Ayers, F. H. et al. (1990), Docmatch: automated input to ADONIS. *Interlending and Document Supply*, vol. 18, no. 3, (July) pp. 92–97.

Barden, P. (1990), ADONIS – The British Library experience. *Interlending and Document Supply*, vol. 18, no. 3, (July) pp. 88–91.

Bowden, R. (1974), *A survey of the opportunities for regional cooperation in library services in developing countries.* MLS dissertation, Loughborough University of Technology.

Bowden, R. (1990), Cooperation, coordination, national planning and national information policies: a plain man's guide, in *Seminar on Information Services and Regional Cooperation, China Society for Library Science, 21–25 May.* In press.

Clement, H. E. A. (1989), The International MARC Network and national libraries. *Alexandria*, vol. 1, no. 1, (May), pp. 23–34.

Coblans, H. (1964), The structure of national documentation and library services. *Aslib Proceedings*, vol. 16, pp. 22–30.

Coblans, H. (1974), *Librarianship and documentation: an international perspective.* Andre Deutsch, London.

Commission of the European Communities, Directorate-General Telecommunications, Information Industries and Innovation (1990), *Your passport to grey literature – System for information on grey literature in Europe.* Scientific and Technical Communications Service. Luxembourg, (January), 10p.

Conference of Directors of National Libraries International MARC Network Advisory Committee (1987), *International transfers of national MARC records: guidelines for agreements relating to the transfer of national MARC records between national bibliographic agencies.* London, IFLA UBCIM Programme.

Donker Duyvis, R. (1940), The International Federation for Documentation. *Journal of Documentary Reproduction*, vol. 3, pp. 176–191.

Helal, A. H. and Weiss, J. W. (1988), *International library cooperation: 10th Anniversary Essen Symposium, 19–22 October, 1987.* (Festschrift in honour of Prof. Dr. Günther Pflug). Universitätsbibliothek Essen.

Jordan, A. (1989), The Association of Caribbean University, Research and Institutional Libraries (ACURIL). *IFLA Journal*, vol. 15, no. 3, pp. 233–236.

Keenan, S. (1978), Development of mechanised documentation. *Journal of Documentation*, vol. 34, no. 4, (December), pp. 333–341.

Khafagi, M. T. (1989), ALECSO and its activities in the field of information. *IFLA Journal* vol. 15, no. 3, pp. 246–250.

Koch, H.-A. (1988), Library cooperation within the Ligue des Bibliothèques Européennes de Recherch (LIBER), in Helal, A. H. and Weiss, J. W. eds. *International library cooperation: 10th Anniversary Essen Symposium, 19–22 October, 1987*. Universitätsbibliothek Essen. pp. 52–68.

Ranganathan, S. R. (1951), Colon classification and its approach to documentation, in Shera, J. H. and Egan, M. E. eds. *Bibliographic organisation: 15th Annual Conference of the Graduate Library School, 24–29 July, 1950*. Chicago University Press, pp. 94–105.

Risseeuw, M. (1990), The International Translations Centre (ITC). *Alexandria*, vol. 2, no. 1, pp. 51–66.

Stern, B. T. and Compier, H. C. J. (1990), *ADONIS – document delivery in the CD-ROM age*. In press.

Swaby, J. E. (1989), Regional cooperation: the role of COMLA in international librarianship. *IFLA Journal*, vol. 15, no. 3, pp. 243–245.

Wolf, D. and Conrad, F. (1986), *International guide to MARC databases and services: national magnetic tape services*. 2nd. ed.

Wood, D. N. (1988), *Universal Availability of Publications. CTA/CARDI refresher course on agricultural information sources, Trinidad, B.W.I.* (unpublished)

3

The European Communities as a focus for library cooperation

MICHAEL HOPKINS

The European Community (EC) is not an organisation that springs immediately to mind in the context of library cooperation. Although the media hype associated with plans to complete the internal market has endowed the year 1992 with a mystique and even a sense of foreboding previously associated only with the year 1984, single market initiatives themselves have had little direct impact upon the organisation and operation of libraries. However, the enormous amount of publicity generated by the 1992 programme has meant that for the first time in nearly twenty years of United Kingdom (UK) membership, the EC has at last made an impact upon the national consciousness. Harmonisation, cross border collaboration and international cooperative action are now more readily accepted as valid policy instruments for dealing with a wide range of issues and common problems previously dealt with on a national or sub-national level.

Ease of access to high quality information and its free flow across national boundaries have long been recognised by the EC as essential pre-requisites for the development of a strong industrial base in Europe. Although libraries have only recently emerged as targets for specific attention by Community institutions the environment in which they operate has been increasingly conditioned by developments initiated and coordinated at a European level, particularly in relation to rapid strides made in the application of information technology.

The purpose of this Chapter is not to assess the impact of the EC on libraries but to highlight the ways in which the EC has already provoked cooperative action amongst libraries on both a national and international level, and to describe a number of the ways in which the EC is likely to stimulate increased collaboration in the future. In broad terms, the EC may be said to act as both catalyst and initiator in relation to library cooperation. On the one hand, membership of the EC has confronted libraries with a set of common problems, challenges and opportunities; it has provided libraries with a reason to cooperate and with an international framework within which to operate. On the other hand, the EC is an organisation dedicated to the creation of a strong and vibrant Europe by means which include ever closer integration, the pooling of resources, and collaborative actions of many kinds. In this context, the EC positively promotes cooperation as an instrument of policy, providing both the infrastructure and often the financial opportunities for major collaborative developments which offer economies of scale and cost-effective use of resources. Each function is addressed in turn in the following pages.

THE EC AS CATALYST FOR COOPERATION

The EC is an interesting case in relation to library cooperation on a purely national scale because it well illustrates how the library and information profession can respond positively and collectively to common problems. At the time of British entry into the EC no cooperative framework existed in the United Kingdom to provide library and information personnel with the support and assistance they required at the operational level to deal with this new, important but almost unknown source of information. Public opinion was largely indifferent and sometimes hostile to the EC and there was widespread ignorance of the role, powers and policies of Community institutions. Although the EC was a prolific source of publications, a lack of familiarity with its institutional structure and law-making processes, combined with the unacceptably low bibliographic standards displayed by EC publications, made life extremely difficult for those librarians who were expected almost overnight to become specialists in EC law and to provide expert assistance in the use of a mass of often complex and confusing legislative documentation. Indeed, problems reached such a pitch that it was claimed that individual citizens were being denied their democratic right to full and free access to information on decisions taken in their names and that

British business was losing contracts and other commercial opportunities as a result of a lack of timely information on European affairs.

The Professional Response

During the years immediately following UK membership a number of initiatives were taken at a professional level to provide a focus for cooperative action in relation to EC documentation. The first concerted professional response took place in 1979 when the Library Association established a Working Party on EC Publications for the principal purpose of establishing a dialogue with senior EC officials. The Working Party included membership from several Library Association groups, Aslib, the Institute of Information Scientists, the British Library and the London Office of the European Commission. Its terms of reference were as follows:

- to establish consultative machinery through which the Library Association may discuss matters of mutual concern, including all aspects of the supply and bibliographical control of Community documentation, with representatives from the European Communities and to provide the Library Association membership thereof
- to act as a forum for the discussion of matters relating to the use of European Communities documentation in the United Kingdom
- to promote the effective exploitation of European Communities documentation in the United Kingdom and to coordinate professional activities with regard to this documentation
- to undertake whatever action is required to further these aims

The Working Party met regularly over a number of years and on several occasions held joint meetings with senior EC officials. Although seminars were organised in response to an expressed demand for training and education in the use of EC documentation, the principal value of the Working Party was as a pressure group, acting at a policy level on behalf of libraries of all types. Constructive comment and professional advice was offered to Brussels and Luxembourg and attention was drawn to deficiencies in the standards of EC publishing practice, with particular regard to distribution and supply, bibliographical control and indexing. The Working Party raised professional awareness of European issues, it provided a forum for the discussion of matters of common concern and established a focus for a coordinated professional response designed to make the most effective impact in dealings with Luxembourg and Brussels.

The Library Association Working Party on EC Publications was an appropriate response to an expressed professional demand for representations to be made to Community institutions for improvements in bibliographical and physical access to EC information. However, by 1985 circumstances had changed. Although much remained to be done, a more business-like approach had been applied to Community publishing, EC information services and sources had been much improved, and there was frequent contact with Community officials. Moreover, circumstances had also changed to the extent that the Working Party was no longer the only professional body active in the field. New professional organisations, such as the Association of EDC Librarians (see below), had been established and others both inside and outside the library and information profession had begun to take a more active interest in questions relating to the availability and use of EC information.

The consequence was that in 1985 the Working Party was transformed into the National Forum on EC Information with an expanded membership and new terms of reference. In order to ease the transition all associations, groups and institutions represented on the Working Party were taken into membership of the new body. However, in addition, such specialist organisations as the Association of EDC Librarians, the British and Irish Association of Law Librarians and the City Information Group were given representation as were information providers outside the library field, such as the Confederation of British Industry (CBI) and the British Sections of the International Union of Local Authorities and Council of European Municipalities and Regions (IULA/CEMR). Also included was representation from the House of Commons Library, the London Offices of both the European Commission and the European Parliament and from HMSO as the national sales agent for EC publications. The terms of reference were as follows:

- to act as the forum for the discussion of matters relating to the provision and use of European Communities information in the United Kingdom

- to coordinate and initiate professional activities designed to promote the effective use of EC information in the United Kingdom
- to represent the views of its members in dealings with Community institutions and other interested parties both nationally and internationally on matters relating to the provision and use of EC information

Continuing the work of its predecessor, the National Forum addressed numerous issues of both a practical and policy nature. In an attempt to promote increased awareness and use of EC information in the United Kingdom, the National Forum undertook a major questionnaire survey of public library holdings of EC publications and organised seminars on the use of EC information, with practitioners in local government and industry a particular target. Consideration was also given to means of improving the ease with which business and industry could obtain access to EC information and numerous practical problems brought to its attention by constituent organisations were also addressed. The National Forum met regularly until the end of 1987 and was dissolved at the end of 1988, ending a ten year period during which first the Working Party and then the National Forum filled a professional vacuum and provided a valuable focus for cooperative action.

At about the same time as steps were in train to create the Library Association Working Party on EC Publications initiatives were also being taken to create a framework for cooperative action in a discrete but related sector of EC information provision. As part of its policy to facilitate and encourage academic teaching and research in the area of European integration the European Commission had granted more than 300 institutions of higher education in member countries and elsewhere the status of European Documentation Centre (EDC), a designation which entitled them to copies of all EC publications and public documents free of charge. In return for this considerable benefit, host institutions were expected to maintain the material in well-organised separate collections, to make it freely available to members of the institution and to promote its academic use. A total of 44 university and polytechnic libraries were designated as EDCs in the United Kingdom, mostly around the time of UK membership in the early 1970s. A further 4 libraries, in this case public and national libraries, were granted the status of Depository Library (DEP), in order to make the same material more easily accessible to members of the public. Full details, including names, special interest areas and brief notes on library holdings of European Documentation Centres, Depositary Libraries and European Reference Centres in the UK and Republic of Ireland have been listed in a recent directory (Directory of European Documentation Centres..., 1989).

EDC librarians faced the same problems that provoked the creation of the Library Association Working Party but more besides. University and polytechnic libraries were faced with a sudden and continuous influx of large numbers of unfamiliar documents, legislative texts and publications which were not amenable to conventional library handling procedures but which nevertheless needed to be organised and made publicly available. The situation was exacerbated by numerous problems concerning the supply and distribution of material to EDCs and by general uncertainty over the exact role EDCs were expected to play and the nature of the obligations they were expected to meet.

In the case of EDCs a cooperative response to common problems was more predictable and more easily accomplished than for the library profession as a whole. EDCs and DEPs were a readily identifiable, small group of privileged users with a common sense of purpose towards whom the EC already recognised an obligation. The London Office of the Commission already organised periodic national meetings of EDC librarians at which there was opportunity to share experience and discuss issues of common concern. It was but a short step first to the arrangement of informal meetings of EDC librarians on a regional basis and then to the creation of a national organisation to represent the interests and views of EDC and DEP librarians, an initiative which in fact took place in 1981 with the creation of the Association of EDC Librarians.

Although the terms of reference reflect the charitable status accorded to the Association in 1986 they differ little from those originally agreed in 1981:

- to provide a forum for the exchange of experience and the dissemination of information among EDC/DEP librarians
- to represent the views of EDC/DEP librarians to the institutions of the European Communities on all matters relating to the EDC/DEP system
- to promote the efficient administration and exploitation of EDC/DEP collections, with particular regard to improved provision for the education and training of EDC/DEP librarians

- to promote improved bibliographic standards and to encourage bibliographical study and research relating to the documents and publications of the European Communities
- to support the activities of and cooperate with charitable organisations wherever situated having similar objectives

In common with both the Library Association Working Party and the National Forum – with each of which it collaborated closely in turn – the Association may be said to display both self-help and pressure group characteristics. In respect of the former it has established a strong publishing programme, a highly successful series of training seminars and conferences, informative visits to the major Community capitals and other education and training activities. As advocate of improved standards and expanded services in relation to the availability and use of EC information the Association has drawn attention to deficiencies in provision and provided constructive criticism and advice whenever appropriate. Indeed, the close working relationship built up over a number of years with key Community officials has been instrumental in clarifying issues and winning many of the bibliographical improvements which have taken place in the past decade.

Characteristics of cooperation

The professional initiatives briefly described above represent three separate responses to a common problem. Both the Working Party and the Association of EDC Librarians were created first as reactive, almost self-defence mechanisms in the face of mounting problems caused by the painful assimilation of a new legal order. All three bodies represented a cooperative professional response to expressions of concern about the state of EC information provision in the United Kingdom and all three have displayed both self-help and pressure group characteristics. However, despite common origins, interests and activities they each display a range of distinctive characteristics which have to some extent determined the nature and scope of the impact they have made.

In structure and composition the principal contrast is between the Working Party and its successor, the National Forum, on the one hand and the Association of EDC Librarians on the other. Both Working Party and National Forum were in effect specialist sub-committees of standing committees of the Library Association, made up of representatives from committees of other bodies and organisations. As a consequence, lines of communication with individual practitioners were tenuous and weak; it was difficult for either to establish a strong sense of identity or to develop a high public profile. Moreover, both initiatives were perceived to be library-based and Library Association oriented, with remits which limited their attention to practical issues concerning the availability, organisation and use of collections of EC publications, leaving more general policy issues concerning the EC, libraries and information to standing committees within parent organisations.

The Association of EDC Librarians, on the other hand, was and still remains a professional organisation independent of both the EC and of mainstream professional associations, with its own membership, committee structure, sources of finance and programme of activities. It was established to satisfy the needs of a defined and small group of academic librarians working in a common educational environment and has benefited enormously from generous practical and financial support from the London Office of the Commission which, without compromising its independence, made it possible for the Association to survive the crucial formative period when resources were slim and the future uncertain. Although annual subventions from the London Office have remained a valuable source of financial support, income generated by the Association itself through annual subscriptions, the organisation of conferences and seminars, the sale of publications and other activities, now provides the sound financial platform upon which its activities are based. As a small, independent professional organisation unencumbered by complex bureaucracy, past history or professional rivalries, able to draw upon its own financial resources and the strength of an enthusiastic and expert membership, the Association has been able to make a considerable contribution in relation to the raising of standards and the quality of provision in the field of EC documentation.

In respect of their activities all three bodies have sought to perform three principal functions, namely self-help, pressure group and coordinating functions. All three have made a useful contribution in relation to education and training by organising seminars and conferences designed to improve understanding and facilitate more effective use of EC documentation. The Association of EDC Librarians in particular, with its stronger financial base and an eager membership, has made a considerable impact, organising an annual programme of training seminars, online demonstrations and conferences open to all and producing a series of informative practical guides and leaflets. Although it is always difficult to pinpoint specific improvements resulting from pressure group activities carried out over a long period, there is good reason to believe that the joint meetings and frequent correspondence entered into with Community officials by all three bodies have drawn attention to grievances strongly felt in the United Kingdom and given a spur to many of the improvements in bibliographic standards that have taken place during the 1980s.

However, in respect of coordination real achievements have proved more difficult to attain. In the early years when professional activity in relation to the EC was minimal, membership of the Working Party did at least provoke a certain amount of discussion and debate on EC affairs in parent committees and help to improve levels of awareness among members of the profession. However, by the mid 1980s it was clear that a working party was no longer an appropriate instrument; there were many more actors on the EC stage and a working party conjured up visions of a small group of experts appointed for a limited period to investigate a particular problem. What was now required was a body with an open-ended watching brief over matters relating to the supply and demand for EC information in the United Kingdom. Consequently, the National Forum was conceived as an umbrella organisation which would bring a degree of coherence and coordination to the work of the ever-increasing number of professional associations and groups by now engaged in the promotion and use of EC information. It was also felt that unless the voice of specialist groups was heard at a national level their needs would be unlikely to receive due consideration from the suppliers and providers of EC information and that there were times when a coordinated response to a particular policy issue, seen to be representative of all shades of professional opinion in the United Kingdom, would have more impact than a series of individual submissions.

In the event, the National Forum was unable to provide the forum within which the issues which form a common link between the principal information providers in the United Kingdom could be effectively dealt with on a cooperative basis. Although its membership did include representation from a number of key information intermediaries outside the traditional library arena, such as the Confederation of British Industry (CBI) and the British Sections of the International Union of Local Authorities and Council of European Municipalities and Regions (IULA/

European Communities

CEMR), as well as the London Offices of both the European Commission and the European Parliament, it still remained a library-based initiative which was unable to harness the rich sources of expertise increasingly active in the private, commercial and business sectors. National coordination of EC information provision remained an elusive goal, awaiting the emergence of a centripetal force which would have sufficient strength and status to attract real collaboration from EC information providers across professional boundaries.

Ironically for organisations concerned with the European Communities, the existing cooperative structures have also been unable to bring a truly European dimension to their activities. As has already been mentioned, it was the original aim of the Library Association Working Party to establish a joint working party with Community officials from Brussels and Luxembourg, using the long-standing Library Association/HMSO Services Working Party as a model. In the event, despite a preparatory meeting in Brussels, representatives from the EC attended just two meetings of the Working Party in November 1980 and March 1981 and one of the National Forum. The fact that neither the Working Party nor the National Forum became truly joint ventures can be attributed not only to practical problems concerning arrangements for meetings but also to a reluctance on the part of the European Commission to expose itself to charges of national favouritism by engaging in regular meetings with third parties from just one member country. Although attempts were later made to internationalise the activities of the Working Party by creating a European Users' Forum, the initiative did not provoke a response strong enough in other member countries to justify further action.

The Association of EDC Librarians has had a similar experience in relation to the creation of a European dimension to its activities. Although the European Commission has organised both national and international meetings of EDC librarians and the Association has been held up as a role model for others to follow, similar initiatives have yet to appear elsewhere in the Community. Bilateral contacts have been established with other EDC librarians but little enthusiasm has so far been expressed for the formation of a European Association of EDC Librarians. It may be that the impending direct involvement of the EC in library affairs – which forms the subject of the second half of this Chapter – will provoke sufficient interest and concern to stimulate the creation of a genuine European level library organisation.

Future cooperative structures

The national scene in relation to EC information has been transformed in recent years, principally as a result of initiatives associated with the programme to complete the internal market by 1992. Current efforts to eliminate the technical, physical and fiscal barriers which prevent the formation of a genuine common market are no more than a renewed attempt to give reality to the four basic freedoms, relating to movement of goods, capital, persons and services, which formed the cornerstone of the Treaty of Rome signed more than 30 years ago. This time, however, the political will to achieve significant progress is much stronger and legislative programmes have been supported by major publicity campaigns which have galvanised British industry and given the EC a higher public profile than ever before. Indeed, such has been the success of the campaign to raise levels of public awareness that there has been an explosion of demand for EC information which has in turn provoked intermediary and representative organisations to take a more positive interest in EC affairs and encouraged new information providers to emerge. Trade unions and employer organisations, trade associations and chambers of commerce, professional and financial institutions, management and private consultants of many descriptions are amongst those who now provide clients and customers, members and users with information on Community affairs.

At the same time, and partly in response to the enormous growth in demand for EC information, the European Commission has begun implementation of a policy of distributed information provision based upon a more selective and targeted approach to information supply, with greater emphasis than previously upon the provision of information through support for alternative relays and information infrastructures rather than by direct provision to the end user. The Offices maintained by the Commission in each member country have adjusted their priorities to give more emphasis to their representational and diplomatic roles than to their previously dominant function as press and information offices and have begun to develop the concept of 'information relay', which it is hoped will fill the gap and ultimately provide more effective channels of communication with defined audiences. European Documentation Centres represent an academic relay network already in place. A very similar network of European Business Information Centres is currently being established in order to provide an EC information service for business and industry, with particular reference to SMEs (small and medium size enterprises) and other potential intermediary organisations, such as public libraries, chambers of commerce and local government, are being considered.

It may be ironic but at the time when the EC has stimulated enormous public interest and when demand for information about the single market and other EC initiatives is at its height the profession is left with just one national – but specialist – organisation specifically concerned with the actual use of EC information. In recognition of the increasing number and diversity of information providers in the field of EC information the Association of EDC Librarians has, in fact, recently decided to review its aims and objectives and to confront once more the need for an overarching organisation to bring a greater degree of coordination to the work of an increasingly diverse group of information providers in the field of EC information. It is likely that moves will soon be undertaken to broaden its remit and membership in order for the Association, perhaps under a new name, to become the acknowledged and broad-based natural focus for professional expertise and assistance on library and information matters concerning the EC in the United Kingdom. At present separate components of the EC information infrastructure work largely in isolation; their closer collaboration would strengthen the national system of information provision and increase their credibility and influence in Brussels.

COOPERATION AS INSTRUMENT OF EC POLICY

The main thrust of EC economic policy is the creation of an industrial entity in Europe which is strong enough to compete in world markets on equal terms with the likes of the United States and Japan. The means chosen for improving the international competitiveness and performance of the European economy include the elimination of the physical, technical and fiscal barriers which currently prevent European industry from realising economies of scale and the pooling of national resources and expertise in such a way as to ensure that the European entity so created has a combined strength much greater than the sum of its individual parts. Integral to this overall strategy has been the development of industrial research, innovation and technological development policies whose aim has been to strengthen the scientific and technological base of European industry by cooperation and collaboration across national boundaries. Research programmes developed as a consequence in such pervasive technologies as telecommunications, data-processing and particularly information technology, have radically affected the environment in which libraries operate and in specific areas have provided an opportunity for libraries to cooperate and become involved in large-scale research and technological development on an international scale. The nature of cooperative activity in this respect forms the subject of this section.

The Information Services Market

The EC has long since recognised the strategic importance of information as a scarce commodity which has an intrinsic commercial value, to which European industry must have quality access if it is to increase its profitability and competitiveness. Much of the work of Directorate-General XIII (Telecommunications, Information Industries and Innovation) within the European Commission has consequently been aimed at stimulating research and development in information technology, with one department (Directorate B: Information Industry and Market) specifically responsible for the development of an information services sector in which information flows freely across national boundaries and which exploits the most recent technological developments. One of the instruments used by the EC to stimulate progress in this as in other policy sectors has been to devise multi-annual action plans in which general objectives have been defined, priorities established and funds made available for external agents, including libraries, to finance research and development projects in relevant areas. The fact that as a general rule EC research funds are used to finance collaborative research projects involving partners from more than one member country has provided libraries not only with a welcome opportunity to engage in research of an international character but also to work closely on cooperative projects with counterparts elsewhere in Europe.

During the period since 1975 work in the information sector has largely been undertaken within the framework of a series of action plans, the principal achievement of the first two of which was the development and successful launch of the Euronet-Diane online information network early in 1980. Although as a physical system Euronet-Diane has now been replaced by interconnections between the packet-switched networks introduced and administered by the national PTTs, it succeeded in providing rapid and reliable transfer of information around Europe at a cost which was reasonable and independent of distance. In its third action plan the EC sought to stimulate the development of high quality, user friendly databases, particularly in areas likely to improve the performance of European industry, and also supported experiments in the field of electronic document delivery and electronic publishing. A fourth action plan for the years 1984 to 1988 identified a number of areas for priority attention, including patent information, biotechnology information, materials databanks, electronic publishing, information for industry and the reduction of regional discrepancies in the availability of high technology information services (Council Decision 84/567/EEC).

In 1987 the European Commission launched a major new initiative in the form of a *Policy and a plan of priority actions for the development of an information services market* to cover the years 1989 and 1990, which was adopted by the Council in July 1988 (Council Decision 88/524/EEC). The intention was to remove the many technical, legal and linguistic barriers that fragment the European information services market and thereby hold back the development of advanced information services in Europe. Later known by the acronym IMPACT I (Information Market Policy Actions), the plan envisaged the creation of a European Information Market Observatory to collect and evaluate data on different sectors of the information market, along with a wide range of additional measures in support of standardisation and the improved quality, coordination and accessibility of services. Extensive consultations are currently under way with experts, specialists and government officials on the content and structure of a follow-up five year IMPACT II programme.

Plan of Action for Libraries in the EC

The environment in which libraries operate and the services they provide have been significantly affected by initiatives taken and developments made possible by the action plans outlined above.

However, it is only relatively recently that the European Commission has taken a specific interest in libraries. In 1985 the Council adopted a Resolution on 'collaboration between libraries in the field of data-processing' after discussions initiated by the European Parliament on the possible creation of a European Library (Resolution on collaboration..., 1985). Having acknowledged that libraries 'constitute a treasure-house of material both culturally and from the viewpoint of scientific, technical and economic development' the Council noted the need for greater cooperation between libraries at a Community level, particularly in relation to the linking of computerized catalogues and urged the Commission to take swift action to help libraries to realise their full potential. As an interim measure libraries were inserted in the 1984 to 1988 action plan as an additional priority and appeared as a separate action line in IMPACT I, with an allocation of 2.5 million ECU (out of a total budget of 36 million ECU) for cooperation between libraries, particularly in relation to the introduction of new information technologies.

The actions intended by the Commission in the light of these initiatives were presented in 1985 in the form of a separate *Plan of action at Community level aimed at library cooperation based on the application of new information technologies.* This original unpublished draft was circulated widely by Directorate B of DG XIII (Telecommunications, Information Industries and Innovation), the feedback from which was later used by the Commission as a basis for a Communication and draft Resolution to the Council (COM(89)234 final. 16.5.1989), further information about which is provided in a recent article (Hopkins, 1989).

The overall objective stated in the *Plan of action* is to encourage libraries 'to improve their services in the interests of the users in such a way that they can respond better to the challenge of the present and the future' and 'to optimize their use of resources in order that these services can be provided economically'. The broad aim of the initiative is to ensure that users in all member countries benefit from modern and cost-effective library services, by means which include the progressive exploitation of new information technologies, standardisation in relation to information exchange and harmonisation of national library policies. The *Plan of action* makes no attempt to change existing library structures; it casts the Commission in the role of catalyst, addressing the international aspects of library cooperation and resource sharing by enabling actions of various kinds, including the provision of funds for collaborative projects. In fact, a number of main action lines are identified as a basis for developments over a five year period. These are intended, amongst other things, to facilitate progress in relation to the increased availability of catalogue/bibliographic records in machine-readable form, improved inter-connection of the automated systems holding such data, better access to the contents of European libraries through enhanced interlibrary loan mechanisms and the modernisation of the skills of library staff.

At the time of writing the *Plan of action* is no more than a proposal from the Commission which has yet to be accepted and allocated funds by the Council, the decision-making institution within the EC structure. Indeed, although it was hoped that funds would be made available during 1990, it now seems likely that the *Plan of action* is to be subsumed within a much larger programme on telematics which has yet to be finalised by the Commission before being sent for consideration by the European Parliament and ultimate decision by the Council. Such is the nature of the decision-making process that it might be a year or more before the process is successfully completed.

Consultation and Cooperation

Contrary to its undeserved reputation as a bloated bureaucracy the European Commission is in fact an institution which has relatively few senior officials to cover an enormous portfolio of policy fields. Consequently, it is well recognised by the Commission that it must make considerable use of outside expertise and experience if it is to fulfil its responsibilities and take due note of external comment and advice if it is to win broad-based support for its proposals. During the formative period when the aim was primarily to define the key issues to be addressed in the *Plan of action* and identify the areas most amenable to a transnational approach, Commission officials built up informal bilateral contacts with a large number of officials from the library and related sectors in all member states and with appropriate professional organisations. This network has been extended during the lengthy period of discussion and debate engendered by widespread circulation of the *Plan of action* in its draft form. A further round of more formal consultations will take place when the *Plan* has been formally adopted by the Commission and presented to the European Parliament for its consideration and to the Council for ultimate decision.

Another mechanism used several times by the Commission has been to arrange set-piece 'hearings', usually in Luxembourg, attended by national delegations together with observers from interested organisations and Commission officials. One such event took place in February 1987 for the purpose of identifying the issues to be given priority attention by the Commission in its policy initiatives on libraries. A similar meeting took place in March 1989 when a 'focus meeting' was held in Luxembourg to consider a second draft of the *Plan of action*. In the case of IMPACT II an alternative approach has been adopted. Rather than invite a relatively small number of representatives to Luxembourg Commission officials have toured European capitals in order to obtain expert opinion and advice from more than a thousand experts, specialists and government officials. The detailed results have now been published (I'M, 1989; I'M, 1990)

The net effect has been twofold. First, the informal consultation process and its attendant publicity and professional debate has provoked an increasing awareness of the wider European dimension to library and information issues previously considered only on a national scale. Secondly, it has drawn attention to the opportunities that exist for joint action on an international scale to improve the environment in which libraries operate and allow them to benefit from the latest advances in information technology. Professional representatives have had the opportunity to meet and compare notes with their counterparts in other European countries and to discuss matters of mutual concern in a common European setting. It is likely that as EC involvement in libraries increases so will major policy issues and technological developments be increasingly considered within a cooperative European framework.

Informal consultation between Commission and profession on policy definition has worked well, largely because Commission officials have sought to win widespread support for their proposals by listening to the voice of the profession and involving it at every stage in the preparatory process. However, such is the nature of decision-making in the Community context that crucial decisions about policy content and about finance are taken not by the Commission but by member governments meeting in the Council of Ministers. Consequently, it is essential that the profession has effective channels of communication and cooperative mechanisms not only with the Commission but with appropriate government officials. The *Plan of action* represents the first concerted attempt on the part of the EC to devise a systematic policy and programme for the development of libraries in a European setting. Not surprisingly, therefore, the initiative has demonstrated that existing mechanisms for consultation and policy-making at a more formal government level are not yet ideal for dealing with European issues.

In the United Kingdom consultation with the library profession has been largely achieved through existing structures and channels of communication. Professional bodies such as the Library Association have played a prominent part in representing the views of British librarians at the major meetings held in Luxembourg and have been instrumental in ensuring that individual members of the profession are kept informed of developments. At government level coordination of professional input and feedback on European library policy issues has been largely arranged through the lead department for libraries, the Office of Arts and Libraries (OAL). The principal vehicle of consultation and professional input used by the OAL has been the National Focus on European Library Collaboration, an advisory body established in 1986 for the purpose of providing professional associations, national institutions and other representative bodies with an opportunity to be informed of current developments and to influence policy formation. However, concern has been expressed about the degree to which professional bodies are kept informed by government on European initiatives and the extent to which they can make a positive contribution to policy formation. In reflection of the potential significance of the *Plan of action* the OAL has recently replaced the National Focus with an Advisory Committee for the European Library Plan, whose membership consists of individuals invited to participate by the Minister for the Arts or nominated by the Secretaries of State for Scotland, Wales and Northern Ireland, together with representation from the Library Association and SCONUL and secretarial services provided by the British Library Research and Development Department. Although an initiative of this kind is welcome, it remains to be seen whether the Advisory Committee, which is also discussed by Beauchamp in Chapter 4, can ensure an adequate level of professional input into decision-making processes.

New management mechanisms with appropriate professional input will become even more essential when the *Plan of action* has obtained official approval and is ready for implementation. Although, if usual practice is followed, the Commission will be assisted by an advisory committee of government officials, a programme steering committee and *ad hoc* groups of experts to advise on the selection and ultimate evaluation of individual projects, it seems possible that project proposals in relation to at least some action lines will have to pass through a national sifting process before being considered by the Commission. In such circumstances a national coordinating body to publicise and provide

Handbook of Library Cooperation

advice to institutions and individuals on research opportunities, to guarantee a suitable level of professional input into selection procedures and to ensure the development of a consistent and coordinated national approach will be essential.

Moreover, despite the fact that the Commission has invested considerable time and effort over the years in building up a complex web of contacts and consultation procedures with professional associations and representative organisations of many kinds, the evidence suggests that new consultative mechanisms are likely to be required if the library and information profession is to make its voice heard effectively, clearly and consistently in Brussels and Luxembourg. The professional response to the *Plan of action* has been predominantly channelled through existing professional organisations and committees on a national level. What is clearly required is a representative body at a European level which is able to enter into a regular dialogue with Community officials, providing both input into policy-forming processes and feedback to the constituent members in each member country on matters of current concern and action. Only then will the voice of the profession be heard effectively not only on research and development issues but also upon an increasing number of additional policy issues which affect libraries such as VAT on books, copyright law and the harmonisation of professional qualifications.

Implementation of the Plan

The *Plan of action* has caused great excitement in the library world and been positively welcomed by the European library profession. Although it has raised expectations which budgetary constraint may yet prove difficult to realise, it will nevertheless provide a welcome source of additional funds for research and related activities and establish trends and patterns of cooperation which will form a basis for future development.

In the first instance, it is likely that the funds ultimately made available through the *Plan of action* will be both limited and over-subscribed. The exact amount of money made available by the EC varies from one research programme to another, with ESPRIT by far the largest current programme with a budget of 1,600 million ECU. IMPACT I had a total budget of 36 million ECU for a two year period, whilst the first draft of the *Plan of action* envisaged a budget of 33 million ECU over five

European Communities

years, later revised upwards to 95 million ECU as a result of professional pleading, only for the latest news to suggest that the eventual outcome is likely to be nearer the original figure after all. It should also be remembered that since EC research and development programmes are principally carried out on the basis of shared cost contracts prospective researchers will be expected in most cases to find half the costs, raising the prospect of the OAL being the principal source of matching funds. Financial powers of this kind would effectively give the OAL a validating function for British research proposals – strengthening the argument for the coordinating body mentioned earlier in this Chapter.

It should also be noted that EC research funds are specifically targeted on research priorities established first in a medium-term strategic plan or 'framework programme' (Council Decision 87/516/EEC), then more precisely in multi-annual programmes, funds from which are subsequently disbursed to individual projects on the basis of international competitive tendering processes. It follows, therefore, that the EC will not become a general source of research funding for libraries; finance will be focussed upon a small number of priority areas relevant to overall policy objectives. The following five action lines were originally proposed as a basis for selecting projects for support within the *Plan of action:*

i) Library source data projects – in the field of machine-readable national bibliography and union catalogues and including the retrospective conversion of catalogues of internationally important collections

ii) Projects to further the international linking of systems holding such source data for specific library functions, and thus foster the development and application of a range of international standards

iii) Projects to stimulate the provision of innovative library services using new information technologies

iv) Projects to encourage the development and production of prototypes of new technology-based products, services and tools specifically for libraries and their more efficient management

v) Projects to stimulate exchanges of experience and dissemination of knowledge between those responsible for libraries in Member States and provision of targeted support for the preparation of projects under the other action plans

However, it should be noted that final decisions on both research priorities and the allocation of funds between them has yet to be decided by the Council. Indeed, at the time of writing it seems likely that the whole initiative will in fact be subsumed within a much broader telematics research programme (which clearly indicates the orientation which the final plan is likely to display) and that projects under the fifth action line will be accommodated within other training and mobility programmes. Whatever the final outcome, it may be assumed that the projects chosen will typically be large-scale projects of international significance concerned with the application of new information technology and carried out by multinational research teams.

Funds have, in fact, already been made available in advance of the main programme for preparatory state-of-the-art studies, comparative reviews and national reports. For instance, a series of national reports on the extent to which new information technologies were being applied in libraries was prepared in the aftermath of the Council Resolution of 1985. Often referred to as LIB-2, the United Kingdom report was prepared jointly by the Library Technology Centre at the Polytechnic of Central London and the Library Association. Additional preparatory studies undertaken at this time included *A study of the library economics of the EC*, by Phillip Ramsdale (Office for Official Publications, 1988. EUR11546).

Further research of this kind will no doubt be financed. However, the majority of funds will probably be directed towards pilot and demonstration projects designed to test the feasibility of new concepts, products and processes made possible by new developments in relation to information technology.

Future trends

Direct EC involvement in libraries is a story which has barely begun. The Commission has made specific proposals which have passed through the initial consultative phase and are currently going through the tortuous and sometimes lengthy EC decision-making process at government level. Given that EC decision-making is largely based upon consensus and compromise, the final outcome is likely to be no more than a modest step in the right direction. However, whatever the ultimate shape of the programme and size of the budget, experience in other areas has demonstrated that EC research and development programmes provide a powerful incentive to international collaboration and cooperation by providing both resources and infrastructure for the conduct of large scale projects of an international dimension which it would otherwise be difficult to finance and organise. The library and information sector is likely to enjoy a similar experience.

Although detailed predictions are not appropriate at a time when the exact composition of the programme has yet to be finalised, it is clear that the upgrading of library and information structures demanded by the new information society is expected to be achieved principally by the application of new technologies in libraries and by enhanced international cooperation and resource sharing. As has already been mentioned earlier, EC concern is not for libraries *per se*, but for their potential contribution to an overriding imperative to improve the competitiveness and profitability of European industry. Consequently, EC involvement is likely to be concentrated in the first instance upon those areas in which information technology can make the most tangible contribution to these wider economic objectives. It is also intended that EC initiatives make a considerable impact upon national and regional disparities in relation to technological development. Library systems which are relatively under-developed in relation to the use of information technology will be given a boost whilst those which are more advanced will be encouraged to exploit information technology for the purpose of introducing innovative library services and developing new technology-based products, services and tools.

Such are the criteria likely to be used in the selection of projects for support that implementation of the *Plan of action* is bound to provide a powerful stimulus to library cooperation. The shared exploitation or pooling of resources in order to enjoy their cost-effective use and economies of scale across national boundaries will be encouraged and joint submissions from cooperating partners in two or more member countries for projects which demonstrably serve cooperation either directly or indirectly will attract particular favour. Libraries may also find themselves involved in projects with partners not only in different member countries but also different library sectors, or with partners who might be publishers, booksellers, library system suppliers or private consultants, thereby building up networks of contacts and new cooperative infrastructures.

Support for technological development and cooperative action will be both welcome and predictable given overall EC research and development policies. However, EC priorities do not necessarily provide an entirely satisfactory basis for the overall development of international library cooperation in Europe. Indeed, such is the notorious independence with which individual directorates-general operate that there are developments which affect libraries taking place elsewhere in the European Commission but which play no part in the *Plan of action for libraries.* DG X (Information, Communication and Culture), for instance, is currently in process of developing a cultural policy which includes the promotion of books and reading, whilst action in other areas includes book prices, copyright and the harmonisation of professional qualifications.

Such is the structure of policy formation within the EC that there is a danger that EC library policy might develop on a partial, uneven and fragmented basis. In this context it is vital that the voice of the profession be heard and that it has the opportunity to participate with EC officials and with member governments in the development of a comprehensive policy framework within which individual policy strands and actions are coordinated and make a valid contribution to the achievement of agreed policy objectives.

It is also clear that national, regional and local library planning will need in future to take due note of the wider European context and that greater consideration will need to be given to the scope for international resource sharing and cooperation in the achievement of long term library and information planning objectives. At a very practical level, for instance, the fact that government funds are likely to be required to match finance provided under the *Plan of action* for library projects in the United Kingdom, means that there must be close correlation between national and EC planning priorities if resources are to be used in the most productive and cost-effective manner. Indeed, the need to consider priorities in a wider European context may well stimulate more effective planning mechanisms at the national level than have hitherto characterised government library and information policy.

However, the full benefits of European involvement in library and information affairs will be dissipated unless there are proper mechanisms able to harness and channel action on both a national and European level. In both parts of this Chapter reference has been made to the lack of a strong central focus for professional involvement and cooperation, be it at the operational level in relation to the provision of information on EC affairs, or at a higher policy level in relation to research and other developmental activities. The eventual adoption of the *Plan of action* and the prospect of an additional source of library finance is likely to provide the trigger that will provoke the emergence of new consultative machinery and other means of cooperation and collaboration between the three principal actors, government, EC and library profession.

At a national level, a coordinating body with sufficient standing and powers to provide strong leadership, a sense of direction and a suitable platform for the views of the profession to have a direct input into decision and policy making processes is required. The Advisory Committee is a useful start but in the long-term a body similar in stature to the Library and Information Services Council (LISC) might be required. Such a body would not only provide a focal point for library cooperation and coordination in relation to the EC, but also have useful by-products in terms of national library structures. Common European interests would in this forum take precedence over purely national differences – which would, for instance, help break down barriers between different library sectors, encourage greater cooperation between professional associations and provoke closer collaboration between government and the library and information profession.

At a European level the onus is on the library and information profession to organise itself in such a way as to be able to open up a regular and effective dialogue with Community officials. Representative bodies of many kinds, including trade, commercial and professional associations, have established outposts in Brussels for the purpose of representing the views of their members to EC officials and relaying information back to national organisations. Most such Euro-groups are small, with limited resources and part-time secretariats dependent on input from national associations at a policy and technical level. However, they play a vital role by informing, lobbying and generally providing expert input into the policy processes which take place on an almost continuous basis. If the library profession is to make an effective impact on EC policy then there is need for the rapid emergence of a European level library voice able to speak to national and EC officials with authority not only in relation to the *Plan of action* but also in an increasing number of associated areas. Such a body would need to include representation from all member countries and, ideally, represent all major shades of opinion and library sectors – the ultimate challenge for library cooperation posed by EC involvement in the affairs of libraries!

REFERENCES

Council Decision 84/567/EEC of 27 November 1984 on a Community programme for the development of the specialised information market in Europe (*Official Journal of the European Communities*, L314, 4.12.1984 p. 19).

Council Decision 87/516/EEC of 28 September 1987 concerning the framework programme for Community activities in the field of research and technological development (1987 to 1991) (*Official Journal of the European Communities*, L302, 24.10.1987, p. 1). Information on the contents of the third framework programme for the years 1990 to 1994 has been published in the *Official Journal of the European Communities*, L117, 8.5.1990, p. 28.

Council Decision 88/524/EEC of 26 July 1988 concerning the establishment of a plan of action for setting up an information services market (*Official Journal of the European Communities*, L288, 21.10.1988, p. 39).

Directory of European Documentation Centres, Depository Libraries and European Reference Centres in the United Kingdom and Republic of Ireland (1989), compiled by Mike Cooper. Association of EDC Librarians.

Hopkins, M. (1989), The EC Plan of Action for Libraries in context. *Outlook on Research Libraries,* vol. 11, no. 8, (August), pp. 2-6.

I'M (1989), *Information Market* 59, October–November. DG XIII (Telecommunications, Information Industries and Innovation).

I'M (1990), *Information Market* 60, December–February. DG XIII (Telecommunications, Information Industries and Innovation).

Resolution on collaboration between libraries in the field of data processing (1985). (*Official Journal of the European Communities*, C271, 23.10.85, p. 1).

4

The Government role in cooperation

Peter Beauchamp

For the observer of Government, recent public library history has been notable on three counts: the prolonged tenure in office of the responsible English Minister (The Rt Hon Richard Luce MP) from 1985–90, a high profile for public libraries, and a greatly increased emphasis by Government on library cooperation.

Of course, the fundamental pressures promoting further cooperation are no different now from what they always were. It has always been a question of making the best use of available resources. Contrary to popular opinion, the problem for public libraries in recent years has not been so much a simple reduction in resources, but the desire, or need, to make available resources stretch over an ever-widening range of services. Cooperation is one of the keys to unlocking this problem.

The purpose of this Chapter is to examine why and how library cooperation assumed a more important role in the eyes of Government. Cooperation cannot provide any simple answers to the problem of inadequate resources, but it may help to stretch them further.

IN THE BEGINNING

There is no simple starting point for the change of emphasis.

For many years in the past, it was assumed that disparities in levels of service, and the growing awareness of the need for inter-dependence, could be satisfied solely by voluntary cooperation. The National Central Library and the Regional Library Bureaux, established following the

Kenyon Report (Board of Education, 1927), were achievements in this tradition. Since the 1940s, however, the inability of the existing patchwork of library services to provide speedy access to scientific and technical information has resulted in increasing Government involvement.

One important product of Government interest was the establishment of a centrally provided and administered service – the National Lending Library for Science and Technology – which subsequently expanded to cover social sciences and the humanities. Other centrally provided services, such as the Office for Scientific and Technical Information (now the British Library Research and Development Department) and the British National Bibliography, also emerged to plug gaps in provision and to support and strengthen existing systems.

The Public Libraries and Museums Act 1964 was a step towards eliminating some of the more glaring disparities in the provision of public library services, while the British Library Act 1972 greatly strengthened the support available to libraries from central institutions. In 1974, the Inter-Departmental Coordinating Committee for Scientific and Technical Information (ICCSTI) was created within Government to harmonise the information activities of departments and agencies, both at home and abroad.

SEEDS OF CHANGE

At the end of the 1970s, three reports were published, from the House of Commons Expenditure Committee (1978), the Library Advisory Council (England) (Future development..., 1982) and the House of Commons Select Committee on Education, Science and the Arts (1980). They resulted in significant changes in the way that Government dealt with library matters, including cooperation.

House of Commons Expenditure Committee

The Eighth Report of the House of Commons Expenditure Committee (1978) discussed, *inter-alia*, provision for libraries, and drew particularly upon evidence which had been submitted by the Library Association and the Standing Conference of National and University Libraries (SCONUL). This evidence suggested inadequate arrangements for cooperation among libraries of all kinds. The Committee's main recommendation was that the Department of Education and Science should establish a committee 'to examine as a matter of urgency the whole relationship between the Department, national, public, university, and other libraries, and library advisory councils'. The role of this body would be to achieve coordination in library policy, resources and services. When the report of the Expenditure Committee was published, the Library Advisory Council for England had already appointed a working party to undertake a comprehensive review of the factors which would influence the future development of the country's library service. The Government decided that, rather than set up an independent committee, it would look to the Library Advisory Council to undertake the study called for by the Expenditure Committee. The task was accepted by the Council.

Library Advisory Council (England)

Subsequently, the Library Advisory Council for England issued its first report on the future development of libraries in 1979 (Future development..., 1982). It was concerned with 'the organisational and policy framework within which libraries of all kinds will be able to cooperate most efficiently and effectively in a coordinated library service, giving particular attention to the roles of central government institutions and the Library Advisory Council'.

The Council's proposals envisaged a greatly strengthened Advisory Council, a more vigorously encouraging attitude by the Government and improved consultations between the Office of Arts and Libraries and relevant organisations. Together, these would make possible the cooperative use of resources, which the Council regarded as essential for the development of improved services.

The Government accepted in principle most of the report's recommendations and undertook to explore the scope for their implementation. It is interesting that the Government's response was first made known at the 1980 joint conference of the Library Association, Aslib and the Institute of Information Scientists (Macfarlane, 1981). This event publicly demonstrated the developments which had led to the reports under consideration; the growing together of library and information services of all kinds, allied with the need for cooperation and coordination to ensure improved services and the best use of existing resources.

Select Committee on Education, Science and the Arts

After the Library Advisory Council's report was published, attention became focussed on the need for a similar measure of coordination throughout the whole field of information provision. A report on this subject, issued in 1980 by the House of Commons Select Committee on Education, Science and the Arts, called for the appointment of a Minister with specific responsibility for information policy, and of a Standing Commission 'to examine on a continuing basis the problems of developing a national information network' and to make proposals (House of Commons: Select Committee on Education, Science and the Arts, 1980).

In response, the Government decided that these responsibilities should be undertaken by the Minister for the Arts (except when they fell within a defined Departmental interest) and by the Library Advisory Council, which already advised the Minister for the Arts on a wide range of matters in the information field. The Government said that it would review and extend as appropriate the membership and functions of the Library Advisory Council, and, accordingly, it was later renamed the Library and Information Services Council (Department of Education and Science, 1981).

Thus, the building bricks were in place and the scene was set for an increased Government interest in library cooperation.

GOVERNMENT OBJECTIVES IN THE 1980s

Under the Public Libraries and Museums Act 1964, library authorities have a duty to provide 'a comprehensive and efficient library service for all persons desiring to make use thereof...' The Minister for the Arts has statutory responsibility under the same Act for the public library service in England and his duties include:

- superintending and promoting the improvement of the public library service (in England)
- securing the proper discharge by local authorities of the functions conferred on them in relation to libraries

There is wide variation in the ways that authorities attempt to fulfil these duties but the general picture is one of expanding demand, and of an expectation on the part of library authorities that they will be enabled to extend the range and quality of their services in response to it. A major strand of the Government's response has been to promote the more efficient use of resources, and the development of improved services through cooperation between libraries of all kinds and through joint ventures with the private sector.

Office of Arts and Libraries (OAL)

In order to achieve these objectives, the Office of Arts and Libraries has developed two short term targets:

- to provide an incentive scheme for promoting new development
- to encourage plans for coordinating the provision of library and information services of different kinds within a geographical area

A medium term target has been to promote collaboration with the private sector.

Library and Information Services Council (LISC)

The Minister for the Arts is advised on library and information matters by the Library and Information Services Council. Its statutory basis is set out in the Public Libraries and Museums Act 1964:

> 'to advise the Secretary of State upon such matters connected with the provision or use of library facilities whether under this Act or otherwise as they think fit and upon any questions referred to them by him.'

In the years that followed, however, the Council had never been given specific and formal terms of reference.

During the 1980s, the developing role of the Council, coupled with the absence of formal terms of reference, led to uncertainty about the Council's scope and powers. As a result, in 1985, the Minister for the Arts set out formal terms of reference for the Council (Report by the Minister for the Arts on library and information matters during 1985, 1986). They included:

- to provide guidance, advice and comment on library and information matters for the providers and users of the relevant services, and to promote consultation and cooperation between them

In the context of the Government's view of the role of the Library and Information Services Council, set out in the Report by the Minister for the Arts on library and information matters during 1983 (1984):

'not only to give me advice on specific issues, but to act as a catalyst to national debate and to articulate concern in a way which can be helpful to all those involved in decision-making at local and national levels'

it will be seen that another powerful voice for cooperation was in place at the centre. And, indeed, it was the Library and Information Services Council that led the way.

WORKING TOGETHER

Challenge of the Library and Information Services Council

As early as 1980, the Council had established a second working party on future development; it was asked to consider the objectives of libraries and information services of all kinds, and the scope for enhancing and supporting the library and information network and for making better use of available resources. This scope was to include the application of new technology, and improved forms of cooperation at local, regional and national levels. The report of the working party was published with the approval of the Minister for the Arts in 1982 (Future development..., 1982).

The underlying philosophy of the report was the achievement of cooperation and coordination through an evolutionary approach, and many recommendations for action to assist in this process were put forward. Most were concerned with local management rather than national policy, but the report also reviewed the future pattern of information services, the impact of new technology – including the development of electronic publishing – and discussed aspects of the funding of library and information services. The report assumed that it would be the policy of Government to continue to respect the existing autonomy of institutions in regard to the allocation of resources in the library and information field, but to expect and encourage them nevertheless to work together to improve their services as a whole. The objectives of such cooperation would be to ensure maximum value from the resources available, and this could involve new methods of sharing.

The report contained an early hint of the Library and Information Plan concept by pointing out that local authorities were particularly well placed to further coordination among the libraries and information services for which they were responsible:

> 'the extent to which these services are at present coordinated varies widely, and we invite local authorities to consider whether it could advantageously be increased.'

The local authority associations invited the assistance of the Office of Arts and Libraries, which responded by commissioning a series of case studies designed to provide detailed information on the actual level of, and arrangements for, current cooperation and coordination of library and information services within a number of library authorities. At the conclusion of the case studies, a summary report was published (Edmonds, 1986).

The good and bad features of existing cooperation and coordination were highlighted by the report, which went on to discuss ways of future development, including the role of the Office of Arts and Libraries and of public library authorities. The report also noted the feeling among a number of librarians that greater publicity should be given to local cooperative activities which might usefully be tried elsewhere, and that it would be beneficial for information on cooperative successes – and failures – to be made more widely available.

Planning and partnership

In 1983, the Library and Information Services Council decided to take forward again its work on the future development of libraries and information services and established another working party – widely known afterwards as FD3 – with wide terms of reference, the essence of which were to consider how library and information services of all kinds could best go forward together.

The report of the working party was published early in 1986 (Future development..., 1986). It expressed the same fundamental convictions as the two earlier reports on future development: that library and information services are a national heritage and require a conscious national effort to maintain them; and that this heritage cannot be fully exploited unless provision is coordinated nationally and locally.

The report had two themes. The first was that those responsible for funding and managing library and information services were more able than central Government to determine the quality and range of provision. The second was that library and information services now needed not merely to supplement informal cooperation by more deliberately planned relationships, but also to contract together within a 'Library and Information Plan' to provide services which would make the maximum possible use of resources.

LIBRARY AND INFORMATION PLANS (LIPs)

A new concept

The Library and Information Plan concept is of a five-year management plan, drawn up by a local authority responsible for library services under the Public Libraries and Museums Act 1964. All the library and information services in the authority's area (the public library, academic libraries and other library and information services in the public sector, as well as the industrial, commercial, professional and other library and information services in the private sector) would review what they currently provided and what they wanted to achieve. With this as a base line, they would agree how they could, in their own individual interests, contract with each other to make the best use of the resources in the area. All would negotiate to get what they wanted, to supply what they wished, free or at a charge, for the benefit of their users.

Purpose

The purpose of a Library and Information Plan is to maximise the benefits obtainable from the total library and information resources in a local library authority area; to concentrate the attention of the services on problems and opportunities which should be dealt with locally; and to identify issues which need to be considered at a higher level.

Benefits of Library and Information Plans

The Library and Information Services Council (Future development..., 1986) envisaged three major benefits arising from the preparation of plans:

- they would cause services to review and decide their priorities in the light of users' needs, the views of their governing bodies, and the total resources available
- they would allow services to rely on the undertakings given them by the other parties to the plan
- they could be the framework for new developments, such as the formation of electronic enquiry networks, or closer business associations between providers of other goods and services in either the public or private sector

Introduction of Library and Information Plans

The Library and Information Plan concept had been successfully tested and introduced in one authority, Cambridgeshire, on behalf of the Library and Information Services Council working party prior to its report. Thereafter, to encourage the production of Library and Information Plans, the Office of Arts and Libraries and the British Library Research and Development Department agreed to provide up to £40,000 each to support a few selected authorities, working under a variety of conditions and representing a geographical spread, to produce plans that could act as case study material. Authorities receiving support were required to at least match the amount of the grant, although the total committed by recipients has in fact been more than double that available from central funds.

Applications were invited from all public library authorities in England – Scotland, Wales and Northern Ireland falling outside the Office of Arts and Libraries' sphere of interest – and a selection panel was established. The panel selected the following authorities to receive grants: Leicestershire County Council, the Northern Regional Library System (with the counties of Cleveland, Durham and Northumberland), and Staffordshire County Council. Work on these three plans began in the spring of 1987.

At the same time, a move to a second round of awards commenced, and local authorities were again asked to indicate their interest. From thirteen positive responses, the panel selected the following authorities for grants: Bradford Metropolitan Council, Hereford and Worcester County Council with Gloucestershire County Council, LADSIRLAC (the Liverpool and District Scientific, Industrial and Research Library Advisory Council), Sheffield City Council, and WANDPETLS (Wandsworth Public, Educational and Technical Library Services).

As well as this main programme, there were other grants to support the establishment of Library and Information Plans. The British Library Research and Development Department has given funds to Bedfordshire and Buckinghamshire and to the Library and Information Services Council (Northern Ireland) for the preparation of plans, and to the Library and Information Services Committee (Scotland) for a feasibility study on a plan in the Fife Region. It has also funded small projects to look at the information needs of ethnic minorities organisations (Leicestershire County Council), and to consider generally the impact of Library and Information Plans on existing cooperative library and information systems (Standing Conference of Cooperative Library and Information Services). There are also, at present, plans being developed in other authorities without outside funding (Berkshire, the Black Country).

Current situation

It is clear that the Library and Information Plan programme has aroused interest among a wide range of information providers and library users; over 20% of England's population is now served by plans. The positive results already appearing are, for example, closer working relationships between bodies in the public and voluntary sectors, directories of local resources, union lists of local serials, and joint staff training courses. From now on, without dedicated central funding, the means and speed of implementing plans will vary even more according to local circumstances. However, the Public Library Development Incentive Scheme (PLDIS) can be used to finance important initiatives arising from Library and Information Plans.

An important example of this is the development of Information North as the agency for taking forward a regional Library and Information Plan. Information North has taken over the existing services of the Northern Regional Library System, but has a much wider remit, and its role is analogous to Northern Arts. Its aim is to encourage and develop the coordination and planning of public and private sector information services in the Northern Region, in order to support general economic growth; stimulate innovation within the information sector; improve the value for money of a wide range of library services for which charges may be made; and enhance the marketing of existing information services bringing together providers and customers.

The broad objectives of Information North are to operate a cooperative venture, jointly entered into by libraries and information providing organisations in all sectors, which maximises access to information by acting as an information broker; to capitalise on strengths, remedy weaknesses and link information providers in creative ways to benefit new groups of users; to collaborate closely with regional agencies concerned with economic regeneration, planning and development; and to provide a model for the coordination of library and information services for other areas.

The intentions of Information North are, at the very least, stirring, and its development should be followed with more than passing interest!

Success or failure

Certainly, the establishment of Information North is an important step in the stabilisation and further development of Library and Information Plans. Nevertheless, they will be judged ultimately by the action which results from them, and the real improvements in service to the user which they stimulate. Despite the large amount of work that has been carried out and is still going on, the development of Library and Information Plans remains at an early stage, and there is little as yet to measure in terms of actual achievement. In such circumstances, it is dangerous to attempt to draw any definite conclusions as to whether or not they are likely to achieve their aims.

It is fair to say, however, that they are raising the profile of information and increasing awareness of the range of resources that are available locally, although much remains to be done. The emphasis on the involvement of organisations from all sectors of the community has been important and has demonstrated the ignorance in many areas of the scope of existing services. In only a few cases has there been resistance to the idea of cooperation.

Perhaps, a major contribution, so far, has been to show that informal cooperation is not the most effective way of proceeding when it lacks any element of coordination. It has been the general experience of all those involved up to now that the planning process is as important as its products. In other words, the bringing together of a wide range of participants in a recognised planning framework, with constructive aims, an agreed timetable, and the ability to explore common problems and opportunities is a worthwhile and beneficial development in itself with a far reaching potential for creating a new culture of resources sharing and partnership.

This is in addition to the immediate practical and tangible benefits resulting from the Library and Information Plan process in terms of enhanced services, improved efficiency and economy, and a better return on the total investment in existing services.

The future – evaluation and development

What happens now? There are, of course, areas of the United Kingdom still unaffected by Library and Information Plans and further geographical development can be expected. There is, for example, now talk of a plan for Wales. Among the most exciting developments, however, are sectoral plans. Law librarians and music librarians are considering Library and Information Plans for their sectors and health information has emerged in almost all geographical plans as an area for concern and attention. Sports information has also received some preliminary attention. Some of these initiatives are considered further in Chapter 9.

Meanwhile, during 1990, there was a general review of the benefits arising from Library and Information Plans. The Library and Information Cooperation Council (LINC) has accepted responsibility for the promotion, monitoring, evaluation and development of plans. The work has been contracted to Information North, initially for one year, and the objectives are (Library and Information Cooperation Council, 1990):

- to encourage the development and growth of local, regional, national and sectoral Library and Information Plans, ensuring that momentum is maintained
- to examine the potential for initiating new Library and Information Plans

– to promote the concepts and achievements of Library and Information Plans in enhancing awareness, access and availability of information and in demonstrating coordinated, cost effective delivery of new services to the library and information community

The current Chair of LINC has contributed Chapter 14 to this volume.

INCENTIVE FUNDING

For a number of years, the Library and Information Services Council and the Library Association pressed the Minister for the Arts to provide funds for the promotion of developments in the public library service. When he spoke at the Library Association Annual General Meeting in October 1987 (Library Association, 1987), the Minister said:

> 'We must ... look for new ways of funding library services, in which partnerships can be created between public and private resources, and some taxpayers' money used for pump-priming, to ensure the development of better services for the customer and better value for money.'

There followed, in December 1987, the establishment of the Public Library Development Incentive Scheme (PLDIS) with funding of £250,000 per year for the three years 1988/89 to 1990/91.

Objectives

At the outset, in order to guide applicants, the Minister indicated his own priorities for awards, although, for two years, they were not exclusive. In the light of experience, and advice from the Advisory Committee to the Scheme, there were slight modifications in the second year of competition; but, the broad thrust remained the same and the thread of cooperation ran strongly through the priorities.

The Minister's priorities for awards in the second year of his Scheme were:

(i) Collaborative developments, involving public libraries and library cooperatives, other libraries, or public sector organisations, which for example:

- enable new services to be offered, or existing services to be provided more efficiently and economically for the benefit of users in more than one local authority
- arise from a single or multi-authority Library and Information Plan
- provide new technical, management, or marketing training courses, chiefly for the staff of public library authorities
- provide, mainly for the benefit of public library services, shared resources or shared facilities for library support operations, marketing and market research, arranging sponsorship or other shared activities

(ii) Feasibility and economic studies for new and transferable improvements, for example:

- the delivery of existing public library services
- the contracting out of elements of public library services, including library support activities
- joint public/private sector enterprises involving public library authorities
- income generating services to be provided by public libraries in collaboration with other libraries or private sector organisations

(Public Library Development Incentive Scheme: the second year:1988/89 progress report, 1989)

In the third year of the competition, for awards in 1990/91, there were considerable changes to reflect the Minister's 'post-Green Paper' priorities for the public library service in England. Happily, cooperation survived! and the revised priorities were as follows:

- investigations of the scope for innovations in the effective use of contractors for public library functions or services
- projects arising from Library and Information Plans
- improving the operational efficiency or effectiveness of services through cooperation between public library authorities or with private sector organisations

– establishing innovative revenue earning services, especially through joint ventures

(Public Library Development Incentive Scheme: the third year: 1990/91 competition, 1989)

Proposals could either be made to establish and implement a new development, or to carry out a feasibility study on a possible new development. They could also include any combination of these priority areas.

Eligibility

For the first time, applications were invited from public or private organisations, such as voluntary groups or commercial enterprises, as well as from library authorities or their cooperative agencies. Applications from public or private organisations had to show that the proposed development would contribute to the quality and cost-effectiveness of public library services nationally, or in a particular region.

Awards

The present Scheme is due to finish after the third year. At the time of writing, the awards for the third year have not been announced. However, in the first two years 23 awards were made to thirteen library authorities, two regional library bureaux, one cooperative and one Library and Information Plan.

Effect of the Scheme

There has been continuing interest in, and enthusiasm for, the Scheme, but it is too early to judge its success and to evaluate the full benefits of projects funded with its help. Useful evaluation cannot begin until enough projects have been completed – this will probably be at the completion of the second year's two year projects.

However, the Advisory Committee has already expressed some disappointment about the range and quality of the initial proposals submitted for the second year. Too many of them were for small, rather parochial, projects with little chance of transferability, which the Committee felt should be funded by local authorities themselves. Others were rather vague 'research' studies with no specific application in mind. Certainly, there were too few real cooperative proposals with other library authorities, or with the private sector, and this is also true of the 23 awards.

Future of the Scheme

If the Scheme is continued without changing some of its operational constraints, it is doubtful whether there will be enough worthwhile proposals coming forward to justify money being set aside by the Office of Arts and Libraries. The difficulties for library authorities, which arise partly from the timetable for applications and the scale and length of projects which the Scheme will support, particularly affects proposals for projects involving cooperation with other authorities and the private sector. As a result, many of the projects supported have been for useful marginal developments which, however, are unlikely to bring about major changes in service provision or efficiency. This does not encourage the more forward looking library authorities to make use of the Scheme and may deflate the potential value (especially transferability) of projects. An announcement about the future of the Scheme was expected late in 1990.

COLLABORATION WITH THE PRIVATE SECTOR

Joint enterprise

In 1985, the Library and Information Services Council and the British Library Research and Development Department established a joint working party to examine the potential for greater interaction between the public and the private sectors in the provision of library and information services.

The resulting report, Joint Enterprise, said that the traditional relationships between the public and the private sectors in the information world had developed into genuine interactive cooperation in many areas of activity (Joint enterprise, 1987). Cooperation could develop further, given favourable conditions and the right climate of opinion.

Green Paper on public libraries

This point was picked up by the Minister for the Arts in his Green Paper on Public Libraries (Financing our public library service..., 1988), which contained proposals on joint ventures between the public and private sectors to provide specialised library and information services, and asked for advice on measures to further joint ventures. It was the hope of the Green Paper that the private sector would contribute the marketing and financing skills which most library authorities seemed to lack, and the Minister explained his thinking further when he gave the 4th CLSI Annual Lecture (Luce, 1988):

> 'I believe that joint ventures, collaborative activities by public and private sector bodies, can enable library authorities to expand the range of their services and to supply both basic and charged services more cost effectively. Some such ventures already exist as some of you may already know ... The potential of the joint venture was well illustrated in the excellent report on this subject, Joint Enterprise ... It demonstrates how carefully thought out partnerships can open up new markets, provide better services and give greater value for money.'

The response to this part of the Green Paper was encouraging, with 76 of the 93 library authorities commenting on joint ventures supporting their wider introduction. The Minister replied by announcing to the House of Commons (House of Commons Official Report, 1989):

> 'I will undertake a programme of case studies, provide pump-priming funds for selected schemes through my Public Library Development Incentive Scheme, and look for other cost effective ways of helping possible partners, including voluntary agencies, to get together.'

Action following the Green Paper

Two sets of case studies had been produced for Joint Enterprise; one covering the publishing activities of libraries, and the second dealing with a selection of other joint public/private sector activities in the library and information field. These studies were published separately from Joint Enterprise (Oakeshott and White, 1987).

As part of the action now to increase and broaden interest in joint ventures, and encourage libraries to participate in them, the Office of Arts and Libraries has commissioned a further set of case studies. They will up-date the earlier work and examine new ventures, and information gained in the exercise may be used to produce guidelines of good practice for libraries to follow when embarking on new ventures.

SUPPORTING THE COOPERATIVE INFRASTRUCTURE

There are a number of other ways in which Government gives support to cooperation through various organisations. Not least is its funding of the British Library, and a newcomer to the scene is the Library and Information Cooperation Council (LINC).

The British Library

In 1989, the British Library published its second strategic plan, *Gateway to knowledge*, covering the years 1989–94 (British Library, 1989). The first plan, *Advancing with knowledge*, had been published in 1985 and gave a statement of the Library's central aim, its functional objectives and its key strategies (British Library, 1985).

While the Library's aims and objectives have changed little since 1985, circumstances have altered, and the 1989 Plan:

> 'is written against a background of Government policy which, despite the investment in St. Pancras, steadily withdraws support from us. We have been told that the real value of the grant-in-aid will continue to decline for the next three years and almost certainly longer. At the same time, we expect salary increases, and a continuing steep rise in book and serial prices. The Library which moves into St. Pancras will inevitably be leaner than the present British Library.'

Certainly, in the ten year period up to 1988–89, the Government's grant-in-aid to the British Library fell by 9.2% in real terms. The Government's Expenditure Plans 1990–91 to 1992–93 hold out little

Government role

hope of improving the situation with the following forecast (in cash terms) for the grant-in-aid (Government's expenditure plans..., 1990):

		£ million
1989–90	estimated outturn	53.6
1990–91	plans	58.0
1991–92	plans	60.0
1992–93	plans	62.4

Nevertheless, included in the British Library's Declaration of Purpose is the need to 'cultivate cooperation with others, in the public and the private sectors, both in this country and abroad'. And, the second strategic plan goes on to say that 'in straitened circumstances, cooperation with others, whether libraries or private sector institutions, is vital if we are to derive maximum value from our combined resources'.

The role of the British Library is dealt with further in Chapter 5.

The Library and Information Cooperation Council

The Library and Information Cooperation Council (LINC) (mentioned earlier in this Chapter) was established in 1989 to replace the National Committee on Regional Library Cooperation, and to continue and develop its work. This arose directly from a recommendation in the Library and Information Services Council report, *Progress through planning and partnership*, that the National Committee should accept the challenge of undertaking a more active and positive role in furthering library and information cooperation (Future development..., 1986).

In the intervening period, both the Office of Arts and Libraries and the British Library provided money to support the necessary review of objectives, and the constitutional and financial arrangements. As a founder member, the Office of Arts and Libraries makes a grant to the Library and Information Cooperation Council to assist with its running costs.

The objective of the Council is to promote cooperation and partnership as a means of improving the effectiveness of the library and information sector in the United Kingdom and Republic of Ireland.

In order to attain its objective, the Library and Information Cooperation Council intends to review, encourage and facilitate all types of library and information cooperation between the British Library, the regional library systems and other organisations and institutions in the library and information community. It proposes to act as a forum for the exchange of views on cooperation by holding meetings and seminars, and to collect and disseminate information on library and information cooperation.

The Council will represent the interests of library and information cooperation to the Office of Arts and Libraries, the Scottish Education Department, the Welsh Office, and the Department of Education Northern Ireland, as well as other interested bodies regionally and nationally.

The establishment of the Council, and its intention, is a significant step forward in the development of national library cooperation. With its wide remit and constituency, the Library and Information Cooperation Council is well placed to develop, encourage, assist and monitor library cooperation at the national level. It should become a leading player on the stage of library cooperation.

As for an immediate programme of work, an action plan for 1990 covers the following areas (Library and Information Cooperation Council, 1990):

- promoting Library and Information Plans
- examining the impact of information technology on interlending
- performance indicators: a review
- cooperative services for ethnic minorities: a review
- the Attenborough report (Arts and disabled people, 1985)
- Joint Fiction Reserve
- cooperation with the International Association of Music Librarians
- European Community initiatives
- new dimensions in audiovisual
- statistics – getting more out of them

Other plans include establishing a database of information on library and information cooperation to facilitate the management of future activities. Information will be disseminated by means of a newsletter, annual report, articles and information in the professional press, and publications. The conclusion to this volume has been contributed by Norman Higham, current Chair of LINC.

Liaison between the national library/information advisory bodies in England, Scotland, Wales and Northern Ireland

It will have been seen that the English Library and Information Services Council has had considerable influence on library cooperation! There are similar advisory bodies concerned with library and information matters in Scotland, Wales and Northern Ireland. The English Council's first report on future development, *The organisational and policy framework*, advocated a closer relationship between all four bodies (Future development..., 1982). In consequence, in the period after 1981, there were regular – once or twice a year – meetings of representatives of the four bodies.

The meetings were successful in promoting an exchange of information, but less so in promoting joint action or the coordination of business. Nevertheless, at a meeting held in 1984, it was unanimously agreed that there was a need for greater, and more regular, cooperation between the four advisory bodies, both as an effective focus for United Kingdom interests, and to avoid duplication of work, while at the same time respecting genuine national interests within the Kingdom. With the assistance of the responsible Government Departments, revised arrangements for future cooperation between the four bodies were agreed. These were to centre on annual meetings of the chairmen and supporting officials in order to discuss future programmes of work and potential cooperation; in addition, observers from each body would be able to attend working parties of the others (Report by the Minister for the Arts on library and information matters during 1985, 1986).

Meetings of the chairmen began in 1985 and have continued since on a regular basis. Progress is slow, but significant. One positive result has been that the English working party on public library objectives, established in 1989, includes representatives of the other countries, and the result should be a manual acceptable to each of the countries.

INTERNATIONAL ASPECTS

One area in which the Minister for the Arts holds a brief to represent the library and information interests of the United Kingdom as a whole is that of international matters, and especially those of the European Community. Consultative arrangements have been traditionally centred on the Inter-Departmental Coordinating Committee for Scientific and Technical Information (ICCSTI), but this body is being overtaken by the Advisory Committee for the European Library Plan (ACELP).

Inter-Departmental Coordinating Committee for Scientific and Technical Information

The Committee was established in 1974 to harmonise in a formal way the responsibilities of Government for scientific and technical information, which had been traditionally spread between various departments and agencies. Until 1981, responsibility for the Committee rested with the science branches of the Department of Education and Science. In that year, however, reflecting the new information role of the Minister for the Arts, responsibility was transferred to the Office of Arts and Libraries. Membership of the Committee consisted primarily of representatives from departments and agencies of Government, but was widened in the mid-1980s to include the Confederation of Information and Communication Industries, the Library Association, Aslib, the Institute of Information Scientists, the Association of Database Producers and the Standing Conference of National and University Libraries. The significance of this was the implicit recognition by Government that it could no longer be the sole provider of briefing about the British interest. In the annual report of the Library and Information Services Council for 1985 (Report by the Minister for the Arts on library and information matters during 1985, 1986), the responsibilities of the Inter-Departmental Coordinating Committee for Scientific and Technical Information were described as:

- to keep under review the ways in which scientific and technical information service functions of Government are performed, and to provide a forum for interdepartmental cooperation
- to help secure the fullest possible benefit to the United Kingdom from international scientific and technical information activities, particularly in the European Community

During the 1980s, however, the Committee devoted its energies almost exclusively to its international role, dealing with the European Community plan for the development of the specialised information market and acting as the briefing forum for the United Kingdom delegates

Government role

to the European Commission Committee on Information and Documentation for Science and Technology (CIDST).

During 1982, the Committee decided to divide itself into two separate committees, dealing respectively with domestic and European affairs. In practice, this seems to have been a formalisation of existing procedures and had little effect on membership. In retrospect, however, it seems also to have been a recognition of the growing importance of the international role and a difficulty in finding domestic issues to discuss; so it proved, and the 'domestic Committee' has not met since the end of 1982. Its very last action, in 1983, was failing to agree on a response to the ITAP report, *Making a business of information* (Cabinet Office, 1983).

Although the 'European Committee' remains formally in being, it has little business at present – mirroring to some extent a similar lack of activity in the Committee on Information and Documentation for Science and Technology – and has been overtaken by the establishment of the Advisory Committee for the European Library Plan.

The Advisory Committee for the European Library Plan

Since 1985, library cooperation has been high on the agenda of the European Community. In that year, Member State Ministers with responsibility for Cultural Affairs passed a resolution on 'Collaboration between libraries in the field of data processing'. This has led to the preparation by the Commission of a draft *Plan of action for libraries in the EC* (1987) which has been widely circulated among the library and information community for comment and advice.

The Plan envisages action in four key areas:

- availability of catalogue/bibliographic records in machine-readable form as a basic resource for international exchanges
- ability to interconnect automated library systems
- better access to documents held in European libraries through enhanced interlibrary loans mechanisms
- modernising the skills of library workers

The Plan has not yet been formally submitted to the Governments of Member States, but it seems to be a useful initiative. It may have to be revised in order to fit into the R & D Framework programme from which it is likely to be funded. There is clearly scope for cooperation between major libraries in the Community on improved access to scarce material, shared responsibility for conservation and better support services. However, the effective advantages to United Kingdom libraries are not quite so clear at this stage and the Government will be looking to the four national library/information advisory bodies for advice.

When the Plan was first developed, the Office of Arts and Libraries established a National Focus specifically to handle and coordinate United Kingdom input to the Plan, and to act as a channel of communication. The Focus was composed of representatives from all identifiable national library cooperative organisations. They have now recommended that the Minister should establish a different kind of body, based largely upon experts, selected for their broad knowledge of library operations and services and the application of new technology to them, rather than institutional representation; there will, however, still be some allowance for institutional representation, namely the Library Association and the Standing Conference of National and University Libraries.

The Minister has accepted the importance of the new machinery being in place as soon as the Plan is formally received by the Government, and the new body, the Advisory Committee for the European Library Plan, is in the process of establishment. Its first responsibilities will be to recommend action by the Minister on the Plan and to produce a more vigorous approach to encouraging ideas about projects which might be funded under the Plan.

The following is a list of the main functions which will need to be carried out to ensure effective United Kingdom participation in the Library Plan:

- ensuring that the major library institutions and others are able to inform themselves of the opportunities open to them through the Plan, the European Commission's criteria for support of projects and any specific calls for proposals that it may publish
- stimulating proposals which will be particularly useful to the United Kingdom and, at the same time, contribute to the Commission's objectives for the Plan; and encouraging United Kingdom organisations to cooperate together in preparing proposals and in approaching libraries in other Member-States about proposals
- briefing and debriefing of the United Kingdom delegates to the main Advisory Committee for the Plan (appointed by the

Government), and of United Kingdom experts participating in the expert groups set up by the Commission. Although the experts will be nominated by the Government, advice will be needed on their selection, and for any other meetings where the Commission seeks advice on who it should invite
- advising, if asked, co-funders on projects, both generally and using criteria drawn up by the Commission
- providing for the Commission a national filtering mechanism for proposals. This may involve them all being sent to a central point and evaluated against an agreed set of criteria reflecting the Commission's own concerns about eligibility. A set of criteria will need to be drawn up, agreed and made available to applicants. Feed-back to unsuccessful applicants will be necessary and an opportunity to resubmit within the timescale of the Commission arranged

The Advisory Committee for the European Library Plan will need to ensure that all of these functions are carried out, but will be free to decide that some of them can be delegated.

Although in the library and information field, nothing much will happen automatically in 1992 in Europe, more and more initiatives in this field are emanating from the European Community. In the words of George Cunningham (1990):

'there can be no doubt that European cooperation is here to stay; that we ignore it at our peril; and that it is better to influence decisions before they are taken than to try to undo them afterwards.'

CONCLUSION

At this stage in 1990, there are a number of loose ends. Apart from the future of the Public Library Development Incentive Scheme and developments arising from the European Library Plan, there is further work in the Library and Information Services Council that may influence the pattern of cooperation.

Role of government

In 1986, the Council established a working party to examine the 'role of government in relation to the coordination of library and information services'. The working party has not found the subject an easy one to investigate because it felt that it would be unrealistic to make any attempt at changing the present pattern of responsibilities for libraries and information services as borne by the Council itself, the Office of Arts and Libraries, and other Government Departments. On the other hand, however, this is exactly what many people expected of the working party.

It was, therefore, not surprising that a draft report from the working party, although accepted by the Library and Information Services Council, has not been well received by those bodies to which it was sent in confidence for comment. The general view seems to be that a valuable opportunity has been lost and that the report does not clarify the role of Government; this is apparently because the main thrust of the report is that acceptance and understanding of the various elements of the present organisational and policy framework is needed if maximum benefit is to be gained from the role of Government.

In these circumstances, it is unlikely that the report on the role of government will be published by the Library and Information Services Council. This is less worrying than it appears because the subject has been partially superseded by another investigation, the 'national framework study'.

National framework

This is an investigation into the feasibility of constructing a model of the interaction between various kinds of library and information organisations. Its starting point is that cooperation is central to the country's library and information network, whereas there is nothing available to show the mutual relationship between various kinds of library and information organisations. How, for example, can any judgement be made about the adequacy of resources for one organisation (or type of organisation) without reference to the (alternative) sources of support?

The model will:

- illustrate (or map) the inter-relationships between library and information organisations, and demonstrate the flow of information between them
- place this map into context by showing transactions with suppliers (including publishers, wholesalers, bookshops and information brokers)
- relate the library and information organisation to the user community served, while recognising different kinds of user, types of use, and geographic locations
- attempt, wherever possible, to quantify these transactions in suitable fiscal or other units of measurement
- provide objective statements concerning the specific purpose and role of each relationship or transaction with rankings or priorities for each, and an indication of uniqueness

This is a potentially exciting development and certainly fundamental to the business of the Library and Information Services Council. Of equal relevance is the 'Glenerin Declaration'.

Glenerin Declaration

This Declaration emerged from the conference on 'Access: information distribution, efficiency and protection' held in 1987 at the Glenerin Inn in Mississauga, Ontario (Access, 1987). It was the third in a series of tri-national meetings convened by the Institute for Research on Public Policy (Canada), the British Library and the National Commission on Libraries and Information Science (USA). The Glenerin Declaration concerns the role of information as a strategic economic resource, requiring unrestricted exchange and some level of equitable distribution. On the matter of cooperation, the Declaration states:

> 'we must foster partnerships amongst all segments of the information sector – workers, information creators, processors, distributors, government and users.'

Thus would individual citizens and society at large be allowed to profit equitably from the development of the information age. Alas, there has been no coherent response in the United Kingdom to the Glenerin initiative, although some attention has been paid to its various themes.

The future?

The next few years will be a testing time for library cooperation. Can the progress and development of the recent decade can be maintained? Can it be built upon? There are loose ends to be tied up, or, perhaps, to form a base for further development. At this stage, it remains to be seen what will be the effect on Government attitudes to library cooperation of the appointment of the new Minister for the Arts, The Rt Hon Tim Renton MP. Political priorities can change rapidly, and there will in any case have to be another General Election no later than the early summer of 1992. It is difficult to imagine, however, that now or then there could be a wholesale reversal of events. And yet in 1979 ...

BIBLIOGRAPHY

Access: information distribution, efficiency and protection. A report on a conference held at The Glenerin Inn, Mississauga, Ontario, May 13–15, 1987. Sponsored by the Institute for Research on Public Policy, the British Library and the US National Commission on Libraries and Information Science, in association with the Department of Communications (Government of Canada), the Canada Institute for Scientific and Technical Information and the National Library of Canada. (unpublished report, available from sponsoring bodies).

Arts and disabled people: report of a committee of inquiry under the chairmanship of Sir Richard Attenborough (1985). Carnegie UK Trust/ Bedford Square Press.

Board of Education: Public Libraries Committee (1927), *Report on public libraries in England and Wales*. (The Kenyon Report). HMSO. (Cmd. 2868)

British Library Act 1972. Chapter 54. HMSO.

British Library (1985), *Advancing with knowledge*. British Library.

British Library (1989), *Gateway to knowledge*. British Library.

Cabinet Office: Information Technology Advisory Panel (1983), *Making a business of information: a survey of new opportunities*. HMSO.

Government role

Capital Planning Information (1988), *An outline Library and Information Plan manual*. British Library. (British Library Research Paper 43). (Note: a revised edition was due to be published in 1990).

Cunningham, G. (1990), Libraries, information and Europe. *Journal of Librarianship*, vol. 22, no. 2, (April), pp. 63–70.

Department of Education and Science (1981), Office of Arts and Libraries *New title for Library Advisory Council*. Department of Education and Science. (Arts and Libraries Press Notice, 6 August 1981).

Edmonds, D. J. (1986), *Current library cooperation and coordination*. (Office of Arts and Libraries, Library and Information Series No. 15). HMSO.

Ferris, D. (1988), *Library and Information Plans*. British Library Research and Development Department/Library and Information Technology Centre. (Library and Information Briefings No. 6).

Financing our public library service: four subjects for debate (1988). HMSO. (Cmnd. 324).

The future development of libraries and information services: 1 the organisational and policy framework; 2 working together within a national framework (1982). (Office of Arts and Libraries, Library and Information Series No. 12). HMSO.

The future development of libraries and information services: progress through planning and partnership. Report by the Library and Information Services Council. (1986). (Office of Arts and Libraries, Library and Information Series No. 14). HMSO.

The Government's expenditure plans 1990–91 to 1992–93 (1990). Chapter 12 – Office of Arts and Libraries. HMSO. (Cmnd. 1012).

House of Commons: Expenditure Committee, Session 1977–78 (1978), *Eighth Report. Chapter IV: provision for museums, galleries and libraries*. HMSO. (HC 600-IV).

House of Commons: Select Committee on Education, Science and the Arts (1980), *Fourth report: information storage and retrieval in the British library service*. HMSO. (HC 767).

House of Commons Official Report (1989), *Parliamentary Debates (Hansard)* Wednesday 8 February. vol. 146, no. 45, col. 987.

Information storage and retrieval in the British library service. Observations by the Government on the second and fourth reports from the Select Committee on Education, Science and the Arts: Session 1979–80 (1981). HMSO. (Cmnd. 8237).

Joint enterprise: roles and relationships of the public and private sectors in the provision of library and information services. Report by the Library and Information Services Council and British Library Research and Development Department Working Party (1987). (Office of Arts and Libraries, Library and Information Series No. 16). HMSO.

Library and Information Cooperation Council (1990), *Newsletter No. 2,* Spring.

Library Association (1987), General meeting – 'Members day: Minister for Arts gives a controversial speech'. *Library Association Record* vol. 89, no. 11, pp. 559–560.

Luce, R (1988), *Libraries – what of the future?* CLSI Publications. (CLSI Annual Lectures on Library Automation No. 4).

Macfarlane, M. (1981), Government policy for the nationwide provision of information at national, regional and local level, in: *The nationwide provision and use of information*: Aslib/IIS/LA Joint Conference, 15–19 September 1980, Sheffield. The Library Association.

Oakeshott, P. and White, B. (1987), *Publishing and information services in the public and private sectors.* Plato Publishing and Brenda White Associates.

Plan of action for libraries in the EC (1987), European Commission. (unpublished discussion paper).

Public Libraries and Museums Act 1964. Chapter 75. HMSO.

Public Library Development Incentive Scheme: the first year: 1987/88 progress report, (1988). British Library Research and Development Department. (unpublished paper, available gratis).

Public Library Development Incentive Scheme: the second year: 1988/89 progress report, (1989). British Library Research and Development Department. (unpublished paper, available gratis).

Public Library Development Incentive Scheme: the third year: 1990/91 competition (1989). British Library Research and Development Department. (unpublished paper, available gratis).

Report by the Minister for the Arts on library and information matters during 1983, (1984). HMSO. (Cmnd 9109).

Report by the Minister for the Arts on library and information matters during 1985, (1986). HMSO. (HC 234).

Report of a one day seminar on the past, present and future of the Public Library Development Incentive Scheme held at the Queen Elizabeth II Conference Centre on Friday 24 November 1989, (1990). British Library Research and Development Department. (unpublished).

Resolution on collaboration between libraries in the field of data processing, (1985). Official Journal of the European Communities, No. C271/1, 23 October. (Resolution 85/C271/01).

White, B. (1989), Library and Information Plans: a review of the literature. *Journal of Librarianship*, vol. 21, no. 1, (January), pp. 49–59.

Note: The list above includes sources which have been heavily drawn upon, and may be useful to the reader, but which do not necessarily receive a specific reference in the text.

5

The role of the British Library in cooperation

ANDY STEPHENS and STUART EDE

The British Library is itself an expression of the principle that through sharing resources and by reducing duplication of effort, libraries may maximise their overall effectiveness and efficiency.

The British Library Act 1972 was economical in its description of the functions and role of the national library. The Act described the Library as 'a national centre for reference, study, and bibliographical and other information services, in relation both to scientific and technological matters and to the humanities', and the British Library was charged with making 'the services of the British Library available in particular to the institutions of education and learning (and) other libraries and industry'. The detailed reasoning behind the establishment of the Library was contained in the *Report of the National Libraries Committee* (National Libraries Committee, 1969) chaired by Dr. F. S. (now Lord) Dainton. The Committee had been appointed to examine the existing national library facilities in the UK, and to consider whether 'in the interests of efficiency and economy such facilities should be brought into a unified framework'. It found that there were large gaps in total coverage and that the problem of keeping pace with the increasing output of world literature given finite resources was likely to become still more formidable. The many different library and information services in the UK, the *Report* argued, 'do not at present form a well-ordered pattern of complementary and cooperating parts'. There was 'remarkably little formal cooperation between the national and other libraries to identify users' needs to coordinate activities'. The recommendations of the National Libraries Committee were, therefore, intended to ensure 'adequate coverage of material and sufficient variety of service to satisfy as economically as possible the needs of all types of user'. In short, the establishment of the British Library was a response to the recognition that no library can be independent and self-sufficient in meeting the needs of its users.

The formal role of the British Library in supporting the whole UK library network is most clearly seen in its provision of central bibliographic services and central lending and photocopying services. In these areas it acts as a library to other libraries and information providers. In the provision of reference services 'of the last resort' the Library provides support to the network by serving directly the special needs of the natural constituents of the academic, public and special library sectors. And by sponsoring research of wide application in the library and information field the Library contributes to the future development of library services. In addition to its statutory responsibilities, the British Library engages in a wide range of cooperative and coordinating activities in support of the UK library network and a review of current initiatives follows. In all this, the composition of the British Library Board, its Advisory Council and various Advisory Committees helps to ensure that the Library is responsive to the needs of the network and to users.

COLLECTIONS

The British Library conducted a review of its acquisition and retention policies in 1987/88. The review (Enright, 1989) demonstrated that the acquisition of an item entails a continuing financial commitment once it is accepted into the collections – the underlying costs contingent upon a purchase decision include cataloguing, storage and preservation – and found substantial mismatches between the role of the British Library as traditionally conceived and the resources available for fulfilling it. There was an implicit conflict between maintaining existing holdings and securing new acquisitions when storage space and the resources for preservation are scarce. The main recommendations advocated greater curatorial control and discrimination as the key to controlling the relationship between acquisition and retention.

In a national context, the review stated that 'selectivity programmes must imply cooperation, shared information on acquisition policies, preservation and disposal. This process of cooperation, in which promising initiatives have been developing relatively quickly, needs to be accelerated. The development of interlibrary cooperation, both national and international, must strengthen the confidence with which the case for adequate funding can be put to government'. One specific outcome of relevance here, is the review's recommendation that current consultation arrangements with the other UK Copyright Libraries should be extended in order to achieve a national sharing of archival responsibility, particularly in respect of 'minor' publications received under legal deposit. A working group has been appointed to develop in detail a feasible scheme.

It is clear that libraries can no longer be independent and self-sufficient in meeting the needs of their users. The worldwide growth in publishing output, together with increasing specialisation of research and the effect that this has upon publications, mean that only a declining proportion of the available important and necessary literature can be acquired by an individual library given limited resources.

In *Gateway to knowledge,* its strategic plan 1989–1994, the British Library states that 'our long-term strategy is to work with others to achieve comprehensive access to recorded knowledge rather than comprehensiveness of collection. In the next five years... we shall seek to make progress both in the better organisation and exploitation of our own resources, and in our cooperative arrangements with other libraries. This means that we shall build on the strengths we already have; and we shall make clear the areas where we shall expect others, better placed than ourselves, to carry the central collecting responsibility' (British Library, 1989). The British Library recognises that while its own resources are limited, it has the responsibility for ensuring the availability of foreign material to meet the needs of research at a national level.

The major pre-requisites for a coordinated approach to collection development and improved access to existing holdings are a reliable guide to the scope of the collections in the major libraries in the system, and knowledge of their priorities for future acquisition expenditure in particular areas. The technique that the Library is promoting nationally to encourage resource sharing and cooperation is Conspectus (Jewitt, 1989; Jewitt, 1989; Matheson, 1989).

Conspectus is a tool which allows libraries to describe the scope and strength of their collections. In describing their collections, libraries assign an 'existing collection strength' value (to indicate the character and strength of inherited collections) and a 'current collecting intensity' value (to express the current selection policies) – both qualified by language code – to each of the 5,500 subject classes within a framework based on the Library of Congress classification scheme. Institutions may also add a more lengthy narrative statement – a 'scope note' – of their resources for each of the 250 broader subject categories within the framework. These may be used to reflect the collection development or preservation policies of the library.

Conspectus provides a map, to a common specification, of library resources within countries, regions, and across national boundaries, and thus has the potential to facilitate the more efficient overall management of resources across a number of collection-related areas of activity. It provides a means of coordinating collection development activities, without surrendering local autonomy. Conspectus is a powerful tool indicating the strengths of library collections to reference librarians, researchers and other users, and directing them to the most comprehensive coverage of the subject area being studied. A group of libraries wishing to cooperate in order to maximise their resources have available a comparative analysis on the basis of which decisions can be taken, leading to more efficient use of acquisition funds particularly with respect to identifying areas of local, national or international weakness in subject coverage. Conspectus makes it possible to designate Primary Collecting Responsibilities to particular institutions – a facility which may be extended to cooperative preservation activities, with Primary Preservation Responsibility being recorded in the same way. Conspectus also has potential for application in interlending and current and retrospective cataloguing.

Conspectus was first adopted in Europe in 1984 when the British Library decided to apply the system to its collections. The programme was implemented in 1985 and 1986. Eleven Scottish research libraries led by the National Library of Scotland, and the National Library of Wales have also completed Conspectus surveys. The data is mounted on a desktop computer system developed at the British Library to form a national database. The Library is now discussing the best way to bring more university libraries into the national system and a National Conspectus Office has been established. In Europe, a National Libraries

Conspectus Group was formed in 1987, following the first meeting of the Conference of European National Librarians. This Group, which is principally concerned with increasing support for the European Conspectus initiative from the European Commission, comprises representatives from the national libraries of France, the Federal Republic of Germany, the Netherlands, Portugal and the United Kingdom. The British Library currently provides the Chair and the Secretariat. The Ligue des Bibliothèques Européennes de Recherche (LIBER) Executive Committee has also established a Conspectus Group, and this has been very active in preparing for the implementation of Conspectus in the member countries.

The principal benefit to the Library from resource sharing in collection development will be in areas where its holdings are weak. In these areas the Library is seeking partners who can offer a secure commitment to a complementary collection development policy. Conspectus provides the broad statements of holdings which will form the basis on which either acquisitions policy may be redefined in relation to others, or discussions on a joint approach to coverage may be undertaken. The Library wishes to work in close collaboration with the other national libraries in the UK, and wishes to see Conspectus adopted by the largest university libraries and by a number of institute libraries and major public libraries. In Europe it hopes to explore the possibility of resource sharing with the major national libraries to see the extent to which they might, in collaboration with others, divide responsibility building on strength. In this the British Library is particularly well placed to provide a bridge between the great research libraries of North America and those of Europe.

PRESERVATION

Dr. F. W. Ratcliffe has described the disaster in Florence in 1966, when flooding led to serious damage of important library holdings, as a dramatic catalyst for growing awareness of the importance of conservation in library management. The great upsurge in use of library materials, and the impact of the introduction of wood pulp in paper production in the mid-nineteenth century – its acidic content leading to embrittlement and significant loss of strength within decades – were less dramatic but no less damaging and urgent problems which needed to be addressed.

Ratcliffe's report, *Preservation policies and conservation in British libraries* (Ratcliffe, 1984), identified 'the need for a focal point for preservation affairs at national level'. Unlike other branches of library and information work in the United Kingdom, there was no coordinating agency relating to conservation through which practices, developments, technology and cooperation could be examined and discussed. Given the British Library's unique 'concentration of experience and expertise', its resources, and its leadership in preservation matters, Ratcliffe argued, it was difficult to envisage a national advisory and research centre for preservation divorced from British Library activities.

In 1985, following subsequent consultation with the library community, the National Preservation Office (NPO) was established within the British Library as a focus for cooperation and guidance. An independent National Preservation Advisory Committee (NPAC) was also formed to advise on the work of the NPO. This is made up of experts from major national, research and public libraries, archives and record offices and advisory bodies such as the Standing Conference of National and University Libraries (SCONUL), the Association of British Library and Information Studies Schools (ABLISS) and the Library and Information Services Council (LISC). The NPO is also supported by a Panel of Conservators who advise on all aspects of physical treatments and storage, and an Education Panel which examines ways in which preservation issues are incorporated into professional library training and into continuing education programmes. In a relatively short period of time the NPO and NPAC have worked together to bring preservation to greater prominence in library management and to ensure that preservation policy is fully integrated into the broader library collection management policy.

The National Preservation Office works at two levels. (Clements and Chapman, 1988). Firstly it acts as a free information, referral and advisory centre – an initial contact point for any question concerned with preservation. The staff in the Office have established lines of communication with centres and individuals with knowledge and expertise spanning the whole gamut of preservation activities. In addition to this primary role of information collection and provision, the Office also seeks to promote and encourage good preservation and security practices, from the basic promotion of careful handling and housekeeping routines through to weightier considerations such as disaster control planning. The Office produces videos and publishes guides on the subject of preservation and security as well as organising training courses and a major annual conference. It also lobbies for the wider use of acid-free paper in publishing, for the recognition of the crafts of bookbinders and conservators, and for cooperation in all areas of preservation and security. Secondly, the National Preservation Office initiates debate on issues through which it seeks to influence policy development at national level. Thus, the NPO is addressing some of the major issues which will influence or determine future policy direction, while at the same time keeping sight of the day-to-day problems which face all library and archive units.

The size of the preservation crisis is such that the costs of preserving all the items that might deserve treatment is beyond the resources of any individual institution. Current funding constraints have merely exacerbated the massive mismatch between the resources available and those required to respond to the problems caused by acid paper and to compensate for past neglect. In the British Library alone, some 2 million of its 16 million holdings are known to have brittle paper, and every year further volumes join the queue of material awaiting treatment, but traditional conservation techniques can cost up to £300 for each individually hand-treated book. Substitution based on microfilming is the most cost-effective solution currently available, but even this costs some £30 per book. A cooperative approach to the preservation of documents issued in multiple copies is therefore essential.

In 1988, the Andrew W Mellon Foundation of New York granted the British Library, the Bodleian, and Cambridge University Library $2.5M for a five-year programme of preservation microfilming. The British Library received $1.5M with which to coordinate, through the National Preservation Office, a cooperative microfilming exercise among British research libraries (Jackson, 1990). In the initial stages of the programme, filming will be from the collections of the other copyright libraries – it is envisaged that other research libraries will be brought into the programme by mid-1991 and at this point consideration will be given to the establishment of a central microfilming unit. The filming process will produce one set of masters for storage in the British Library and a duplicate negative together with a positive for the originating library's users. The end result of the five-year enterprise will not however simply be more reels of microfilm, but also an internationally accessible database recording the items that have been filmed. All libraries participating in the Mellon programme will supply records containing location data for the Register of Preservation Microforms which was mounted online on the Library's BLAISE-LINE service in 1989. This database will ensure that, internationally, microfilming effort is not duplicated, and at the same time, ensure access to records of microform masters for acquisition purposes. Copies of the Register have been sent to the Research Libraries Group in the United States and mounted on the Research Libraries Information Network (RLIN). Plans are under way to establish a European Register with European Commission funding.

The great majority of filming undertaken within the Mellon Programme is expected to be of printed books and serials. Newspapers were deliberately excluded because of NEWSPLAN. The aim of this programme is to preserve on microfilm all newspapers published in the UK, with film of all titles being available both locally and in the British Library Newspaper Library in London, and with a securely kept master negative from which additional copies can be made. NEWSPLAN is a cooperative programme with the British Library, the library regions, local libraries and the other national libraries working in partnership. It provides the framework for research into the surviving files of local newspapers, and the extent of preservation effort to date. On the basis of this detailed information, priorities for microfilming, the means by which they are filmed, and programme costings can be determined for implementation and funding. To date NEWSPLAN reports have been published for the South Western, Northern and East Midlands regions. (Wells, 1986; Parry, 1989; Gordon, 1989).

Two further practical examples of cooperation are worthy of mention. Trained conservators from the British Library's bindery and conservation workshops share expertise generously both in the UK and overseas (particularly in developing countries), and work is undertaken on behalf of a wide range of other libraries and museums. The British Library also administers applications for grants for preservation and purchase from other institutions on behalf of the Trustees of the Wolfson Foundation. The Library's Preservation Service undertakes visits to examine the collections for repair, and these provide a valuable means of contact on the preservation issues faced by libraries and archives.

BIBLIOGRAPHIC SERVICES

Cooperation in the area of bibliographic services has been well established for many years and is fully explored by Peter Stubley in Chapter 11.

The British Library has played a major role principally through the provision of catalogue records. The duplication of effort in so many libraries cataloguing the same books had long been recognised, and in the 1950s and 1960s the printed *British National Bibliography* (BNB) and its associated catalogue card service were the main means by which libraries contained their costs in this area. The advent of BNBMARC and the growth of library automation cooperatives enabled cooperation to really take off, allowing libraries to make better use of scarce human resources.

BNBMARC records and Library of Congress records, which the British Library provides in UKMARC format, are distributed in a variety of media: as complete files on tape (often to bibliographic utilities for further redistribution), by selective off-line retrieval, on-line from BLAISE-LINE (for immediate downloading or despatch via tape) and now – for BNB data – on CD-ROM. While their predominant use is for cataloguing, these records are also used for ordering, especially the Cataloguing-in-Publication records which appear on the files.

In addition, the catalogues of many of the collections of the British Library are both published and mounted on BLAISE-LINE. They provide a source of records for overseas or special materials not covered by the BNB and Library of Congress files, and in making knowledge of the Library's collections more widely available they contribute towards resource sharing with regard to acquisition, referral and document supply.

Of particular note is the catalogue of the former British Museum Library which contains 3.5 million records spanning several centuries. This invaluable resource is in the process of being retrospectively converted to machine-readable form ready for the occupation of the new British Library building at St. Pancras. Part of the *British Library Catalogue* is already available on CD-ROM (published jointly by Saztec and Chadwyck-Healey) and on BLAISE-LINE. These files will dramatically improve access to the Library's collections and provide a major tool for the retrospective conversion of other libraries.

The major measures of the usefulness of these bibliographic services are the coverage of the records coupled with their quality and timeliness. For the user to obtain the maximum cost benefit, the records must be available at the time the user wants to order or catalogue a book. Timeliness has proved problematic especially during the 1980s, because the British Library has had to face a dramatic growth in the output of UK titles while the resources available to it have been diminishing.

However, *Currency with Coverage*, (British Library, 1987), the Library's cataloguing action plan, addressed this problem. As a result of the actions taken major improvements have been seen in the timeliness of records as measured by the BNBMARC hit-rate compiled by the Centre for Bibliographic Management.

However, the problem of increasing numbers of titles will remain, and the battle to maintain currency with coverage must continue. In which case how can adequate resources be found? This question has prompted the Copyright Libraries Shared Cataloguing Project. The Copyright Libraries of Britain and Ireland have signed a memorandum of understanding to share the burden of cataloguing the UK publishing output. A pilot scheme became operational in the 1991 publishing year. If successful, it should make a major contribution to performance.

Cooperation with the private sector was targetted by *Gateway to knowledge* (British Library, 1989) as another means of achieving more with less. Recent years have seen a trend towards more private sector agencies, including library booksellers, providing bibliographic record services. One area where there is such an example of cooperation is in the collection of information on forthcoming titles, where Book Data gathers the information from its subscribers and presents it in a prescribed way to the British Library. For the 1991 publication year Book Data will provide these records in machine readable form, and J. Whitaker and Sons Limited will take up the baton from the 1992 publication year.

Quality is a much more subjective measure, and one that poses an interesting problem for cooperation in the future. The MARC format was designed when linear output on cards, paper or microform was the order of the day. As a consequence the format is quite complex, it embodies various features to facilitate filing and contains some redundancy and duplication of data. Economic pressures have in many cases led libraries to adopt shorter records or simplification in certain areas. What is more, the advent of online public access catalogues (OPACs) has led to the questioning of whether the present MARC format is appropriate. Readers may well require less-structured records but with greater content, for example, subject data, contents pages and even book indexes.

Considerable research will be necessary into the many different demands that will be placed upon the format in future, not just from libraries and their readers but also from the book trade. When a clearer picture of these demands has emerged then it should be possible to see whether and how the MARC format should evolve. Clearly a new generation of MARC should be compatible with the present generation so that the vast worldwide investment in machine-readable files will not have been wasted. An exercise of this type will, by its very nature, have to involve an enormous cooperative effort both nationally and internationally. It will also require leadership and coordination which suggests an important role for the British Library.

Technological change will act as a catalyst on other developments. One will probably be the growth of electronic and other non-book publications. The question of how these publications can be controlled and recorded will have to be resolved. As an important step towards better control, the Library and other national bodies have urged the UK government to arrange for a serious public review of the case for extending the statutory provisions for legal deposit to audiovisual, electronic and other new materials.

Networking of individual library catalogues is already occurring, for example, over the Joint Academic Network (JANET). If cataloguing records are increasingly exchanged between libraries over networks, then there will be implications for the return that central bibliographic agencies receive for their records. This prospect led the British Library to introduce its licensing scheme whereby redistributors of records pay an annual fee for the use of BNBMARC records. Other national libraries are also exploring the issue of licensing schemes, and the question is now the subject of international debate through the Committee of Directors of National Libraries.

The rise of CD-ROM offers yet another way of distributing records, and provides an excellent example of international cooperation in technological development. The *BNB on CD-ROM*, and the national bibliographies of France and Germany on CD-ROM were foreshadowed as commercial products by cooperative pilot disc experiments partly funded by the European Commission. Now the Commission is again providing support for a consortium of European National Libraries to develop new national bibliographies on CD-ROM, especially from the smaller and less advanced countries, and trans-national bibliographies in such subjects as music which transcends national boundaries.

The objective is to promote the sharing of records throughout Europe, and this has, of course, to go hand-in-hand with the second objective to explore the issue of standardisation which is essential if this sharing is to be realised. The third main aim is to integrate the medium of CD-ROM into existing information systems, for instance by the development of interfaces with local library systems and with on-line hosts. In this way it is hoped this exciting new medium will facilitate international cooperation in the future.

INFORMATION SERVICES

Through referral, informal cooperation involving the British Library has flourished for many years; but there have been fewer examples of more formal schemes. This situation has begun to change in recent years and new initiatives are taking shape.

The Patents Information Network (PIN) is a partnership between the British Library, the Patent Office and thirteen selected libraries with the aim of making key patent documentation and related sources of information publicly available from regional centres spread across the United Kingdom. The Network, which was created in 1980, now comprises six 'Patent Information Libraries' (which have substantial holdings of patent documentation) and seven 'Patent Information Centres' (which have basic collections of patent documentation). With one exception these centres are all based on local public reference libraries.

The British Library's Science Reference and Information Service has funded the supply of all non-national documentation and also provides substantial support to the Network in the form of training, marketing and promotion, and in answering complex information requests. The Patent Office is responsible for the supply of national material and maintains a watching brief over the Network. The host library authorities house and staff the patents documentation collections; they ensure that free access to the collections is provided and that staff with knowledge of patent documentation are available for a reasonable proportion of the libraries' opening hours.

The British Library has also identified the need to consider formalised cooperative arrangements in other areas, particularly in business information, where there has been substantial growth in specialised services offered by public libraries in recent years. The Science Reference and Information Service has, therefore, initiated the creation of a Business Information Network of publicly funded library and information services with the broad aim of promoting the exploitation of business information resources in the UK and providing an effective focus for the development of business information products and services. The Network is seen as complementing the Library and Information Plan (LIP) initiatives – more efficient and effective services nationwide will be facilitated through formal arrangements for cooperation and joint action.

DOCUMENT SUPPLY

There is a long history in the UK of cooperation in interlibrary lending and document supply (Roberts, 1984; Jefferson, 1984). In the 1920s and 1930s, the National Central Library, one of the predecessors of the British Library Document Supply Centre (BLDSC), was actively involved in cooperation with university and public libraries in promoting the development of union catalogues of both books and journals to allow libraries to share their resources across the nation (Filon, 1977). The National Central Library in London maintained a national union catalogue of books in selected public, academic and special libraries, and was subsequently deeply involved in the production of the British Union Catalogue of Periodicals (BUCOP). Over time, the NCL began to build up its own substantial collection of books, many received through the Gift and Exchange programme which it ran, and which allowed other libraries to dispose of material they no longer required for adding to the NCL stock or for redistribution to other interested organisations.

However, in the 1950s it became clear that this cooperative system was failing to cope with the needs of the scientific community to obtain access to the growing volume of research information. This led to the Government's decision to set up what became the National Lending Library for Science and Technology at Boston Spa (Houghton, 1972), which joined with the National Central Library in 1973 to become the British Library Lending Division (renamed in 1985 the Document Supply Centre).

Now when libraries or other information units in the UK are unable to provide an item which their customer or reader requires, they have a high expectation of success in being able to obtain that item through the Document Supply Centre, as evidenced by the rise in demand from 200,000 requests in 1962 to over 3 million requests in 1989. No other country in the world has a system which provides so fast and comprehensive a document supply service as the UK, and the existence of the BLDSC allows libraries to concentrate their collecting policies on areas of high local demand. BLDSC thus plays an implicit but nonetheless key role in UK library cooperation.

Of course, cooperative interlending still has an important role in providing access to materials where it is not cost effective to maintain a central collection, or to materials which pre-date current collection policies. To supplement its collections the BLDSC continues to maintain union catalogues for categories of material which it does not collect comprehensively itself. At present these union catalogues cover foreign language monographs, pre-1973 English language monographs and music scores. In addition the BLDSC cooperates closely with the Regional Library Systems in the maintenance of union catalogues of their holdings which until recently have mainly been based on simple ISBN records. The VISCOUNT system, developed by LASER (see also Chapter 12), which is now gradually superseding these ISBN catalogues, has been developed with active cooperation from the BLDSC, and BLDSC's own post-1979 book holdings are included on the VISCOUNT database.

In areas where the BLDSC does not collect material, it will in some cases attempt to assist with the development or support of union catalogues or guides in order to improve cooperative national provision. Examples of this are the *British Union Catalogue of Orchestral Sets*, now edited by the Library, and the *Union Catalogue of Asian Publications* for which financial support was provided over a number of years.

Providing that those requesting items from the BLDSC have indicated that they would like to have an extended search for items they require, the BLDSC will either suggest other locations in the UK through its union catalogue or through specialist knowledge, or will refer the request to one of its 'back-up libraries'. These include all the legal deposit libraries and a number of other specialist libraries which in many cases were not involved in interlibrary lending until the early 1970s.

While there is no national acquisitions policy, BLDSC collecting policies have influenced those of individual libraries, as witnessed by librarians' protests made when diminishing grant-in-aid has necessitated cuts in the Library's acquisitions budget.

In developing its own collection policy, the BLDSC has been guided by many factors. Above all, it wishes to cooperate with other libraries, by allowing them to develop collections which best suit local needs in the knowledge that back-up support is available from the central collection at Boston Spa. The BLDSC was never intended to supplant local provision. In broad terms the BLDSC's collecting policy can be divided into that for material in relatively high demand and that for material in relatively low demand. The former, which includes much of the world's English language output of scientific, technical and medical journals, and current British and American monographs in all subject fields, is acquired because the UK library system could not cope with the total demand for this material without severe conflict developing between remote provision and provision to local users. Much of this material is already held in libraries in the UK, but it is intensively used within those libraries, and would often only be available to other libraries after very lengthy delays. A central collection of such material is therefore a key element in cooperative resource sharing.

The lower-use material includes, in particular, grey literature and foreign language serials. In these areas no library in Britain could justify collecting comprehensively just for the sake of their own readers or customers. Central provision is essential if good service is to be provided. By acquiring extensively material in such fields as conference proceedings, British theses, official publications, scientific and technical reports and translations, the BLDSC is allowing other libraries to concentrate their resources on material of most immediate importance to their local users.

In the last twelve months there has been some debate as to how far developments in new technology and networking remove the need for a central document supply service of BLDSC's size. It is argued that, with much easier access to one another's catalogues, libraries can obtain items from each other, thereby decreasing their reliance upon the Document Supply Centre. The BLDSC has been a willing participant in this debate, as it is anxious only to collect those categories of material which it needs to collect. If good cost-effective alternative systems of supply are available, the BLDSC is ready and willing to opt out from collecting in those areas. The demand which would be placed on other libraries if the BLDSC ceased collecting, for example, English language humanities monographs would however be enormous, and it is not clear how far libraries have considered the full implications of such a change. In addition, the costs of both borrowing and supplying an item are as yet far from clear. In 1989, the BLDSC commissioned a report on the costing of interlending, and it is hoped that the computer model developed in connection with this report (Pilling & Bonk, 1990) will help libraries of all types to become more aware of the costs of borrowing and supplying items, and so better enable them to judge what the most cost effective national system of document supply is.

Internationally, the Document Supply Centre has long been involved in library cooperation. The BLDSC houses the Office for the IFLA Core Programme for the Universal Availability of Publications and also its Office for International Lending. The latter is entirely financed by the British Library while the former is mainly financed by IFLA, with substantial administrative support from the British Library. Both offices are centrally concerned about the promotion of international library cooperation in the fields of interlibrary lending and resource sharing.

Other international cooperative activities include international exchanges of publications, which are an important method of acquiring material, particularly serials, from some countries.

The BLDSC is also heavily involved with ITC, the International Translations Centre. Over a quarter of all requests received at BLDSC come from outside Britain, and this inevitably brings the BLDSC into close contact with library organisations throughout the world. Several hundred visitors come to the BLDSC each year, and the BLDSC has close links with the British Council both in Britain and with its offices overseas.

On the European front, the BLDSC has been involved in many projects with the support of the European Commission. Two projects deserving particular mention are SIGLE, which provides access to grey literature in Europe, and where the BLDSC is the single largest contributor of records, and ADONIS, where the BLDSC in conjunction with several major scientific publishers was involved for two years in an experiment to test out the feasibility of providing document supply from CD-ROMs. The latter initiative reflects the wide interest of the BLDSC in cooperation in the area of advanced technology. The BLDSC has also been in the forefront of cooperative experimentation in areas such as Group IV facsimile, full text scanning, and satellite transmission of documents.

RESEARCH & DEVELOPMENT

The British Library Research and Development Department, as the main UK funding agency for research in the library and information field, contributes to library cooperation both directly and indirectly. The Department endeavours to assist, through the work it supports, the library and information profession, and to be responsive to its needs. Ultimately, all research – not merely those projects of direct relevance to library cooperation – will benefit and support the wider library community both in the decisions it is having to make and in the development of new services. Two recent projects illustrate this point. Project Quartet (Tuck, 1990) investigated electronic information exchange within the academic research community in the technological environment of the 1990s. The PIRATE Project (Public Information in Rural Areas: Technology Experiment) (Dover, 1988; Clarke, 1989) was concerned with examining ways of overcoming the difficult problems of access to public information in rural areas. Clearly, both projects have broad applicability across the library and information sector as a whole.

Looking towards the future, the Department is currently funding the Information UK 2000 programme to explore likely trends in the way that information will be generated, handled, stored and used over the next decade, and beyond. The programme will generate forecasts and scenarios covering particular issues and technologies that are likely to be significant over the next decade, and the results of the study will be of particular significance for the library and information services community and its users.

Turning now to direct research on interlibrary cooperation, Moore described various projects in his 1987 review (Moore, 1987). Since then, and following the publication of LISC's third report, *The future development of libraries: progress through planning and partnership*, a major cooperative programme supported by the Department has been the development of Library and Information Plans (LIPs). The report proposed that local authorities responsible for library services should draw up five-year management plans for their areas to ensure that the best uses were made of all the information resources within each area. These plans are more fully discussed in Chapter 4. The various LIPs funded by the Department have now been completed or are under way, and responsibility for monitoring and encouraging the plans has been taken on by the Library and Information Cooperation Council (LINC).

The British Library continues to support the Centre for Bibliographic Management at Bath University, which aims to help libraries and other agencies in the book world to improve the generation, storage and retrieval of bibliographic records. It also supports the UK Office for Library Networking which both promotes effective use of existing and developing networking infrastructure in the UK and overseas and represents the needs of libraries to the computing and telecommunications industry.

At present, the Department is giving high priority to the European Community *Plan of action for libraries in the EC* (1987). This was the first proposed action at Community level dedicated to library cooperation, and the history and current situation are set out in Chapter 3 by Michael Hopkins.

The Library's R&D Department is actively involved in this significant initiative for European library cooperation and harmonisation. The Department provides the Deputy Chairman and Secretariat for the UK Advisory Committee for the Plan mentioned by Peter Beauchamp in Chapter 4. This body will provide within the UK: a mechanism for disseminating information about the Plan; a means of stimulating proposals; a source of advice for potential co-funders; and a national filtering process for proposals submitted under certain 'action lines'.

In order to assist libraries and other information sector organisations prepare proposals and establish European partnerships, the Research & Development Department has awarded grants both for overseas study visits and for preliminary studies in the UK. The motive for this support is to encourage the development of well thought-through proposals, thus ensuring that the UK plays a full part in European cooperative development.

TO CONCLUDE

In *Gateway to knowledge* (British Library, 1989), the Library's strategic plan for 1989–1994, two factors are identified which will lead to greater participation in, and cultivation of, cooperative activities. Firstly, the financial realities, where the Library has to both prepare for the occupation of the new library building at St. Pancras, and undertake a major new investment programme in basic computer applications against a backdrop of a grant-in-aid which is declining in real terms year-by-year. At the same time, the budgets of other libraries have also shrunk thus increasing their dependence on the British Library's central services. The second factor is the key developments in information technology, telecommunications, and networking which will improve access, communication, and data exchange and enable practical and significant advances in library cooperation to be realised.

The British Library's strategy for the 1990s will be to achieve comprehensive access, rather than comprehensiveness of collection; the goal will be to guide users swiftly and accurately to the information they need. Information technology will also be central to the sharing of the collection development, record creation and preservation effort. The Library cannot foretell the ways in which technology will develop, but it will seek to keep abreast of developments which promise benefit for the library and information community.

REFERENCES

British Library (1987), *Currency with coverage.* Consultative paper.
British Library (1989), *Gateway to knowledge: the British Library strategic plan 1989–1994.* British Library.
British Library Act 1972. HMSO.
Clarke, J. E. (1989), *Public Information in Rural Areas: Technology Experiment (PIRATE) – phase II.* British Library. (LIR Report 74).
Clements, D. and Chapman, P. (1988), The role of the National Preservation Office, in: *Conservation and collection management.* (National Preservation Office Seminar Papers 2) British Library.
Dover, M. (1988), *Public Information in Rural Areas: Technology Experiment (PIRATE) – phase I.* (LIR Report 64) British Library.
Enright, B. J. (1989), *Selection for survival: a review of acquisition and retention policies.* British Library.
Filon, S. P. L. (1977), *The National Central Library: an experiment in library cooperation.* London, Library Association.
The future development of libraries and information services: progress through planning and partnership. Report by the Library and Information Service Council (1986). (Office of Arts and Libraries, Library and Information Series No. 14). HMSO.
Gordon, R. (1989), *Newsplan: report of the Newsplan project in the East Midlands.* British Library.
Houghton, B. (1972), *Out of the dinosaurs: the evolution of the National Lending Library for Science and Technology.* London, Clive Bingley.
Jackson, M. (1990), The Mellon Microfilming Project, in: *Preservation policies: the choices.* (National Preservation Office Seminar Papers 5) British Library.
Jefferson, G. (1984), Interlibrary lending in England and Wales from 1945. *Interlending and Document Supply*, vol. 12, no. 4, pp. 119–128.

Jewitt, C. (1989), Conspectus: a means to library cooperation. *Library Conservation News*, no. 22, (January), pp. 4–6.

Jewitt, C. (1989), Developing Conspectus. *Library Conservation News*, no. 23, (April), pp. 2–3, 6.

Matheson, A. (1989), Conspectus in the United Kingdom. *Alexandria*, vol. 1, no. 1, (May), pp. 51–59.

Moore, N. (1987), *Research and practice: 21 years of library research in the UK*. (LIR report 55) British Library.

National Libraries Committee Report (1969), HMSO. (Cmnd 4028).

Parry, D. (1989), *Newsplan: report of the Newsplan project in the Northern region*. British Library.

Pilling, D. and Bonk, S. (1990), *Modelling the economics of interlibrary lending*. Boston Spa, British Library. (in press).

Plan of action for libraries in the EC (1987), European Commission. (unpublished discussion paper).

Ratcliffe, F. W. (1984), *Preservation policies and conservation in British Libraries*. (LIR Report 25) British Library.

Roberts, N. (1984), Interlibrary lending in England and Wales 1900–1945. *Interlending and Document Supply*, vol. 12, no. 3, pp. 87–94.

Tuck, B, *et al.* (1990), *Project Quartet*. (LIR Report 76). British Library.

Wells, R. (1986), *Newsplan: report of the pilot project in the south-west*. (LIR report 38) British Library.

6

The role of professional associations in cooperation

JACK MEADOWS

It is said that the first action of any group of Britishers marooned on a desert island is to form themselves into as many different societies as possible. A survey of the library and information scene does certainly suggest that the formation of specialist groups is a major British hobby. Such fragmentation makes it difficult to decide just which bodies should be counted as the 'professional associations' within the UK. It also makes it difficult to determine what influence any individual professional body has on the progress of library cooperation within the UK. One final difficulty is that professional bodies of various kinds necessarily figure in other Chapters in this book. This Chapter will therefore concentrate mainly on the relevant activities of what might be called 'the big three' of the professional associations – the Library Association (LA), the Institute of Information Scientists (IIS) and Aslib, the Association for Information Management. It will be illustrative rather than exhaustive, and will concentrate on developments during the past decade.

Even limiting attention to these three associations still leaves a fairly complex picture, since all three have special interest groups and regional groupings along with their central organisations. Such groups can independently promote cooperation when it affects their interests. For example, the Local Studies and Rare Books Groups of the LA did all they could to encourage members to support the British Library's 18th-Century Short Title Catalogue Project during the 1980s. Again, a regional

Professional associations

grouping, such as the Scottish Library Association, can exert a significant influence on cooperative activities within the area it covers.

Such fragmentation of influence is somewhat balanced by the plurality of groups to which many librarians adhere. At one level, this may simply mean membership of a special interest group along with membership of the main organisation. At another level, it may mean active participation in the activities of all three of the main professional bodies. It is usually senior members of the profession who are involved in such participation, and who are therefore concerned with library cooperation across the different professional groupings.

In assessing the relevance of professional bodies to library cooperation, the first need is obviously to define the meaning of the phrase. The definition used here will be that, 'cooperation is the reciprocally beneficial sharing of resources, developed or pre-existing, by two or more bodies' (Edmonds, 1986). This definition implies that the interest of professional bodies in library cooperation is basically indirect, rather than direct: that is, they are concerned with the factors affecting the exchange of material, rather than with the actual process of exchanging material. Professional bodies have typically had their own library resources to call on, often as an historical consequence of members' problems in acquiring relevant items of literature. This is true both of the LA and Aslib. However, such access is nowadays usually more easily obtained via other routes, and many professional associations' collections are primarily of interest for historical reasons. To some extent, this trend has affected the LA and Aslib, but the libraries of both are still in regular use. In the case of the LA, this has been ensured by reaching an agreement with the British Library, so that what used to be the Library Association Library is now the British Library Information Sciences Service (BLISS). The new title is a reminder that both the LA library and the Aslib library support other information activities of the bodies concerned, as well as being available for use by members. However, it remains true that the library resources of the professional associations (the IIS has none) are much less important for library cooperation than the influence which the associations can bring to bear.

LIBRARY COOPERATION AND THE ASSOCIATIONS

The theme of this Chapter will therefore be the role of the associations in facilitating and monitoring the sharing of resources between libraries.

Handbook of Library Cooperation

One question needs to be disposed of at the start. Why should the associations regard cooperation both as a valuable activity and one in which they must play a part? The answer harks back, in part, to the reasons for their foundation. In each case, there was an acceptance of cooperation as an activity to be fostered by the association. During the 1980s, an additional urgency has arisen from the internal and external pressures which are affecting cooperative activities. This has led to an increasing expectation that the associations will coordinate their members' views about cooperation and reflect them to the world outside. It might be argued that they are better able to do this because they are not major actors themselves in the actual provision of materials.

The changing world of the 1980s has forced the associations to reconsider their aims and responsibilities with regard to cooperation. The LA, which is by far the largest of the three in terms of finance and membership, made its views explicit in 1986 during the revision of its Royal Charter. At least four of the headings listed under the Statement of Purposes and Powers in the amended Royal Charter can be considered relevant to cooperation:

- to scrutinise any legislation affecting the provision of library and information services and to promote such further legislation as may be considered necessary to this end
- to promote and encourage the maintenance of adequate and appropriate provision of library and information services of various kinds throughout the United Kingdom, the Channel Islands and the Isle of Man
- to promote the better management of library and information services
- to work with similar associations overseas and with appropriate international bodies to promote the widespread provision of adequate and appropriate library and information services

Most of the LA Special Interest Groups are based on either a subject, or a library categorisation (for example, cataloguing and indexing; public libraries). These can become involved in promoting cooperative activities as part of their natural development. For example, the Information Technology Group has set up a number of regional circles to put people in touch at the local level, to provide advice and to organise training. The group has also experimented with a computer-based index of expertise to provide a further advisory back-up. A look at the aims and objectives of most of the LA groups confirms that they emphasise the importance of promoting and fostering cooperation.

The IIS originated in a post-Second World War demand for education and qualifications in what was then called 'documentation', as distinct from traditional librarianship. Hence, the Institute was not originally concerned with cooperation in library and information services. However, the Institute's aims broadened subsequently to include this. It certainly sees itself now as having an interest in facilitating the acquisition and provision of information by its members. It is noticeable, in this connection, that the UK Online User Group is easily the most popular of its Special Interest Groups.

When ASLIB was founded in the 1920s (as the Association of Special Libraries and Information Bureaux), a major aim was to facilitate 'the coordination of, and systematic use of resources of knowledge and information in all public affairs and in industry and commerce and in all the arts and sciences'. Hence, library cooperation clearly came under its brief from the beginning. Its reorientation in the 1980s as Aslib, the Association for Information Management, underlined the importance of the newer forms of automated library and information services for cooperative purposes. The Information Resources Centre, which Aslib set up in 1986, was intended to encourage good management practices in general, including, where appropriate, cooperative library and information activities.

Aslib differs from the LA and the IIS in being predominantly an organisation with a corporate membership. It is therefore necessarily as concerned with cooperation between institutions as between individuals. As with the other two bodies, Aslib runs a number of specialist interest groups to cater for the particular requirements of its members. In terms of facilitating cooperation, both Aslib and the IIS may be most useful in the area of one-man-bands and small businesses, where they provide a forum for contact and advice which would not otherwise be readily available.

POLICY CONCERNS

The question is – which general activities of the professional associations are directly linked to cooperation? For example, all of them are concerned with training. Certainly, some of their training sessions relate to activities involving cooperation, and contacts made at such sessions may subsequently lead to improved cooperation. But the enhancement of cooperation, in the sense of improving the sharing of resources between the participants, is only occasionally the main objective of the training. Consequently, although training deserves a mention in the context of the professional associations and library cooperation, it does not deserve an extended analysis. Rather, the important contribution of the associations tends usually to be in policy-related matters.

An example of such involvement in policy-making occurred at the beginning of the 1980s with the debate over the reorganisation of the library services in the UK. A memorandum from the LA at the end of 1979 tackled, in particular, the problems which had arisen from trying to run library cooperation on voluntary lines. One paragraph ably sums up the position on cooperation as seen by a professional association (Library Association, 1979):

> 'Libraries exist to provide services to particular groups of users but the growth in recorded knowledge coupled with the decline in the economic situation makes it increasingly impossible for even the most wealthy or specialised libraries to be self-sufficient. Libraries are therefore increasingly dependent on one another and on a range of centrally provided support services. The converse is the contribution to the national resource that a comparatively excellently stocked library, for instance in a region otherwise relatively poorly provided for, can make when this library adopts outward going policies of local support. In this new complex situation existing mechanisms for cooperation and consultation are proving inadequate. Many are cumbersome and insufficiently flexible to meet rapidly changing needs; others can be weakened by the withdrawal of the strongest members for political or financial reasons; staffing and financial resources are lacking; and others are inhibited by the uncertain legal basis on which they are founded. And yet they continue to proliferate in an attempt to fill the gap and this proliferation results in further confusion, waste and duplication.'

This assessment of the position facing the profession in the 1980s led the LA to press for the creation of a central planning and coordinating

Professional associations

body in the UK. Of the various functions suggested for such a body, four were directly concerned with library cooperation:

- the rationalisation and standardisation of the automation of library processes
- the creation of a national network of reference libraries involving the designation of regional reference libraries and the development of centres of excellence
- the development and maintenance of a national system of transport for library materials
- a national plan for the storage in regional and national centres of little-used library materials

The question of a national information policy was pursued at a tripartite meeting of the LA, IIS and Aslib, which led to a reconstitution of the Joint Consultative Committee (JCC) – to be mentioned again below.

The idea that efficient and full cooperation requires planning at the national level has remained potent throughout the 1980s. Thus, a document produced within the LA in the mid-1980s comments:

> 'Each library ... needs to provide, to the best of its ability, the optimum amount of material to satisfy the demands of its users, no matter in what form that material may be available. No collection, however, can be complete in its coverage and will be dependent on the resources of other centres. Cooperation and, if necessary, coordination will be imperative if the requirements of most users are to be met. For this reason, the problem can only be solved nationally and with international implications.'

The professional associations expect, and usually take, the opportunity to comment on proposed legislation, or on official reports affecting the development of the profession. During the 1980s, a number of these have had implications for library cooperation. An example is the Green Paper, issued on *Financing our public library service: four subjects for debate* (1988). (It is noteworthy that the general outline of this document had already been presented by the Minister to the LA Annual General Meeting some months previously.) One proposal in this document particularly concerned cooperation between libraries, for it invited public library authorities to consider the pros and cons of, 'charging other library authorities and institutions in both the public and private sectors for all the elements of the services they provide to them'. As the LA soon pointed out, pursuit of this aim could threaten cooperation in the transfer of material, both between public and non-public libraries and between authorities with different attitudes to charging. A blanket application of the suggestion would therefore almost certainly reduce the access of readers to materials now made available through cooperative interchange.

Reports of national interest, such as those produced by the Library and Information Services Councils (LISCs), can also influence cooperation. A recent relevant example is provided by the deliberations of a LISC (England) working party on the 'Role of Government in Relation to the Cooperation of Library and Information Services'– see page 92. The LA, in its comments, disputes some of the points raised in the report – for example, that the library and information community is now fragmenting into an unmanageable complex. However, it agrees wholeheartedly with the working party that government is not yet seen to be coordinating library and information activities effectively, and that this lack of coordination is evident both in the UK and the EC. One comment by the LA on this report reflects a feeling shared by the professional associations throughout the 1980s. This concerns the tendency of government to treat library and information services in different parts of the UK – England, Wales, Scotland and Northern Ireland – as separate entities. The associations see this division as ensuring that some forms of cooperation and coordination often cannot easily be initiated or maintained.

It is not only the Office of Arts and Libraries and the Library and Information Services Council reports which require scrutiny nowadays. The spread of information technology means that reports from such bodies as the Department of Trade also need to be monitored. One area of concern for the professional associations concerns standards to be applied to new systems – something which requires consultation not only between themselves, but also with such bodies as the British Standards Institution. It is not only technical standards which have come to the fore in the 1980s. Technological change has affected legislation in other areas: a prime example in the past decade being copyright and related law.

In the first half of the decade, a good deal of effort was put into the question of how data protection affected library and information services.

Professional associations

This led, for example, to the compilation of guidelines by the Joint Consultative Committee. In the latter half of the decade, more energy went into the new copyright legislation, some parts of which certainly affected the transfer of materials. When it was first introduced in 1987, the Copyright, Designs and Patents Bill excluded commercial research from the fair dealing clause (i.e. the ability to make a single copy for personal research). Many members of the LA, IIS and Aslib were affected by this provision. A consequent joint campaign led to the deletion of this proposal while the Bill was before the House of Lords. As in this case, the professional associations have developed political contacts to allow their voices to be heard in matters which relate to library cooperation.

Professional concern with the policy aspect of library cooperation extends to the international arena. The professional bodies are naturally seen as a major focus in the UK for international contacts. An example involving aspects of library cooperation is the Unesco General Information Programme. Despite the British withdrawal from Unesco, the LA managed to persuade the Foreign and Commonwealth Office that the UK should continue to be represented on the programme – by an LA representative attending its Council. International activity is now increasingly coming under the banner of the European Community. The exchange of library personnel is an obvious way of fostering cooperation. This will certainly increase in the 1990s with the establishment of the Single Market. The LA is already concerned in these developments, as it has been designated the professional body for vetting applications before entrants from other EC countries can take up jobs in the UK.

Although the Commission of the EC has been involved in encouraging cooperative activities since its early days, library cooperation has only recently become a particular concern, for example, the *Plan of action for libraries in the EC* (1987) appeared as a discussion document in 1988 (see Chapter 3). Its guidelines stressed that a particular intention is to promote harmonisation. Three of its proposed objectives overlapped with the interests of the British professional bodies in terms of cooperation – promotion of the availability and accessibility of modern library services; promotion of standardisation; harmonisation and convergence of library policies. Such European developments underline the need for the professional associations' attitude to library cooperation to be placed increasingly within an international context.

OTHER PROFESSIONAL BODIES

The original concerns of the EC *Plan of action* reflect the pressures which act now on all bodies concerned with libraries and cooperation. As noted above, such pressures led to the reactivation of the Joint Consultative Committee, which then brought together, along with the LA, IIS and Aslib, the Society of Archivists, the Standing Conference of National and University Libraries (SCONUL) and, subsequently, the Council of Polytechnic Librarians (COPOL). The activities of the Society of Archivists may not come under a discussion of library cooperation, although there is an increasingly overlapping area of interest in the field of records management. However, both SCONUL and COPOL can be considered professional bodies, in the sense that they are concerned with the professional work of a specific sub-set of librarians. Both bodies are naturally concerned with any matters which affect interchange of materials between their members. The topic tends to surface more frequently at SCONUL because of the presence of the national librarians on its committees. Apart from the actual exchange of material, SCONUL and COPOL produce annual statistics and reports which give some insight into their cooperative library activities.

The number of specialist library groups within the UK which have some involvement in library cooperation is large. It therefore makes best sense to indicate what sorts of groups exist, with examples, rather than to attempt a complete listing.

Several of these groups, as has been noted, are either constituent parts of, or are affiliated to, the main professional associations. One example is the Association of Assistant Librarians (AAL) which, although a part of the LA, has its own Council and infrastructure. In this case, since its membership amounts to nearly half that of the LA as a whole, it can be expected to make its voice heard on matters affecting assistant librarians. Its members are involved in the actual day-to-day running of interlibrary cooperation schemes, as distinct from the policy aspects, and so have their own perspective on changes affecting such cooperation. Another example in this category is the Library and Information Research Group (LIRG) which, although affiliated to the LA, includes members from elsewhere, especially from the IIS. So far as library cooperation is concerned, LIRG's main concern lies in the exchange of experience and in the encouragement of research on the topic, as discussed by Diana Edmonds in Chapter 10.

Professional associations

A second category of groups are those like SCONUL and COPOL which bring together professionals from a particular type of library. An example specifically relating to library cooperation was the establishment of the Consortium of University Research Libraries (CURL) in 1985. Its declared intention was to facilitate cooperative activity in order to develop access to the collections of the seven largest university libraries in the UK. In this case, CURL obviously has overlapping interests with SCONUL and the LA (see Chapter 8). Such overlap is common with specialist or regional groups. Thus, when the Government's Green Paper on *Financing our public library service* (1988) appeared, one reaction was to organise a joint seminar of the Federation of Local Authority Chief Librarians (FOLACL) and the LA, since it was seen as of equal concern to both.

Some of the local or regional bodies that have been established have specifically been concerned with interchange of material. Their activities range from the organisation of transport for such material to the setting-up of networks for the exchange of information and identification of relevant material. Such joint action also extends to facilitating further developments – for example, by organising joint training relevant to library cooperation.

A final group consists of those bodies which are concerned with particular subject areas, formats or particular types of library activity, and so become involved in library cooperation. These may overlap with some of the special interest groups of the main professional bodies, but lead a separate existence. One example is the British and Irish Association of Law Librarians examined in Chapter 9. During the 1980s, this body devoted an appreciable amount of time to considering future cooperation in library provision for law in response to the new pressures which were arising. Another example is the UK Serials Group which was set up to promote the discussion of serials between all the relevant parties in the information industry. One effect of the growth of automation has been to put electronic links between librarians, subscription agents and publishers increasingly on the agenda (see Chapter 11). These developments are likely to extend the scope of what is meant by library cooperation in the future.

WIDER OUTREACH

One aspect of library cooperation which is worth a brief mention concerns the production of literature – newsletters, journals, etc. The newsletters, in particular, are intended to provide for the exchange of experience and opinion, and often have the explicit purpose of promoting cooperation. Over the past 10–15 years, newsletters from the various professional groups have proliferated. Thus, from the mid-1970s to the latter part of the 1980s, some twenty LA group newsletters were either founded or drastically redeveloped. In addition, the reference works published by the professional associations – such as *Library and Information Science Abstracts* which was produced by the LA, or the *Technical Translations Bulletin* produced by Aslib – clearly help facilitate library cooperation in the exchange of material.

More recently, the professional bodies have become concerned with cooperation via electronic networks. The early running was made by Aslib, but the main system currently operating is LA-Net. The idea of electronically linking members either individually or in groups can obviously enhance cooperation in general, but some of the possibilities are more immediately aimed at this end. For example, the central provision of forms which can be downloaded and printed out via the network is a useful step in the direction of standardisation.

The increasing importance of information technology, both within the library world and without, means that there is a growing overlap with the interests of professional bodies in other disciplines. An obvious example is the British Computer Society's developing interest in all forms of automated information handling. Less obviously, the emphasis on information management in the 1980s has led to an increasing overlap between library and information professionals and the British Institute of Management. So far, much of the mutual interaction with these other professional bodies has occurred at the level of the individual, rather than the profession as a whole. More progress at the latter level has been made with professions traditionally allied to librarianship, such as the publishing industry. One sign of this expansion of mutual interest appeared in 1984 with the formation of the Confederation of Information Communication Industries (CICI). This brought together the trade associations and professional bodies from all the main areas of the information industry. Along with the LA, IIS and Aslib, CICI includes such bodies as the British Library, the Publishers Association, the BBC and the Independent Broadcasting Authority (IBA). This provides a potentially powerful grouping for the promotion of cooperation and for influencing government thinking on the matter. However, because of the differing nature of the bodies represented, there is still some doubt whether it can become more than a talking shop. In addition, it has been criticised as bringing together only senior management, so that topics of mutual interest can only be discussed at a general policy level. This is, in fact, a criticism which has also been made by members of the library and information community of discussions between the LA, IIS and Aslib.

It would certainly be unfair to level such a criticism at the current widespread discussions concerning the Saunders Report (1989). In a sense, this report sums up the cooperative trends in the 1980s. As the professional bodies have worked increasingly together, so the query has grown whether a single professional body might be more effective than the present diffused responsibility. From the first, this debate has seen improved cooperation as one of the desirable consequences of forming a single body. Saunders (1989) pinpoints this as an important stimulus in the preparation of the report: 'discussions have taken place between the chief executive officers of the LA, Aslib and the Institute, since early in 1987, to assess whether there are areas of their work and services in which greater cooperation or coordination could take place'.

Whether the advantages of unification in terms of cooperation and coordination will weigh heavily enough with the members of all three associations to overcome the fears which some of their members have expressed remains to be seen. The former Director of Aslib has voiced his own doubts concerning the feasibility of such a merger. Whether unification occurs or not, it is already evident that the involvement of the professional associations in library cooperation is likely to increase in the 1990s, as the forms of this cooperation continue to diversify.

REFERENCES

Edmonds, D. J. (1986), *Current library cooperation and coordination. an investigation* (Office of Arts and Libraries, Library and Information Series No. 15). HMSO.

Financing our public library service: four subjects for debate (1988). HMSO. (Cmnd. 324).

Library Association (1979), *A National Review of Library and Information Services*. The Library Association.

Plan of action for libraries in the EC (1987), European Commission. (unpublished discussion paper).

Saunders, W. L. (1989), *Towards a unified professional organisation for library and information science and services: a personal view.* (Viewpoints in LIS No. 3). The Library Association.

7

Public library cooperation

STUART BREWER

The phrase 'public library cooperation' has in recent years taken on a wider dimension than was previously the case. The involvement of public libraries in cooperation was generally understood to entail membership of a regional library system, or possibly of a local cooperative organisation such as Hampshire Technical, Research, Industrial and Commercial Service (HATRICS) or Sheffield Interchange Organisation (SINTO), or of an automated cataloguing network such as BLCMP or SLS, or perhaps a collaborative arrangement between neighbouring library authorities in the provision of specialist services.

Less formal and possibly short-term cooperation might also be arranged between library authorities e.g. joint provision of training programmes.

Moreover, for public libraries, the sense in which cooperation was generally understood was relatively restricted: 'The term interlibrary cooperation is used to mean chiefly interlibrary lending' (Filon, 1967); Filon goes on to say that the term 'refers in fact to any kind of cooperation between a number of libraries with the object of giving a better service to their readers'. Significantly, however, his article is concerned almost entirely with aspects of interlending.

The same writer also noted that 'schemes of library cooperation in Britain mainly arise through local initiative, or independent action taken by groups of libraries with common interests...This tendency for cooperative schemes to begin on a local or 'sectarian' basis has made it very difficult to produce any kind of harmonious and consistent national scheme' (Filon, 1967).

Filon's view is a clear illustration of the fact that cooperation is, perhaps inevitably, a function of that 'enlightened self-interest' (Enright) which is effected more easily between close neighbours than among organisations which are located, geographically or functionally, at some distance from each other. The 'self-interest' factor may also help to throw light on the current efforts to establish Library and Information Plans (LIPs), whether on geographical or sectoral bases, and on the lack of progress toward the establishment of a National Information Plan.

A decade later, however, the Director of a Regional Library System was able to write: 'We have in fact already progressed far beyond the original concept of interlibrary lending as the sole component of library cooperation. Library cooperation now encompasses many library functions and exists at local, regional...and national levels' (Plaister, 1976).

Jean Plaister also suggested that 'librarians accept that library cooperation is practical and apparently economic and will show benefits in the use of library and personnel resources extending beyond the purely cost-effective' (Plaister, 1976).

The prevailing view today would be less optimistic and more probing. A climate of increasing financial stringency, budget reductions and service cuts has triggered a more rigorous attitude toward the costs and the benefits to be derived from cooperation. A paper on the recently formed Business Information Network commented that the interested parties 'all agreed (that) subscriptions were necessary and they had no intention of involving themselves in that bane of the librarian's life, the traditional voluntary cooperative scheme which relies upon so many professional officers' goodwill and spare time' (Gomersall, 1990).

Nevertheless, during the 1980s the boundaries of public library cooperation significantly expanded, not so much between public libraries themselves, but between public libraries and other types of library and, especially, other types of organisation in the 'non-traditional' sectors, whether public, private, voluntary or charitable.

As the boundaries widened, so also did the types of cooperation which emerged; and, to reflect the trends and modes of cooperation which were now developing, different words began to be used to describe the kinds of relationships which were being essayed by library and information managers, e.g. partnership, joint venture, contract, agreement, collaboration, coordination, coalition, and networks.

CURRENT SITUATION

The aim of this Chapter, then, is to chart some of these shifts in the theory and practice of cooperation in which public libraries are involved, illustrated with examples of some of the new horizons which are opening up, to consider why such developments and initiatives have evolved, to offer some views as to their effectiveness, and to consider the future potential for the widening spectrum of cooperative processes and mechanisms. A number of key documents have contributed to this changing scene:

(i) *The future development of libraries and information services: progress through planning and partnership.* (Future development..., 1986) proposed local Library and Information Plans (LIPs), i.e. five-year management plans involving all library and information services within a given local authority or other given geographical area (e.g. White, 1990, on the Northern Ireland LIP).

It also recommended that 'all concerned with the funding and management of library and information services should accept greater responsibility for exploiting the opportunities and dealing with the challenges facing them'.

The subsequent growth of LIP initiatives has spread widely throughout the United Kingdom, and is bound to have a significant impact on library cooperation. The LIP concept is notable for seeking to embrace public, private and voluntary sector organisations and, thereby, potentially many information providers which normally operate outside the traditional library framework.

LIPs may be the most demanding form of cooperation known to the library and information world, because of their emphasis on policy, planning and partnership.

(ii) *Current library cooperation and coordination: an investigation* (Edmonds, 1986) is a summary report of a series of case studies within six library authority areas, highlighting some of the good and bad features of existing cooperation and coordination. The report recommended that:

– local authorities encourage cooperation between, rather than the coordination of, the libraries and information services for which they are responsible

- libraries review the potential for developing cooperative initiatives with local organisations
- major libraries in a local area cooperate in reviewing the potential for cooperative activity, perhaps with a formal plan
- the Office of Arts and Libraries give encouragement to the development of local library cooperation, and actively encourage the dissemination of information about cooperative activities

One can see in these recommendations not only a chronological but also a conceptual link with *The future development of libraries and information services: progress through planning and partnership.*

(iii) *Joint enterprise: roles and relationships of the public and private sectors in the provision of library and information services* (Joint enterprise..., 1987), noted that 'the downward pressure on public resources alongside the changes taking place in the information industry is leading to deliberate experiment in the provision of revenue-raising services by public bodies'. It summarises the findings of two sets of case studies which showed that public/private sector interaction 'is taking place, often beneficially, without distorting basic service commitments or infringing current conventions about charging for services'; the development of joint ventures is seen as an 'effective way of expanding the range of services available to consumers'. The report recommended that:

- new thinking and new attitudes should be assumed by public sector managers
- responsible people in both sectors should together explore ways of developing communications in order to create an environment in which creative ideas can begin to flow

It has recently been announced that the Office of Arts and Libraries (OAL) has commissioned an update of these case studies and a search for further examples of joint ventures.

(iv) The Green Paper *Financing our public library service...* (1988) emphasised the Government's commitment to the free basic library service, and summarised ways in which library authorities could raise their gross annual income to a total of over £50 million (few people believed this claim, which has yet to be substantiated). The Paper also suggested there might be more charged public library services, proposed joint ventures between the public and private sectors as an effective way for library authorities to expand the range of their services, and outlined possibilities for releasing money through greater use of competitive tendering and contracting out of services. Although somewhat heavy-footed and simultaneously utopian in its thinking, the Green Paper galvanised the library world and played a key part in encouraging discussion on the place of public libraries in what had now become known in many quarters as the enterprise society.

A key player in encouraging new forms of cooperative activity has been the OAL, advised particularly by the Library and Information Services Council (England) (LISC). A strong thread of government support for the concept and practice of cooperation is therefore apparent throughout the 1980s, together with an increasing emphasis on the potential for raising income. The tension between these two dimensions, plus the budget cuts and service reductions which many public libraries have had to implement during the decade, will provide a fascinating matrix of issues for study by future historians and analysts.

PUBLIC LIBRARY DEVELOPMENT INCENTIVE SCHEME (PLDIS)

Among the evidence available to them will be the Public Library Development Incentive Scheme, which was announced by the Minister for the Arts in December 1987, with £250,000 being made available per year (*Public Library Development Incentive Scheme: the third year: 1989/90,* 1990). The aim of the Scheme is to extend and improve public library services in England through activities likely to promote cooperation between public libraries and other libraries or organisations in the public or private sector. The Scheme is managed by the British Library Research and Development Department which monitors the progress of successful applications. A mid-term evaluation of the Scheme is being published in 1991.

The Minister's specific priorities for PLDIS grants have changed a little during the life of the Scheme; currently they are:

- investigations of the scope for innovations in the effective use of contractors
- projects arising from Library and Information Plans
- improving the operational efficiency or effectiveness of services through cooperation between public library authorities or with private sector organisations
- innovative revenue earning services, especially through joint ventures

A total of thirty one grants were made during the first three years of the Scheme. The Advisory Committee to the Scheme has found that the quality of applications overall has highlighted a very real need for training to assist applicants with preparing proposals for funding and formulating business plans. Consultants are available through the Scheme to help the preparation of applications although, at the same time, many libraries have welcomed the opportunity to use the PLDIS projects to develop the skills (project management, business planning, marketing, negotiating, etc.) of their own staff. The 1989/90 Progress Report of the Scheme notes that 'some highly successful ventures have been undertaken...projects which could not have taken place without PLDIS funding...the effect of an award in 'levering' sponsorship or other funding...benefits such as staff development and raising the profile of library services'.

Financial partners for public library authorities in PLDIS applications have included health authorities, academic institutions, ICL, Linguaphone, GEAC, DBS, Reed International, local authority departments, the Northern Region Councils Association, the European Commission, the Hong Kong Government, Inner Area Partnership, a bookseller and a publisher. Support and cooperation has also come from voluntary self-help groups, general practitioners, Gateshead Metrocentre, Chambers of Commerce, the Poetry Society and West Midlands Arts.

The extent to which PLDIS has facilitated the development and promotion of public library services will be a matter for the planned long-term evaluation to consider. Some of the projects and feasibility studies carried out are undoubtedly pioneering and innovative; how far they are transferable into other library authority areas is less clear, since energy and commitment and skills are often very localised factors, as indeed is the actual 'chemistry' of the project, partnership or joint venture. On the other hand, the Scheme does enable risk-taking operations to be established, enabling public libraries to break new ground.

It is sometimes suggested that the Scheme is too poorly funded to provide lasting benefit, and that only long-term and in-depth research can effectively ensure practical service development: 'A strong infrastructure of properly funded research activity – and not just a glossy patina of short-term 'development incentive schemes' – is necessary to the continued health of the public library service' (McKee, 1989).

One interesting feature of PLDIS and 'joint venture' concepts is that the ensuing partnerships with the private sector are often pump-primed with grants from one or other government department or agency; and in many cases it is proving difficult to keep the project going without further injection of public sector funding. A certain irony is also built into PLDIS in that its emphasis on *ad hoc* development is set in a framework of severe and continuous financial difficulty for many library authorities. Growth is accompanied by decline.

COALITIONS AND CAMPAIGNS

Another form of cooperation, or partnership, in which public libraries may therefore get involved is that of coalitions – or campaigns. The concept is perhaps more familiar in the United States where coalitions are recognised as an essential medium for explaining and advocating the vital role of the library. 'Coalitions are essential for the 1980s because if you lack clout, you're out' (Josey, 1987).

A coalition may be defined as an alliance, a coming together, of persons, institutions and groups formed for the purpose of joint action. An alliance may be local, regional or national, temporary or permanent. It is just as important to realise that, although coalitions are essential for the self-interest and protection of libraries, they in turn have much to offer to other organisations which are engaged in work of mutual concern, and for which the existence of a strong and healthy public library may be essential if their own work is to flourish. Building coalitions may, in some circumstances, be the only way to counter threats to the public library system and to raise its profile.

One such example occurred in Detroit, where the Friends of the Detroit Public Library (DPL) successfully identified groups willing to join them in a campaign to keep the financially distressed DPL from sinking.

This kind of campaigning is generally foreign to the way things are done in Britain although, even in the USA, 'on the whole, libraries do not yet appear to be strongly oriented towards actively reaching out to – and working effectively with – other organised groups of institutions working on broad public-interest questions' (Josey, 1987).

In Britain, such activism is not second nature to librarians, who are all too easily persuaded that campaigning and lobbying are too 'political' and too risky to be attempted. Library cooperation tends to operate at an operational or service level; cooperative advocacy and lobbying come less naturally to us. Organisations of 'friends' of public libraries have emerged from time to time, usually in response to threat of budget and service cuts, but they have rarely become established as permanent lobbies for the public library.

The closest parallel is the Library Campaign, founded in 1984 as an independent, voluntary organisation. The objectives of the organisation, set out in its Manifesto, are:

- the defence of all publicly funded library and information services from cuts, whether national or local
- the improvement of services provided by publicly funded library and information services, and wider promotion amongst the public and library workers of the range and depth of services currently funded and needed
- the right of access to library materials and information without charge
- the provision of a free library and information service as an essential ingredient of a democratic society
- the support of other campaigns engaged in fights against public expenditure cuts, especially where such cuts worsen the services and benefits due to already disadvantaged groups

In seeking to achieve these objectives, the Library Campaign aims to:

- stimulate the establishment of local campaign groups by the provision of information, publicity materials and other resources
- support campaigning activities undertaken by trades unions and other independent action groups
- disseminate information on local initiatives through *The Library Campaigner*, regional conferences and other means
- campaign politically whilst remaining independent from all political parties (*The Library Campaigner*, 1990)

As well as individual members the Campaign has a small number of affiliated members such as trades union branches, national Trades Unions (e.g. Nalgo), national organisations (e.g. Society of Authors, Age Concern England), and Local Authorities, although disappointingly these number less than twenty.

The Library Campaign is clearly a national coalition of the kind described above, and it has done well to survive, to publish regularly *The Library Campaigner*, and to make an occasional impact e.g. with Library Promotion Month 1989 when it collaborated, to mutual benefit, with The Library Association. However, it has always had to contend with very limited financial support (it currently operates on an annual budget of about £17,000), and with a general climate which, despite the commitment of a number of local enthusiasts, can best be described as a passive benevolence towards public libraries.

The core plan of the Campaign, 'to raise the profile of libraries in political, trade union, commercial and civic life to the extent that public and political support will halt and reverse the tide of regression' is ambitious but, as yet, unattained (*The Campaigner*, 1987).

An interesting comparison is the National Campaign for the Arts (NCA), itself a reciprocal member of The Library Campaign, but an organisation which enjoys larger resources and a considerably higher profile. The NCA was founded, also in 1984, as 'the independent voice of the arts'. Its manifesto is:

- a real increase in central and local government funding
- the improvement of tax incentives for private benefactors
- the advancement of equal opportunities in the arts
- the promotion of the arts in schools
- a higher priority for the arts on the political agenda

The NCA aims to provide 'sustained lobbying and campaigning' and is able to do so through its full-time staffing of a Director, a Research Officer and an Administrator. Its services include a regular periodical, occasional papers and briefings. Individual membership was 485 in 1989, with a corporate membership of 313, including over 40 local authority members (National Campaign for the Arts, 1989).

In some respects the NCA carries out functions which are similar to those of The Library Association, reflecting the fact that there is no established professional body for arts practitioners, administrators and organisations which would equate with The Library Association and its role in the world of library and information management. Nevertheless, the relatively high profile achieved by the NCA, and its sustained efforts to enlist support for the arts, contrast significantly with the somewhat tentative air that still pervades the promotion of libraries.

Libraries' involvement with the arts, therefore, is well worth studying and has recently been well documented (Heeks, 1989; Hinton, 1990). The scope for partnership and collaboration is extensive and potentially invaluable for mutual widening of horizons, enhancement of services, and contribution to community development. Also, the arts world often speaks a similar language to that of libraries: incentive schemes and challenge funding are part of the scene, and Greater London Arts' recent *Arts Plan for London* calls for 'agreement and partnership from all local authorities, practitioners, arts bodies and sponsors to ensure that the future challenges to and potential of the sector as a whole will be faced and satisfied' (Austwick, 1990).

OBJECTIVES, OPPORTUNITIES AND DIFFICULTIES

Now that several examples of new kinds of cooperation have been outlined, it will be helpful to consider the reasons as to why such developments have occurred, and to consider some management issues of cost, benefit and ease – or otherwise – of implementation.

Reasons for public libraries to seek cooperation with each other, and with other organisations, include:

- to improve services
- to create new services
- to share expertise
- to facilitate staff development
- to achieve together what cannot be achieved alone
- to meet customer wants/needs/demands
- to satisfy higher authority
- to respond to government pressures to establish partnerships and joint ventures
- to satisfy professional aspirations
- to take account of the realisation that no library is an 'island entire of itself'

- to counter the threat of budget cuts
- to save money

As librarians tend to be cooperative (rather than competitive) people, they have perhaps a natural tendency to cooperate with others. However, our traditional comfortable feelings about library cooperation are now being challenged by three factors: the need to learn to cooperate with 'non-traditional', often non-public sector, partners; pressures to enhance the quality and targeting of our services; and a sharpening awareness of the costs, direct and indirect, which are involved in cooperative activity.

The wide spectrum of partners with whom the managers of public library services are now involved is evident from the examples previously given in this Chapter, e.g. those arising from the Public Library Development Incentive Scheme. But collaboration of this kind is not easy; it can entail much time, effort and frustration in trying to identify, to clarify and then to harmonise the differing philosophies, attitudes, aims, objectives, operational practices and accountancy arrangements of the respective partners. There is also a cost involved, in terms of the expenditure of human, intellectual and financial resources.

Moreover, one of the partners having had the original idea for the proposed collaboration, it will have to spend time and money in 'selling' the idea to other potential partners (from whom, to make things more difficult, it may wish to elicit financial commitment). Some risks are involved here, since the efforts made may turn out to be abortive; or, if the 'selling' is successful, the project may eventually flounder because of unforeseen or unavoidable difficulties.

Also, public libraries are relatively comfortable with the notion of attempting a collaborative venture with one of their own kind; after all, they speak the same 'language'. They are less comfortable when approached by a completely different animal with proposals which, perhaps, have persuasive political or financial backing from organisations or agencies which have their own 'agendas'. Collaboration within a local authority, with colleagues from different professional disciplines, whether archivists or engineers, can also be a minefield, e.g. if untested assumptions are made, on either side, about other persons' attitudes and expertise.

Joint ventures with Government Departments and quangos are not the least prone to meeting such problems. Newcastle Central Library's Marketing Advice Centre provides a significant example of the complexities, tensions and misunderstandings which may have to be resolved before a joint project can be successfully implemented. 'The Marketing Advice Centre's story illustrates how public libraries can find themselves at the epicentre of conflicting government policies' (Wressell, 1990).

The problem has not gone unnoticed by the Audit Commission which has recently suggested that 'government support programmes are seen as a patchwork quilt of complexity and idiosyncrasy. They baffle local authorities and business alike. The rules of the game seem over-complex and sometimes capricious. They encourage compartmentalised policy approaches rather than a coherent strategy'. The Commission noted four particular problems (Audit Commission, 1989):

- government rhetoric has contributed to a climate which is less favourable for cooperation than it might be
- the multiplicity of governmental agencies and schemes generates confusion
- the structures and procedures of individual programmes do not harness the energies of local authorities as effectively as they could
- inadequate coordination of local strategies

Even when a joint project has been successfully implemented, the withdrawal or 'time expiry' of financial support (whether of the pump-priming, incentive, challenge or some other variety) can leave the public library, and the local authority of which it is a part, with a major challenge if the project is to be adequately funded, maintained and developed. The politics of cooperation is therefore a skill which public library managers have to master if they are to be effective in establishing relationships, negotiating deals and implementing joint ventures.

Nor is the private sector necessarily unsympathetic to the problem. Many businessmen are happy to acknowledge the strengths of the public sector (including those of the public library service). They also recognise that the principle of partnership is one which the Government is keen to foster within the public sector.

The view of one businessman is that 'the only stumbling block is that such partnerships are not easy to arrange': business people may not know whom to approach, and public sector officials may lack understanding as to how commercial relationships are established. He goes on to suggest 'the need for some public partnership centre, an organisation staffed both by people knowledgeable about the principles of partnership, and skilled in the ways of the public sector...There are many cases where the public sector possesses assets, but the private sector possesses the means of their exploitation. Cooperation must be encouraged' (Knight, 1990).

The clear implication here for public library managers is that, in order to forge new partnerships and to win over potential funding bodies, they need to be not merely cooperative but also competitive and entrepreneurial. Similar considerations have led The Library Association to propose 'the establishment of an agency to maximise professional and managerial growth within library and information service provision... a specific focus on the necessity to update knowledge and enhance skills in order to ensure that proactive and effective information services are created in the market economy' (Library Association, 1990).

An alternative and immediately available way to bring the relevant business skills into public library management is through the creation of specialist posts (e.g. marketing, publicity, research, automation), and through the use of secondments and short-term contracts. Evidence of a trend in this direction can increasingly be seen in the work of public library authorities, Regional Library Systems, and Library and Information Plan agencies (*Information North Newsletter,* 1988–). Many examples of such arrangements can be seen in the world of the arts and in the cultural and leisure industries generally. The trend is steadily increasing, and local government itself is clearly going in the same direction.

Other potential sources of concern and discomfort for public library managers are management committees, advisory groups and user panels. Often required as part of new projects which involve a number of partners, they can be regarded as threats to that sense of independence which librarians tend to feel is part of the natural order of things. However, there is no doubt that attitudes in this respect are changing, together with a growing recognition that effective feedback of the views of our readers, users and clients is an essential ingredient of high quality, customer orientated services. Moreover, the strengths to be gained from the shared 'ownership' of a joint project, on the part of the agencies involved, is likely in a well managed situation to far outweigh any perceived loss of autonomy or control on the part of the public library.

SOME EXAMPLES IN PRACTICE

The concept of accountability is therefore coming to be better understood and appreciated by managers, in relation both to customers and to partners who are putting resources into a joint initiative. Cooperation implies benefits and improvements; it also entails duties and obligations. The provision of tourist information services provides a good example.

The English Tourist Board oversees a network of over five hundred accredited Tourist Information Centres (TICs), of which around one fifth are provided by public library authorities. The key point here is that, to become and to remain accredited, a TIC has to undergo annual monitoring and assessment by the relevant Regional Tourist Board. The Board, having completed its *TIC Visit Check List*, sends the TIC management a copy together with comments and notes on action required by the Board. The sanction is therefore available to the Tourist Board, if it is not satisfied with the TIC's performance, to withdraw its accreditation together with the very tangible benefits enjoyed by members of the network (Brewer, 1990).

TICs therefore are regularly assessed, against a declared set of criteria, in a way that is quite unlike the normal management practices in public library provision. Regular reports, monitoring and feedback mechanisms are also required in connection with grants made via Inner City Partnership, Public Library Development Incentive Scheme, British Library and other funding agencies. The practice will no doubt increase as public libraries become more heavily involved in new partnership and sponsorship ventures.

In any case, membership of a formal network is bound to entail some constraints on library management's scope for making independent decisions.

With the Patents Information Network (PIN), for example, overseen by the Patent Office and the British Library Science Reference and Information Service, the major regional reference libraries enjoy the continuous receipt of United Kingdom and European patent literature, free of charge; on the other hand, more than one hundred yards of shelf-run is required each year for this literature to be housed. Also, as with the TICs network but less rigorously applied, membership of PIN entails meeting certain requirements regarding public access to and promotion of these patent deposit collections.

Public libraries

The benefits and advantages of belonging to a network of this kind, therefore, are counterbalanced by duties and obligations – and also by costs. In the case of PIN, these include the direct staffing and shelving equipment costs, as well as the overheads of accommodation, heating and opportunity costs.

The emergent Business Information Network (BIN) will also be offering a mixture of costs and benefits. The general aims are:

- to promote exploitation of business information resources in the UK
- to improve the overall standard of business information provision
- to provide an effective focus for the development of business information products and services (Gomersall, 1990)

Unlike PIN, members of BIN will pay a subscription and the Network will be self-managing, not supervised by 'higher authority'. The appointment of an executive officer is envisaged, in order for the aims of the Network to be met in capitalising on the resources and skills available in libraries throughout the country. However, as well as sharing in such potential benefits as joint publicity and promotion, a referral database and reduced subscriptions to online hosts and expensive directories, BIN members are likely, in due course, to be establishing standards and criteria for the performance which they, and by extension their users, will be expecting of each other.

Not all potential members are convinced that they should join BIN; some are anxious, for example, that undue demands could be made on the already stretched resources of the major business information services in the public sector. Such concerns help to illuminate a major factor which underpins – and, some would say, undermines – all library cooperation, *viz*: it's all an act of faith, and one that is rarely tested at a later stage in order to assess whether the act of faith has turned out to be justified.

Similar thoughts may be particularly relevant to automated networks for catalogues and bibliographical records, where the capital investment and continuation costs may be substantial. All the more important is it, therefore, to assess the potential benefits of commitment to a particular project. It was for this reason that Information North recently decided against participating, at least for the time being, in LASER's VISCOUNT scheme, preferring to take stock of its own manual, 'steam age', regional union catalogue and to review what other methods might be feasible for meeting its members' current and potential interlending needs.

Cooperative acquisition has also been a traditional favourite among public libraries, but reassessment of its virtues is again in hand, prompted by the usual factors of space, time and money, by the ever increasing number of titles being published, and by a sharper understanding of the life cycle costs involved in acquiring, managing and 'decommissioning' books and periodicals (Enright, 1989). At Westminster City Libraries, 'we have amassed thousands of books under various cooperative and centralised acquisition schemes. One striking feature to emerge is the necessity for a strict acquisitions policy. Had one been in existence years ago, today's problems would be less daunting' (Williams, 1990).

COOPERATION IN TRAINING

Staff training is another area in which marked progress has been made in recent years in establishing and developing cooperatives and networks. In some cases a number of public libraries have joined forces to create their own cooperatives on a regional basis, e.g. the Central Scotland Training Group (CSTG), and the Eastern Region Training Officers' Group (ERTOG).

In other cases public libraries have formed more localised training groups in partnership with university, polytechnic and other libraries and with schools of library and information studies, e.g. the Staff Development Group of the Newcastle upon Tyne Libraries Joint Working Party, and the Welsh Libraries Training Group

According to a recent account of thirteen cooperative training schemes, their growth in popularity has come about for a number of reasons: 'a principal motive may have been a recognition that coordination of activities offers a better standard of overall training provision and a reduction in unit costs per trainee. Many other advantages and unforeseen spin-offs have occurred: better understanding of needs, efficiency of provision, improvements in methods, prevention of isolation and stagnation have been seen to offer additional social and professional inducements to share problems and solutions' (MacDougall and Prytherch, 1989).

As mentioned earlier, one of the recent PLDIS projects comprised a feasibility study for a public/private collaborative training scheme.

LASER, with International Computers Ltd. (ICL) and four public library authorities, investigated training needs and the possibilities for cooperation between different types of libraries and between libraries and the private sector. It recommended that public library authorities devise plans to address key issues, particularly in terms of human resource development, and examine the possibility of devising training modules on a public/private collaborative basis.

To stay with the private sector for a moment, another businessman has written that 'successful joint venturing requires common objectives, a clear statement of purpose, agreed priorities and a management structure which allows for changes in initial hypotheses and programmes. One survey suggests that three times as much senior management effort goes into setting up joint ventures as into running them' (Daniell, 1990). Effective management skills are therefore essential.

VALUES, COSTS AND STRATEGIES

Given all the caveats expressed above about the relative costs and benefits of public library cooperation, it is hardly surprising to find that not all library managers are totally in favour of it. Indeed, some are positively sceptical. I have already referred to the concept of 'enlightened self-interest'; and, although some would argue that poverty shared is poverty halved, the notion has the same kind of limited value with regard to library management as it has in domestic and social situations.

Clearly, few librarians would want to seem actually uncooperative and, as Michael Wills points out, the pleasure of travelling around and being cooperative 'sure beats working'. Moreover, 'cooperation is positively encouraged, nay demanded, by libraries' funding bodies, which have the idea that it is the key to saving money'. Wills therefore suggests that 'effective cooperation has a lot going against it...the ineffectiveness of cooperation is not generally realised because, while the costs of doing something cooperatively or otherwise may be compared, the costs of cooperation itself are rarely considered' (Wills, 1990).

Unfortunately, like the rest of us, Wills is unable to point to any satisfactory research that would help us to answer the question: is it worthwhile? Perhaps the Office of Arts and Libraries and the Library and Information Services Council (England), having so persuasively championed the cause of cooperation and partnership for a number of years, should now be asked to look for ways of evaluating and assessing the current state of the art. Evaluation of the PLDIS may provide an opportunity to start the process.

Arguably the issue is also one that should be addressed by the Library and Information Cooperation Council (LINC). Recently born out of the long established National Committee on Regional Library Cooperation, the object of LINC is 'to promote cooperation and partnership as a means of improving the effectiveness of the library and information sector in the United Kingdom and the Republic of Ireland'. Specific aims of LINC therefore include reviewing, encouraging and facilitating all types of library cooperation, collecting and disseminating information on cooperation, and reviewing the progress of local and regional cooperation (LINC, 1989). These aims give plenty of scope for LINC to initiate some badly needed research into the efficiency, effectiveness and economy of public and other library cooperation.

In the light of all the above comments, three specific points need to be made about library cooperation. First, it is seductive. Second, it should be approached as a business proposition. Third, its ultimate purpose, and justification, is the improvement of service for the customer.

All three points are relevant when considering the question of making charges. Regardless of whether cooperation does save money, or whether budgetary constraints actually make cooperation more difficult, the issue of whether money can be made from cooperation is bound to arise. Expectations of being able to do so have perhaps been raised by some of the discussion surrounding such publications as the Green Paper and *Joint enterprise*.

Some of the discussion has been over optimistic about the potential for income generation in public libraries. Certainly there are opportunities for developing fee-paying, value added, services, possibly in collaboration with agencies from other sectors, but I am not aware of any firm evidence to show that identifiable net profits are available from such initiatives. Some light on this topic is provided by a British Library Research Paper on levels of service, related costs and charging systems (Hyde, 1988). Useful definitions are given for such terms as visible costs, overheads, cost recovery, handling charges, surpluses and profits, all of which can help to clarify library managers' thinking on financial management and costing exercises.

Less formal modes of networking can provide relatively cheap forms of cooperation, and informal groupings of chief librarians are not

Public libraries

uncommon among public libraries, e.g. the Northern Metropolitan and County Chief Librarians (NMCCL) and the Council of City Research and Information Libraries (COCRIL). NMCCL includes the public library authorities of Cleveland, Cumbria, Durham, Gateshead, Newcastle, North Tyneside, North Yorkshire, Northumberland, South Tyneside and Sunderland. The chief librarians meet every other month; the venue rotates around the ten authorities, as do the chair and responsibility for minutes. One of the group acts as convenor for a term of around two years.

The group is valuable for information exchange, discussion of current issues, mutual support and for one-off joint action. Any workload or commitment arising from decisions made at NMCCL meetings is deliberately kept in check. Continuity, and staff development, are facilitated by the attendance of deputies when necessary. There are also two or three off-shoot working parties, including the Northern Training Group mentioned earlier.

COCRIL is slightly more formal: it has a set of objectives (including to promote and publicise the cause of regional reference libraries) and an Executive Secretary; it occasionally lobbies in appropriate quarters (e.g. British Library, Office of Arts and Libraries) for a stronger recognition of the role of the regional reference libraries. Otherwise it is similar to NMCCL in the way it functions; venues and the chair rotate among the membership (Belfast, Birmingham, Edinburgh, Glasgow, Leeds, Liverpool, City of London, Manchester, Newcastle upon Tyne, Sheffield and Westminster). COCRIL meets twice a year and allows for the attendance of deputies.

The Newcastle Libraries Joint Working Party (JWP) is a variation on the same theme of informal networks which are voluntary, flexible and contained. It includes public, academic and educational organisations, and is something of a misnomer since libraries outwith Newcastle itself are welcome to join and some have done so, including the universities and polytechnics of north east England. The chair is also the convenor; this combined role does not rotate, but the venues do, three times a year. The rationale of the JWP is basically similar to NMCCL and COCRIL; it also keeps a close eye on government and the British Library, occasionally communicating on behalf of its members; working groups are sometimes set up and discontinued when their work is done.

A particularly interesting development within the JWP has been the Newcastle Libraries Agreement 1989 (see the Appendix to this Chapter).

This arose from a concern among the four major public sector libraries in Newcastle that, although their cooperation was well established after two decades of pioneering work, there was a weakness in that their achievement had not been clearly articulated, particularly for the benefit of the four libraries' governing bodies. The Agreement is unusual: it embraces the virtues of library cooperation, and it documents in some detail the signatories' commitment to working together; but it also respects the limitations of cooperation, and allows for each partner to set its own boundaries, e.g. with regard to channelling and controlling use of its services by external readers, and to work to its own strengths. There is therefore an underlying hardheadedness to the Agreement, reflecting the JWP's preference always to look to the cost as well as to the benefit of cooperation.

CONCLUSIONS

To summarise and conclude, I have attempted an outline of some of the many types of library cooperation involving public libraries to have emerged in recent years. I have deliberately used the phrase 'library cooperation' as an umbrella term for a wide spectrum of cooperative processes and mechanisms. I have suggested that these have evolved in response to government policies, budgetary constraints, and fresh attitudes to service delivery, to quality management and to customer care. I have noted that the benefits of cooperation need to be weighed against the costs.

In addition, it has become increasingly obvious that the provision of a 'comprehensive' library service, as required by the Public Libraries and Museums Act 1964, cannot in fact be achieved, certainly not by any single library authority from its own resources. Collaborations and partnerships will therefore continue to be created by public libraries, with each other, with other local government services and departments, and with a wide range of outside bodies – all of whom are affected by the same kind of social, political and economic changes as the public library service.

All these trends will continue through the 1990s during which the major factors will include:

- change
- complexity
- flexibility
- diversification
- segmentation
- policy planning

Cooperation will continue to be an essential part of the public library world, where too many aspirations will still be chasing too few resources.

REFERENCES

Audit Commission (1989), *Urban regeneration and economic development: the local government dimension.* HMSO. pp. 1, 16.

Austwick, D. (1990), Arts for London. *The Leisure Manager*, (May), pp. 18–19.

Brewer, S. (1990), Tourist information and public libraries. *Public Libraries Journal*, vol. 5, no. 2, (March/April), pp. 52–54.

The Campaigner (1987), vol. 19, (October), p. 4.

Daniell, M. (1990), Webs we weave. *Management Today*, (February), p. 82.

Edmonds, D. J. (1986), *Current library cooperation and coordination: an investigation* (Office of Arts and Libraries, Library and Information Series No. 15). HMSO.

Enright, B. J. – I owe the phrase 'enlightened self-interest' to a number of stimulating conversations over the years with the late Dr. Brian Enright; the phrase, a child of realism, seems to be gaining in currency.

Enright. B. J. (1989), *Selection for survival: a review of acquisition and retention policies.* British Library.

Filon, S. P. L. (1967), Library cooperation, in Saunders, W. L., *Librarianship in Britain today.* The Library Association. pp. 13–14, 23.

Financing our public library service: four subjects for debate (1988). HMSO. (Cmnd. 324).

The future development of libraries and information services: progress through planning and partnership. Report by the Library and Information Services Council. (1986). (Office of Arts and Libraries, Library and Information Series No. 14). HMSO.

Gomersall, A. (1990), A BIN or a BLIP: a proposed national business information initiative. *Refer*, vol. 6, no. 2, (Summer), pp. 1–6.

Heeks, P. (1989), *Public libraries and the arts: an evolving partnership*. The Library Association.

Hinton, B. (1990), *Marshalled arts: a handbook for arts in libraries*. Association of Assistant Librarians.

Hyde, M. (1988), *Library and information services to business and industry: study on levels of service, related costs and charging systems*. British Library Research Paper 48. British Library Research and Development Department.

Information North Newsletter. 1988– , *passim*.

Joint enterprise: roles and relationships of the public and private sectors in the provision of library and information services. Report by the Library and Information Services Council and British Library Research and Development Department Working Party (1987). (Office of Arts and Libraries, Library and Information Series No. 16). HMSO.

Josey, E. J. (1987), *Librarians, coalitions and the public good*. Neal-Schuman, New York, pp. 109, xi.

Knight, D. (1990), What's in a name. *Management Today*, (May), p. 136.

Library Association (1990), *A Development agency for information services managers (DAISM)*. Paper submitted to the Minister for the Arts, April. The Library Association. (Unpublished).

Library and Information Cooperation Council (1989), *Constitution*.

The Library Campaigner (1990), vol. 34, (Autumn), p. 12.

MacDougall, A. and Prytherch, R. (1989), *Cooperative training in libraries*. Aldershot, Gower.

McKee, R. (1989), Book review, *International Journal of Information and Library Research*, vol. 1, no. 1, p. 86.

National Campaign for the Arts (1989), *Annual Report 1 April 1988–31 March 1989*. NCA.

Plaister, J. M. (1976), Future library cooperation and the British Library, in Harrison, K.C., *Prospects for British librarianship*. Library Association. pp. 205, 203.

Public Library Development Incentive Scheme: the third year: 1989/90 (1990). British Library Research and Development Department. (unpublished paper, available gratis).

White, B. (1990), A Library and Information Plan for Northern Ireland. *Library Association Record*, vol. 92, no. 6, (June), pp. 441, 442, 445.

Williams, L. (1990), Going, going, gone..., *Library Association Record*, vol. 92, no. 9, (September), pp. 667–668.

Wills, M. (1990), Lust: or 'cooperation', *Library Association Record*, vol. 92, no. 4, (April), p. 292.

Wressell, P. (1990), Marketing advice: a new role for libraries? *Library Association Record*, vol. 92, no. 3, (March), pp. 189–191, 192.

APPENDIX

The Newcastle Libraries Agreement 1989

1. Participating Libraries

1.1 The signatories of this agreement at the date of issue are the Chief Librarians of:
- Newcastle City Libraries
- Newcastle College Library
- Newcastle Polytechnic Library
- Newcastle University Library

1.2 Other Libraries in the Northern Region may become Participating Libraries by agreement with the existing members.

2. Scope and Background of the Agreement

2.1 This Agreement deals with:
- Basic Principles of Stock Cooperation
- Collection Policies
- Identification of Collection Specialisms
- Access to Library Catalogues
- Access by Reader Visits
- Interlibrary Lending
- Gift and Exchange of Stock
- Publicity

2.2 The Agreement is based on two decades of interlibrary cooperation, positive development and disaster avoidance through the Newcastle Libraries Joint Working Party and other agencies. The Agreement is intended as a statement of intent and as practical guidelines rather than a legally binding agreement. Examples of successful existing arrangements are provided.

3. Basic Principles

3.1 The aim of this Agreement is to foster and enhance the richness, diversity and economy of library provision through stock cooperation measures. The cooperation covers books, periodicals, computer, electronic, and other non-book materials.

3.2 The Libraries are committed to working together to obtain the best possible value in library services for their users and for the community at large.

3.3 It is recognised that each Library operates collection policies designed to achieve maximum benefit for its primary clientele. This leads naturally to a richness, diversity and relevance of provision.

3.4 A prerequisite of stock cooperation is a clear understanding of the nature and extent of access which will result. Each Library offers a particular balance of facilities of its funding organisation. Even a public library has a primary duty to the citizens of its own authority area.

It is therefore recognised that each Library has a duty to channel and control external use arising from library cooperation, in order to minimise conflict between the demands of external users and those of the primary clientele of the library concerned.

3.5 The Libraries agree that charges to recover the marginal costs of use by external readers arising from this Agreement may be made at the discretion of the providing Library provided advance notice is given.

4. Collection Policies

4.1 The Libraries agree to share knowledge of their collection policies and to seek to enhance the complementarity of those policies.

Public libraries

4.2 The Libraries agree to share the results of studies which seek to ascertain the existence of any undesired overlaps or gaps in provision, while recognising that studies have repeatedly shown that overlap between libraries is low, except where it is justified by the nature of demand.

5. Allocation of Collection Specialisms

5.1 It is agreed that collection specialisms will relate to natural specialisms for the libraries concerned. The allocation of subject areas on a random basis in order to achieve comprehensiveness is rejected, because it aggravates conflicts between local needs and cooperative obligations.

5.2 The agreed approach is to exploit the areas of natural focus for mutual benefit. Where access to another library with complementary collections is available, each library buys less in peripheral areas and deepens and strengthens its mainstream collections instead. This is a cooperation which strengthens the richness and diversity of the total collections in the area in harmony with the needs of individual clienteles.

5.3 The Libraries undertake to seek to establish and extend reciprocal or community-wide arrangements for collection specialisms.

5.4 The Libraries agree jointly to maintain a register of such arrangements and to make it available to Library staff and to readers in each Library.

5.5 The Libraries undertake to foster the crucial factors of good personal relationships and regular communication between the staff in the different Libraries to ensure that all the agencies concerned receive and feel that they are receiving good value from the bargain.

5.6 The following existing successful examples are provided as illustration:
— Health: medicine by Newcastle University; paramedicine by Newcastle Polytechnic (both with some funding from the Northern Regional Health Authority)
— Technical Standards: shared across the region
— Student provision (for any students resident or working in Newcastle): further education students by Newcastle College; polytechnic students by Newcastle Polytechnic;

university students by Newcastle University; (freeing Newcastle City Library from such obligations)
— Newcastle local history by Newcastle City; teaching packs by Newcastle College
— European documents by Newcastle Polytechnic
— Historical Collections by the Newcastle Literary & Philosophical Society (with some funding by other libraries) and Newcastle University
— Patents and foreign directories by Newcastle City
— Law by Newcastle Polytechnic (with some funding from the Newcastle Law Society and Newcastle Civic Centre)

6. Access to Library Catalogues

6.1 The Libraries undertake to make available copies of their Library Catalogues to the other signatory Libraries whenever possible, at no charge or at marginal costs.

6.2 It is anticipated that this will normally apply where a Library maintains its Catalogue in printed or microfiche form. In addition, where a Library has a computerised catalogue available on-line on a dial-up basis, then access will be permitted to other Libraries.

7. Access by Reader Visits

7.1 A reader will always be given access to a particular publication if one Library holds the only reasonably accessible appropriate source.

7.2 In the interests of all library users, access to libraries other than public libraries is recognised to be a conditional privilege, not an absolute right, but every effort will be made to maximise the resources accessible.

7.3 Normal access arrangements are as agreed between the libraries or organisations concerned on a reciprocal or payment basis which takes account of respective needs, relative resources, geographical location etc.

7.4 Referral procedures are agreed where readers do not have direct access under a reciprocal agreement. The purpose of the referral procedures is to filter enquiries so as to minimise the possibility of disappointment or difficulty for the reader through misunderstanding, poor information or unavailability.

8. Interlibrary Lending

8.1 The Libraries agree to lend appropriate items between libraries, thereby bringing individual items of stock to the reader in response to specific expressed demands.

8.2 For this purpose the established local and national networks are used, together with any extensions to these networks which may be devised.

9. Gift and Exchange of Stock

9.1 The Libraries seek to support each other by gift and exchange of stock no longer required by the present holding library, where appropriate.

9.2 This clause is not intended to preclude arrangements made by Libraries to sell unwanted stock or with other agencies such as the British Library Gift and Exchange Service, the Ranfurly Library Service etc.

10. Publicity

10.1 The Libraries agree that it is vital that the carefully constructed network of cooperative links outlined above is accurately communicated to the readers for whom it is intended. They undertake jointly and individually to give publicity to the cooperative provision available.

10.2 The Libraries also agree to seek to promote and publicise such cooperative arrangements regionally through the Regional Library and Information Plan to which Newcastle libraries have already committed considerable effort.

Signed .... Newcastle City Library
 .... Newcastle College Library
 .... Newcastle Polytechnic Library
 .... Newcastle University Library
Date ....

8

Academic library cooperation

JOHN FLETCHER

The term 'academic library' covers a very wide range of size, type, and service provision, from the national libraries, through large university libraries and polytechnics to small specialist colleges. The clienteles which these libraries serve is equally diverse: advanced researchers, postgraduate and undergraduate students, sub-degree, professional qualifications, and access course students. The services offered vary too, from full bibliographic and teaching support for staff and researchers to simple textbook provision for students. Nevertheless, there is a similarity of approach, the support of teaching and research in educational establishments, though the emphasis will change with the institution's objectives.

Librarianship in the United Kingdom is a relatively small profession, and the work which its members perform is primarily the provision of information. Their ability to do this well is to a large extent dependent on cooperation between them, for no library can ever be self-sufficient. In order to provide a satisfactory service, it is essential that librarians cooperate with each other, and this tends to be through publications, but more importantly through personal contact. The importance of meetings, exchange of experience seminars, training sessions, and conferences can not be overemphasised in this context. The social network is the lifeline for many information providers in libraries. These meetings are organised by a variety of librarians' organisations, so a quick survey of the more important ones for academic librarians is a good foundation for this Chapter.

NATIONAL ORGANISATIONS

There are three major groups of academic librarians on a national basis: the Standing Conference of National and University Libraries (SCONUL), the Consortium of University Research Libraries (CURL), and the Council of Polytechnic Librarians (COPOL). Within the Library Association two groups cater for the interests of members in academic libraries: the Colleges of Further and Higher Education Group (COFHE), and the University, College and Research Section (UC&R).

Standing Conference of National and University Libraries

As its name implies, SCONUL membership includes the various divisions of the British Library, the National Libraries of Scotland and Wales, and most, but not all, of the universities and university colleges of the United Kingdom and Ireland. The larger university libraries, such as Manchester and Edinburgh, are also members of the Consortium of University Research Libraries (CURL). At the other end of the size scale are Lampeter College, and some of the constituent colleges of the University of London. Most libraries are general, though with varying strengths and weaknesses reflecting their institutions' teaching and research interests. Some are more specialised because of this: the British Library of Political and Economic Science (at the London School of Economics), and the library of the School of Oriental and African Studies, for example. SCONUL is an independent corporate body, and the librarians attending the Conference, the main forum of SCONUL, are their institutions' representatives.

SCONUL has many sub-groups, called Advisory Committees, comprising representatives, and other interested and involved individuals. Some Advisory Committees are on topics which are of interest to all libraries, such as Buildings, Research Collections, Automation Policy, and Information Services, and these tend to advise the SCONUL Council on matters in their remit. Others are subject-oriented: American Studies, Orientalist, Medical Materials, and Slavonic and East European Materials, for example. The latter Committees, and to a smaller extent the first group, encourage cooperation between members with similar interests, by providing a forum for discussion and exchange of experience.

Consortium of University Research Libraries

The Consortium of University Research Libraries (CURL) was formed in 1982; its members are those universities with substantial research collections which identified certain opportunities for cooperation that could not be explored through existing bodies. Membership comprises the university libraries of Cambridge, Edinburgh, Glasgow, Leeds, London, Manchester and Oxford. A major project at present well advanced seeks to create a database using bibliographic records of the seven members, with access via the Joint Academic Network (JANET). This initiative is more fully described by Peter Stubley in Chapter 11.

Council of Polytechnic Librarians

It is significant that whereas SCONUL is a conference of 'libraries', COPOL is a council of 'librarians'. This is a much smaller group, representing libraries which are much less diverse than those in SCONUL. Its membership comprises the librarians of all twenty nine English and the one Welsh polytechnics, six of the larger Scottish Central Institutions, and, since 1989, six of the larger English Colleges or Institutes of Higher Education which are similar in character and size.

All the polytechnics were founded in the early 1970s, by the amalgamation of a variety of local colleges, and whilst there is some diversity in size, and to a lesser degree in subject coverage, their libraries' aims and objectives, and services are much more homogeneous. Lacking a permanent secretariat, COPOL has fewer committees, and cooperation among its members is fostered by the twice yearly meeting of the full Council, and seminars on specific topics of common interest. COPOL also supported the foundation of two special interest groups, for acquisitions librarians, the National Acquisitions Group (NAG) and for interlibrary loans librarians, Forum for Interlending (FIL), both of which have developed as independent bodies.

Library Association (LA) Groups

The LA is an association of professional librarians, and to serve its aim of fostering cooperation between them has several groups. Two of these are specifically for academic library staff. Colleges of Further and Higher Education Group covers what might be termed the third level of tertiary

Academic libraries

education, the staff of local authority colleges of further and higher education, and, to some extent, that of smaller libraries within larger systems. The University, College and Research Section of the Library Association caters for the staff of universities, polytechnics and colleges at all levels, in addition to staff of research libraries. Both the LA groups have regional subgroups, and these and the national groups hold meetings, conferences, and training sessions for members.

It is worth noting that cooperation between these national professional organisations is assisted by their representatives meeting as the Joint Consultative Committee (JCC) where matters of common interest can be discussed, and a more united policy on professional matters can be prepared. The work of the JCC is examined in Chapter 6.

SPECIAL INTEREST GROUPS

In addition to the national, general, overarching organisations noted above, librarians with an interest in a special subject area, or type of library work, have frequently formed groups to meet their perceived needs for cooperation. Some of these are completely independent of the national organisations, and some have close affiliations with them. An incomplete list of the more important and active subject interest groups would include:

- British and Irish Association of Law Librarians (BIALL) (see Chapter 9)
- Art Libraries Society (ARLIS)
- University Medical Schools' Librarians' Group (Chapter 9)
- Association of E(uropean) D(ocumentation) C(entre) Librarians
- British Business Schools' Librarians' Group (which has links with the European Business Schools' Librarians' Group)
- Aslib, the Association for Information Management, also has special subject interest groups on such areas as transport, business information, and social sciences, whose members include academic librarians as well as the industrial and commercial librarians who make up the majority of the Association's membership

COOPERATION IN COLLECTION DEVELOPMENT

From outside academic libraries there would seem to be a clear case for cooperation between libraries on purchasing and holding book and periodical stock. Very expensive reference tools, and periodical subscriptions need not be purchased by two libraries geographically close to each other. In practice, there is less scope for this than one would imagine, and most attempts have achieved only limited success. There are several factors militating against such cooperation: the reluctance of readers to travel even short distances to use material in other libraries, and restrictive rules on access to collections by readers from outside the parent institution are the most obvious. The dominance of the collections of the British Library Document Supply Centre has also conspired to diminish the viability of cooperation in acquisition and stock.

There has been greater success in cooperation in retention of specialist stock. Some libraries agree to keep permanently certain types of material, titles, or subject areas, on a regional or national basis. Two useful, perhaps even essential, prerequisites to such cooperation are the wider use of computer networked access to other libraries' catalogues, and Conspectus. The former will be discussed below under cooperation in automated systems. Conspectus is a methodology first applied in individual libraries in the United States who wished to assess their relative strengths and weaknesses by subject area. The methodology has been promoted by the British Library and is fully explained in Chapter 5. The results of work in Scotland are encouraging, though there was some scepticism about them. It is probably the most advanced collection development cooperation which has taken place in the United Kingdom. It has certainly helped to bring together the libraries, their collections, their staffs, and their computer systems.

With changes in the academic profiles of institutions, the growth of some subjects and the diminution of others, there is scope for library book and periodical stock to be transferred between libraries. This is not a simple matter of shifting stock. The costs of removing items from one catalogue and adding them to another are high. Nevertheless, cooperation between academic libraries in this situation has been good. SCONUL's Advisory Committees on Research Collections, on Interlibrary Loans and Access to Materials, and on Preservation all keep this movement under their watchful eye.

The widespread development of computerised catalogues has diminished the value of union catalogues of even specialised materials, and the last few years have seen the demise of several such ventures. However, there is still room for cooperation among specialist subject librarians in the production of guides to such material. The SCONUL Advisory Committee on Latin American Material has supported the publication of a guide to census material for their area.

COOPERATION IN INTERLIBRARY LENDING

The dominant position of the British Library Document Supply Centre (BLDSC) in the provision of interlibrary loans to British libraries has substantially affected the level of direct interlending. In addition to its own stock, BLDSC also has knowledge of the holdings of a number of research libraries which are prepared to act as backup for interlibrary loan requests. The Scottish experiment with Conspectus also allows for the possibility of direct interlibrary loans. Nevertheless, there is a certain truth in the suggestion that it may be less expensive, and more efficient, for a library to request a loan from BLDSC than to attempt to obtain the same item from another library, even a local one. This may not be true, however, where a reader wishes to consult a range of volumes of a periodical, or is willing to travel to the alternative source library.

COOPERATION IN BIBLIOGRAPHIC CONTROL

For the creation of bibliographic records for British publications, the work of the British Library Bibliographic Services Division (BLBSD) has dominated the scene since the early 1950s. With greater financial constraint on the Library, and the ever increasing flood of new publications, in 1988 BLBSD sought the help of the Copyright Agency libraries in processing some specialised material in which they had particular strengths, and material outside the Cataloguing-in-Publication programme of the BLBSD. A memorandum of understanding was signed by the copyright libraries early in 1990, and a pilot scheme is now planned. It will require much detailed discussion on how these agency libraries could best help the whole library community, but the product should be better and timelier coverage of British material in the British

National Bibliography. Chapters 5 and 11 offer a fuller picture of cooperation in this area.

COOPERATION IN WIDENING ACCESS TO COLLECTIONS

With some exceptions, academic libraries allow reference access to their collections to members of the public, and this includes students of other institutions. The conditions attached to such outside access vary considerably, but there is agreement among most university libraries to allow students from other universities this facility, at least during vacations. All polytechnic and college libraries allow free reference use of their collections to outsiders, with few conditions.

Borrowing privileges are offered to non-members of their institutions by most university and polytechnic libraries, and most now charge a fee for this service. The fee may be waived for certain categories of reader, such as graduates and retired staff of the institution, local teachers, health service employees, etc. In districts where there is both a university and a polytechnic, it is normal for each to allow staff and research students of the other to register as borrowers, without charge.

Members of COPOL have an agreement whereby sandwich course students of one polytechnic on placement in the catchment area of another, may, if they are supported by their 'home' librarian, be allowed borrowing privileges in the 'away' library. Several universities with sandwich courses have also agreed to follow the same reciprocal arrangement, which benefits the students, and causes few problems for the libraries.

With the growth in the number of part-time students, in all sections of higher education, there is increasing pressure for libraries to extend borrowing facilities to part-time students of other institutions. This is being met in many areas, by local agreement between the librarians of the universities, polytechnics and colleges concerned. Many higher education institutions have arrangements for local further education colleges to run 'access' courses, to bring potential students' qualifications up to the standard required for entry into higher education. These students are usually given free borrowing facilities at the senior institution. Similarly, agreements and contracts are being struck between specialist colleges (of nursing, for example) and higher education institutions whereby the latter validate the former's students' qualification. This

Academic libraries

often results in some form of association between the institutions which includes freeing up access to each other's library.

COOPERATION IN LIBRARY STAFF TRAINING

The recent volume, *Cooperative Training in Libraries* (MacDougall and Prytherch, 1989) includes several essays detailing the history of cooperation in training between academic libraries. One of the longest established examples of cooperation among university libraries is the SCONUL Trainee Scheme. Under this scheme, those members of SCONUL which have posts for graduates wishing to gain one year's library experience before progressing to a postgraduate course in librarianship, advertise them together in a publication issued by SCONUL and sent to all careers offices in universities and polytechnics. SCONUL lays down minimum requirements for the posts, the training and experience the trainee will receive, and acts as a clearing house for applications. From 1990 this service is offered to polytechnic libraries willing to meet the same conditions.

In recent years there has been a greater awareness among chief librarians of the importance of the continuing education and training of library staff at all levels. This is intended to increase their efficiency and effectiveness in their current posts, and to prepare them for promotion within or outside their library. There is great scope for cooperation between academic libraries in library staff training and development, at both national, and regional/local level. Mounting such courses is expensive, and cooperation with other libraries can afford considerable savings in cost, and additionally enhance the training experience by mixing together staff from different libraries.

Staff training may be of a general nature, such as courses on personnel or financial management, team building, interviewing techniques, and time management. Some meetings are more specialist, on topics such as science reference work, art bibliography, sources of economic statistics, and access to unpublished materials.

The national organisations of academic libraries, and librarians, run many courses, conferences and seminars for library staff through their various committees. Some recent examples include:

- New technology for interlibrary lending (SCONUL)

- Training together (COPOL)
- Historical bibliography (SCONUL)
- Harmony through networking (LA)
- User surveys (SCONUL)
- Library services for part-time students (COPOL)
- Use of CD-ROM (SCONUL)

In addition, most of the specialist committees and groups mentioned above hold annual conferences and seminars, often with a particular theme, and these are usually open to librarians from all types of academic library.

Locally, joint training initiatives linking two or more academic libraries arrange training sessions for staff on a range of topics of common interest, for example, overseas students, disabled students, dealing with awkward customers, and using microcomputers. These meetings may be organised by individual librarians in cooperation with each other, or under the auspices of local or regional professional groups, such as the regional library bureaux.

COOPERATION IN LIBRARY MANAGEMENT

The national groups of libraries and librarians described above see as one of their major roles that of working together to present a 'public face' of academic librarianship. They also form an informed pressure group to present that face publicly in the most effective way. This is achieved through exchange of experience at general conferences, and through their respective committees and councils. Increasingly the various groups are working together to further these common aims, and joint or open meetings are becoming more frequent.

Cooperation in the collection and dissemination of statistical information about their libraries, and their services, is now usual. Thus one of SCONUL's Advisory Committees defines in great detail the data which it collects from all members. COPOL has a parallel Committee, and there is one librarian common to both groups, to assist in the mammoth task of bringing (and keeping) the two statistical databases on similar lines, and thus attempting to make the data comparable. These annual statistical exercises began with the relatively straightforward area of expenditure, then expanded into the more difficult, but more interesting, topics of library services. Finally they are now tackling the delicate questions of library performance indicators. Close cooperation among librarians is essential in these tasks in order to ensure comparability of the data they produce. Increasingly the statistical output of SCONUL and COPOL is being accepted by government and quasi-government bodies as the best source of data about academic libraries and their services.

Some years ago, groups of university purchasing officers formed consortia to enable them to work together in the bulk purchasing of commonly used items, and to bring pressure to bear on suppliers for the best possible prices and service. With polytechnics now independent of their local education authorities, such purchasing consortia are a distinct possibility in the future. There has been minimal impact on libraries, but it is a possible area for consideration.

COOPERATION WITH INDUSTRY AND COMMERCE

A particularly successful example of local cooperation has been based on the library at Hatfield Polytechnic; HERTIS (originally the Hertfordshire County Council Technical Information Service) was founded in 1956 and was at first a cooperative of local academic libraries and the county library technical information department. It now has 180 members, mainly industrial and commercial firms, who depend on HERTIS for a range of library and information services which include training of staff in information handling, and the provision and staffing of reference services on members' premises on a contract basis. HERTIS has become widely known for its energetic moves towards European cooperation, and its success in winning new, income-earning contracts outside its immediate area.

COOPERATION IN LIBRARY AUTOMATION

This is one area of library activity in which cooperation has been most marked, and most successful in recent years. The benefits to both libraries and their readers are clear, and can be expected to continue.

Joint ventures in research into, leading to commercial operation of, library computer systems, produced the two major library automation cooperatives in the United Kingdom. BLCMP (formerly Birmingham Libraries Cooperative Mechanisation Project) brought together the libraries of the Universities of Aston and Birmingham, and the public library of the City of Birmingham, to create a centralised catalogue and cooperative cataloguing. A similar cooperative development by the libraries of the Universities of Exeter, Bristol, Bath and University College of Wales at Cardiff produced the South West Academic Libraries Cooperative Automation Project (SWALCAP), now SLS Ltd., which achieved a similar objective. National computer networking, and the development of the systems, enabled their owners to 'go commercial' and offer them to other academic and public libraries throughout the country. The names change, as do the technical methods by which the results are produced, but the basis of these commercial organisations is the cooperative efforts of their customers.

At the core of the cooperative scheme was the union catalogue of all the participating libraries, with bibliographic records emanating from the British Library, and from the libraries themselves. The next developments in library automation tended to undermine the cooperative origins of these schemes. Other system suppliers offered more advanced and sophisticated standalone systems, which did not require the user libraries to cooperate with each other. BLCMP and SWALCAP were forced to follow the market trend towards greater independence of their members, but retained the cooperative catalogue aspect of their original scheme.

Apart from these cooperative schemes cooperation between academic (and to some degree public) libraries in the field of library automation systems has developed into exchange of experience between users of the same system. There are thus user groups representing libraries with each of the now wide range of standalone library automation systems paralleling the cooperative groups. Although cooperation does take place, there is much less pressure on members to standardise, or rationalise their methods of working.

The second computer development to have a great impact on academic library cooperation came from the computing services of their institutions. The Joint Academic Network (JANET) links the computing systems of all the universities, and now most polytechnics of the United Kingdom. JANET allows computer users, on password, to gain access to the systems and databases of other institutions. Academic librarians were not slow to appreciate the great benefit this could bestow on their staff, and readers. At very little cost, they could consult the library catalogues of local, or distant, libraries. This is an enormous boon to interlibrary loans librarians seeking a location for a wanted item. Having traced it they can request a loan, or alert the reader to the other location. A user group for JANET was set up, and soon after, a JANET User Group for Libraries (JUGL) was founded. Once again, cooperation between academic librarians has been fostered by technological developments.

THE INTERNATIONAL DIMENSION

Universities and polytechnics have long had close relations with similar institutions overseas. Some are for the exchange of students, for cooperative ventures, and more recently, for development assistance to newly established colleges and universities in developing countries. These have tended to be bilateral agreements between institutions, often at the instigation of individual members of staff with personal contact with, or knowledge of, the other partner. Other cooperative arrangements have been made through the auspices of the British Council, and involve librarians from the United Kingdom spending time in the newly developing institution abroad, advising on professional matters relating to the library scene. One of SCONUL's most successful recent conferences was a joint meeting with members of the American Association of Research Libraries. From this meeting both groups anticipate closer cooperation as groups, on specific topics, and between individual members.

Within Europe, the pace of development of relationships between academic institutions will increase, and we can expect greater pressure for cooperation between their libraries. Some moves in this direction have already been made. Both SCONUL and COPOL have arranged visits to continental European countries to enable members to see the libraries of higher education institutions. SCONUL has also opened its annual conference to delegates from Europe and further afield.

The political pressure for the success of the ERASMUS programme (European Community Action Scheme for the Mobility of University Students) and the new European Credit Transfer Scheme (ECTS) will force an increase in institutional cooperation in the exchange of students between European countries. There is mounting pressure on their librarians to meet, exchange experience, and cooperate in the provision of services to this growing band of students with very special needs. Little seems to have been achieved so far, but there is a clear need for much closer cooperation in this area of library activity, and both SCONUL and COPOL are looking to find the best means of progressing.

In specialist subject areas of the profession some progress is being made on closer contacts, especially with European counterparts. Members of the SCONUL Advisory Committee on Medical Materials have welcomed the formation of the European Association of Health Information and Libraries (EAHIL), which they see as a major step forward on international cooperation.

A CHECKLIST OF ACADEMIC LIBRARY COOPERATION

It may be useful to provide a list of the areas of professional activity which have featured in cooperation between academic libraries in some localities. The list is not complete, it never could be, but is an indication of some of the activities which have featured in library cooperation. Some of these involve the public library services as well as academic ones, some only chief librarians, others staff at all levels. It is unlikely that any area achieves full cooperation in all of them.

> *Collection development*: this includes books, periodicals, and non-book media. Cooperation may cover the identification of specialist collections, subject strengths, special materials, such as standards, patents, or European Community material; agreement on collection and acquisition policies, coverage of periodical titles abstracted in specified secondary services; transfer of unwanted or little-used stock, and disposals.
>
> *Library services*: acknowledgment of each library's staff expertise in specific subjects or types of material; agreement to use each other's specialised services such as in-house bindery, photographic service, or graphic designer. Are there any examples of joint appointments of specialist staff by two or more libraries? If not, why not?
>
> *Access*: probably the most visibly beneficial form of cooperation between libraries from the users' viewpoint. Cooperation includes exchange of, or access to each others' catalogues, interlibrary lending, reference access, and its concomitant, enquiry assistance; borrower registration may be unlimited, restricted by distance between the parent institutions, by level of study, or to part-time

students, sandwich students on placement, or Open University students. Joint approaches to local industrial and commercial firms with a package of information services designed to meet their needs.

Staff development and training: joint training courses, lectures, conferences, exchanges of experience, and of staff; reviews of each other's libraries.

Management: exchange of management information, and of experience between senior staff of the cooperating libraries.

Publicity: especially within a confined local area, publicity about other libraries' facilities for the benefit of all the libraries' users.

International links: cooperation between libraries of a similar type, or in a geographical area, to set up links with similar groups or institutions abroad.

Professional involvement: agreement that staff of different libraries should represent the group of libraries, not merely themselves or their own library, in national forums.

WHAT OF THE FUTURE?

What follows can only be a personal view and the reader must accept this inevitable bias. It seems clear that a great deal of effort has gone into cooperation between academic libraries over a very long period of time. If, however, one seeks the concrete product of this, and tries to assess it from the viewpoint of the final arbiter, the libraries' users, the benefits seem to be very small. Maybe experiments have not been publicised in the professional literature, but it appears there are very few, and in some instances no, examples of the following:

- all students of one institution automatically having full borrowing rights at others
- librarians not buying periodicals, or books, because another library close by has already done so
- long-term (i.e. six months or longer) regular exchanges of staff at all levels between libraries
- joint appointments of specialist staff, such as conservationists, or subject specialists

- joint ventures in setting up binderies, photographic services, off-campus stores, or graphic design studios
- cooperative purchasing agreements to reduce the costs of commonly used items

I am under no illusions about why cooperation between librarians fails, or succeeds. If the interests of the library's clientele are not served, if there is no visible benefit to the parent institution, then the effort is doomed to failure. In other words, 'professional altruism is dead: long live self-interest!' This is in conflict with the traditional philosophy of librarianship: service to the reader, which always had the added rider, whoever he or she may be.

Academic librarians are now receiving conflicting messages from their institutional executives and government: open up your libraries to all who need them, access not holding; on the other hand, all institutions are in competition with each other for students, courses, and funds. Resolving this dilemma, with the pressures from above and below, will exercise all the academic librarians' ingenuity for the next few years, for it seems unlikely that the national education policy in this respect will change.

To take a hypothetical example: a polytechnic and its nearby university both bid to mount a specialised course for a local industrial company. It is a lucrative contract, and could have beneficial knock-on effects on the range of courses mounted by the successful institution. The university pares its costs to the bone, and is successful, and the contract is signed. The polytechnic library is, however, better equipped to meet the information needs of the course members. What does the polytechnic librarian reply when asked by the university librarian to allow these course members to use the polytechnic library?

How will this competitive philosophy affect the willingness of institutional executives to allow what could be sensitive data to be published? The Department of Education and Science, and the two funding councils will require financial and statistical data about the higher education sector, but will this be in the same detail as previously? Will the Polytechnic Finance Officers' Group be able to publish financial tables on the polytechnics' activities in the same detail in the future as in the past? Are academic institutions' annual reports going to become like company annual reports: lots of figures which never tell you what you really want to know?

To end on a more optimistic note, it seems probable that academic librarians will continue to talk to each other, to share problems, and experiences, to work together for the benefit of their readers. They have always exchanged sensitive information, knowing that their confidence will be respected. I think, and hope, that this will continue.

So far as the library organisations are concerned, I see signs of some movement. Academic libraries range in size and complexity from the large research university libraries to the small further education college libraries. There is clearly little point in trying to bring such a disparate group into one organisation since the members would have too little in common. It seems possible that the very large research libraries may form their own group, together with the national libraries. At the other end of the size scale, the smaller colleges of further and higher education look set to continue their liaison in groups such as the Library Association Colleges of Further and Higher Education Group. Some will merge to create larger colleges, some of which are already aspiring to become polytechnics, and they may well join COPOL.

This leaves the polytechnics, the medium-size and small universities, and the larger Scottish Central Institutions, most of which are already members of either SCONUL or COPOL. Closer working relationships between these two organisations seems sensible, inevitable, and productive. The funding councils for the two types of academic institution will, during 1991, share accommodation. There are already strong suggestions that, in the course of the next five years, they will merge into one. On the library front, exploratory discussions are already under way on how best SCONUL and COPOL can cooperate. The differences of levels and sources of funding between universities and polytechnics are being eroded. Polytechnics and universities are becoming increasingly alike in the balance of subjects taught, and of part-time and full-time students, and courses for specific industrial, commercial and professional purposes.

Certainly the next decade will see closer liaison between the libraries, and librarians, of the institutions. Whether this will produce more active cooperation in the provision of services to users, remains to be seen.

REFERENCES

MacDougall, A. and Prytherch, R. (1989), *Cooperative training in libraries*. Aldershot: Gower.

9

Subject cooperation

Cooperation between libraries and information services that deal in the same or similar subject areas is an obvious feature of the profession. Many groups have formed in recent years, and developments in networking and other technical advances have made such cooperation both easier to plan and more essential to implement.

Coverage of subject cooperation in this volume can only be offered selectively: there are too many groups for individual attention, and simple listings of groups and activities cannot offer any sense of development and achievement. We have therefore selected four subject areas – law, medicine and health-care, audiovisual materials, sport and recreation – and asked a leading figure from each field to discuss cooperation as they see it.

The four contributions present insights into the advantages and problems of subject cooperation; activity in audiovisual librarianship ranges from local to national, and international, where there is an especial opportunity for growth and a different scale of difficulties; in the medical and health-care field we see a prolific development of many diverse groupings, reflecting different shades of emphasis in an area where provision is complex. In law libraries, individual initiatives appear as a catalyst, and confidentiality and fee-based service structures could become a barrier to cooperation; sport and recreation information is a newly emerging field where informality is now just leading to a more formal structure, building up a wider role in the subject area and making substantial advances from a recent, small-scale initiative.

These sections demonstrate the rapid growth of activity, the various structures of cooperation, and the potential for further national and international development. We could have selected many other subject areas: these examples are intended as representative, not as models.

Law

BARBARA TEARLE

The law library sector in the British Isles has changed dramatically in the last thirty years; in the late 1960s academic law libraries predominated, with the professional libraries (the Inns of Court and the Law Societies) having an important role. In 1990 law firm libraries are numerically dominant. Academic libraries (universities, polytechnics and some colleges of higher education) are still important because of breadth and long runs of their holdings, but they have cut back on staff, subscriptions and book purchasing in the last decade. The British Library has vast legal holdings scattered throughout the library and therefore difficult to use. Court libraries, government law libraries, local authority legal information units, public libraries, and law libraries in industry and (de)nationalised industries have developed in size and strength since 1960. The structure of libraries sponsored by the European Communities (European Documentation Centres (EDCs), European Reference Centres (ERCs), and Euro Info Centres) provide access to European Community law for everyone more thoroughly than provision to the public of access to domestic law.

Funding comes from across the whole spectrum, i.e. central and local government, including the educational sector, (de)nationalised industries, commercial firms and private societies. Besides affecting the amount of money available to the library, the source of funding affects the class of reader who may use the library, for example, law firm libraries are only open to members of that firm.

Institutional readership (practitioner and academic) is well catered for. Provision for the general public, who may have a practical need for legal materials or just a general interest, is patchy. Many law libraries are not open to such people. The non-lawyer using a law library, especially the litigant in person, is underprivileged in as far as access to legal materials is concerned. The law librarian must avoid crossing the bridge between providing bibliographic legal information and giving legal advice.

Lawyers primarily require the basic sources, journals and textbooks of their own jurisdiction. There are six jurisdictions within the British

Isles to which European Community law has been added. During the last thirty years lawyers in all sectors have started to look at law from other jurisdictions, at first from other common law countries (mainly USA, Canada, Australia and New Zealand) but recently, with the growing involvement in Europe and international trade, they also require materials from potentially any other country of the world, principally from Europe, East and West, and the Far East. As each country has its own distinct legal literature, which is at least as extensive as that of England and Wales, and its own language, demands on law libraries may be massive.

The literature itself has changed in the last 30 years. There are now many more publications to cater for the growth in specialist areas of the law. Many textbooks have changed format from the traditional bound volume in a new edition every few years to the looseleaf which is updated frequently. Lawyers use both recent material, often demanding it before it has been published, and also older, 18th and 19th century law reports. They expect them to be on the library's shelves, not outhoused with a 24 hour delay in delivery.

RECENT AND CURRENT COOPERATION NEEDS

The foregoing points to some factors affecting law libraries and the provision of legal material (see Logan, 1987 for a fuller discussion of law libraries).

There are distinct law library sectors which are independent of each other. Provision for one group of readers (the general public) is inadequate, although it has improved over the 30 year period. Law library holdings are inadequate to cater for the growing range of readers' interests. Practitioners, especially, require information very quickly.

The national library scene does not alleviate these problems. As a matter of policy, the British Library Document Supply Centre does not hold law reports. The law collection of the British Library in London is strong in British and Irish law and also in foreign law, but there is no law reading room after the pattern of the Library of Congress Law Library and the material is scattered throughout the collections. The British Library does not file looseleaf supplements so that borrowing such volumes from Boston Spa or consulting them in London is not practical.

This would indicate the potential for cooperation to provide the services that readers require. Law librarians must cooperate to achieve lending (or provision of photocopies), cross-sector access to libraries, planned provision of foreign law.

The initiative for cooperation may come from the top at the institutional level or from the bottom from individual librarians. In law librarianship it has come from the bottom. Law librarians acting together have attempted, with little success so far, to push institutions into cooperative initiatives.

RECENT AND CURRENT COOPERATIVE ACTIVITIES

Librarians

Associations

Foremost amongst the cooperative activities in the last 20 years has been the establishment of law library associations: first, in 1969 the British and Irish Association of Law Librarians (BIALL), later, the City Law Librarians Group (CLLG) and lastly the Scottish Law Librarians Group (SLLG) in 1988. Membership amongst the three overlaps as the last two are smaller, less formal groups set up for specific local purposes, whereas BIALL was set up for all law librarians within the British Isles. Its programme of activities includes all sectors and all regions. It is no accident that all three groups use the term 'librarians' in their title rather than 'libraries'. They are essentially associations for individual library professionals and their members act as such, rather than representing their employing institutions.

BIALL has been involved in several cooperative efforts. The Association early recognised the need for cooperation and its first act was to set up a committee on cooperation which reported in 1971 (British and Irish Association of Law Librarians, 1971) recommending the importance of central collections, support for standards for provision in law libraries, cross-sector access, exchange of duplicates, preparation of a legal thesaurus, cooperation in automation and use of automation for union lists, and training for law librarians. Some of the recommendations have been fulfilled (exchange of duplicates, training and a legal thesaurus, although this was not achieved by cooperative effort), some have been overtaken by subsequent developments, others are still to accomplish (automated union lists).

Publications

The obvious publications lacking in the early 1970s were a directory of law libraries in the British Isles, a librarian's guide to the bibliography of legal literature and guidance on running a law library. This last is important because then, as now, many law libraries are one-man-bands often with unqualified or newly qualified librarians, who suffer from professional isolation. BIALL decided to combine the two needs into one volume. Its *Manual of Law Librarianship* now in a second edition (Moys, 1987) was produced with contributions from members and non-members. BIALL's directory of law libraries is now in its third edition. For communication among law librarians BIALL started a journal, *The Law Librarian,* which aims to cover the whole range of legal bibliography, management of law libraries and legal collections from both the individual librarian's perspective and in the national (and international) context. For domestic news, a *Newsletter* is distributed to British and Irish members.

All these publications are produced by volunteers with contributions and support from members.

Training

It was quickly realised that there were insufficient law libraries and law librarians in the British Isles to support full scale professional law library training of a similar kind to that available in the United States. At first modest attempts at weekend or one day courses were started, and it was not until the 1980s that a consistent approach was established on three fronts. In response to the growth of law firm libraries and the need for their staff to understand something of the law as well as legal literature, the Polytechnic of Central London in conjunction with BIALL organises a course on 'Law for Librarians', which covers the core legal topics and legal bibliography. It is over-subscribed each year. The Department of Information and Library Studies, University of Wales at Aberystwyth has a joint law and librarianship degree, which BIALL supports by sponsoring a student at its annual conference and by assisting with summer vacation placements. BIALL itself now runs regular one day courses on legal materials at introductory level and occasional courses and seminars on specific topics.

Subject cooperation

Contact with overseas law librarians and libraries

Contact with overseas law librarians has developed significantly in the last decade. Law librarians have participated in overseas law library conferences (in particular in the USA and Canada) often with BIALL sponsorship. Contacts have then been strengthened on an individual basis when help is needed. Organisational contacts have been made by a few job exchanges, placements and visits, although they are difficult to organise satisfactorily because of the disparity in size and resources between British and American or Canadian law libraries. Law firms having offices in several countries have encouraged their librarians to develop contact.

Considerable attention has been paid to BIALL's activities. The Association has been the catalyst for self-help cooperation by bringing law librarians together, identifying their needs, and harnessing their professional expertise and energy for the benefit of the law library community.

Libraries

Union Lists

In the decade after it was established in 1947, the Institute of Advanced Legal Studies (IALS) of the University of London published five union lists, some in several editions: serials, United States law, Commonwealth law, Western European law, and air and space law. With the exception of the air and space list, they concentrate on serial publications. A new union list, of law reports, is being planned. Although the creation of a union list of necessity calls for cooperation amongst participants, the initiative came from one library, taking upon itself the task of acting for all law libraries.

More recently union lists have been compiled both by law libraries in an area for example, Liverpool and Staffordshire, and by groups of libraries whose holdings include law for example, Sheffield as part of its local cooperative scheme, and the University of London.

At an informal level, the CLLG, groupings of law firms, and the lunch time meetings of provincial law librarians have compiled union lists of materials held within their group. These lists are intended for internal use only. The second edition of the CLLG's union list places a greater emphasis on foreign legal materials in recognition of the rapid growth in the need for foreign law.

Acquisitions

Cooperative acquisitions policies have been attempted through existing cooperative schemes. An early example was the subject specialisation scheme amongst public libraries, in which Hammersmith Public Library was for some years responsible for law in the south east area (Hammersmith..., 1986) followed by Buckinghamshire since 1976.

When IALS was founded, some legal material was transferred from colleges or schools of London University and arrangements for sharing acquisition between the five law-teaching institutions and the Institute were laid down. As well as a jurisdictional demarcation, the arrangement provides for language specialisation, for example, the library of the School of Oriental and African Studies is responsible for legal material in the vernacular languages of the countries which it covers while the Institute of Advanced Legal Studies takes legal material from the same countries but which is published in Western European languages. The arrangement was re-affirmed in 1986 (University of London, IALS, 1986) and accepted by the Library Resources Coordinating Committee of the University of London thus ensuring the formal agreement of the other libraries involved.

Formal cooperation in the early 1970s amongst the four Inns of Court and the Law Society enabled the European Communities collection to be set up in the Middle Temple Library, funded by the five libraries and open to barristers, whatever their Inn, and solicitors. The Law Society Library withdrew from the agreement in 1990.

Cross-sector cooperation is more difficult to achieve, but exists. Within Sheffield, the law librarians of the University, Polytechnic and the Public Library consult over the purchase of expensive material.

It seems that less attention is given to consultation over cancellation of subscriptions.

The modest success of published union lists and cooperative acquisitions policies is clearly related to institutional backing.

Disposal

In the 1970s BIALL set up an exchange of duplicates' scheme because law librarians were not satisfied with the long general listings emanating from the British Library. The scheme operates with a minimum of cost and administration to BIALL: participating libraries, which need not be members, bear the brunt of the cost (producing multiple copies of duplicates' lists) and reap the benefit of re-circulated legal material, which ranges from individual issues of recent journals and law reports to long runs of reports and foreign material. Some libraries such as the Supreme Court Library and the Middle Temple also circulate duplicates' lists when they have items for disposal, which probably owes more to librarians' dislike of discarding anything which might find a good home, rather than to a conscious intention to cooperate.

Sharing of information

All the activities so far described could be called 'sharing of information', but they were not established for that general purpose. But the information systems being devised by law firm groupings, such as M5 Ltd., Eversheds, and Legal Resources Group, have a brief to share (some) information. To that end, M5 Ltd. has organised its information technology network to include information of common use to the participating firms. These groupings of large firms of solicitors agree to share such resources as financial information, staff training and library facilities.

NATIONAL EFFORTS AT COOPERATION

Early cooperative efforts which included law were the subject specialisation schemes amongst public libraries, already mentioned.

During the early 1980s the British Library focussed its attention, amongst other subjects, on provision of law materials. The report of the Working Party (British Library, 1982) ably highlighted the problem areas, especially the lack of a national legal information policy. It proposed a framework for national law library provision with central funding, and the encouragement of provision of law materials and access through (institutional) cooperation. This 'top down' plan foundered on a change in attitude to public finance (Anderson, 1986).

The current 'bottom up' approach advocated by the Library and Information Services Council (LISC) has substituted a partial solution which will satisfy one need – for local access. Library and Information

Plans (LIPs) published to date cover few areas having a significant law library sector other than the local university or polytechnic and do not include any private law firm sector law libraries. Nevertheless where libraries with law collections are covered, comments have been made about the need for union lists of legal holdings (Bradford, 1989).

The various EDCs, ERCs and Euro Info Centres provide information and material on the European Communities, including its law. They should be integrated with local LIPs.

CRITIQUE OF PRESENT COOPERATION

The overall level of cooperation amongst law librarians is high, but it operates at a personal level. It is aimed at helping readers (and fellow law librarians), rather than as an institutional policy, although that can be seen to be developing. The current trend towards fee-based services may have adverse affects on informal cooperation. If they become common, the relationship between law librarians may need re-thinking on a business footing. Librarians may charge not only outside enquirers for services, but also fellow law librarians, if it is thought that the information will be passed on to an outside enquirer for profit.

A constraint on cooperation amongst law firm librarians is the commercial confidentiality of their employers' business.

The two major cooperative successes have been union lists and associations of law librarians. The success of union lists can be measured in terms of both the willingness of librarians to contribute and the usefulness of the lists once published. The success of associations of law librarians has been in creating the network upon which informal cooperation depends.

Although examples of cooperation in the law firm and academic sectors and through LIPs have been given, generally there is little formal cooperation sponsored by the institutions to which law libraries belong. This can be attributed to the fact that the law library is usually only a section of the institution's library. Institutional cooperation is more likely to occur where the institution's library is solely devoted to law (for example, the Law Society and Inns of Court, the Lord Chancellor's Department, the groupings of provincial law firms). The exigency of limited finance is beginning to affect the educational sector to the extent that parent bodies are setting up formal cooperative arrangements. Thus the law library is carried along as part of an overall plan (for example, the recent endorsement of the University of London arrangements). Contrasts can be seen with the American experience, where university law libraries are part of the law faculty rather than the university library. This has enabled local consortia to be established (Duckett, 1987).

There is also little formal cross-sector cooperation. Coupled with little central or national provision of legal material and the limited nature of public library legal holdings (although they are often thorough within their own definitions) this lack of cooperation reinforces the exclusiveness of access to legal materials and the difficulty of access for the person in the street.

FUTURE COOPERATION

During the next five years the major concerns of law libraries will remain the same but formal, institutionally imposed cooperation will play an increasing role rather than the informal arrangements hitherto. Informal and personal cooperation will always be necessary.

Access to a growing range of legal materials, especially the law of the member states of the European Communities and other trading partners, will be of increasing importance. No doubt library holdings will develop to some extent to reflect this need, but the major source for foreign legal materials will be from the countries themselves. It will be important to form links with, for example, continental European law libraries, but with a direct programme of cooperation under the auspices of the European Community, rather than mirroring the informal contacts with American and Canadian law librarians.

Despite the proliferation of online catalogues, they will not replace subject based union lists. The present stumbling block in compiling union lists is the cost. The two-tier approach – ordinary legal sources at the local cross-sector level and specialist sources at the national level – will become firmly established. In future possible methods of funding may be by grant, sponsorship or subscription in which participating libraries subscribe to be included or (more likely) pay an annual subscription to access the union list online.

Provision of legal material, information and advice will increasingly be coordinated for the local community by cooperation amongst publicly-funded services, starting with the local public and educational libraries, legal advice centres, Citizens' Advice Bureaux (CABs), EDCs, ERCs, and Euro Info Centres, but also extending to the local law society, bar or court library. This will probably be organised under the auspices of LIPs as part of general local library and information cooperation, but it might possibly occur through a government department drawing in government sponsored law libraries and other providers of legal information services.

In the academic sector, cooperative acquisitions policies will be forced on many libraries through lack of funds. Thus law libraries will have institutional blessing for cooperative acquisitions agreements. They might assign subject or jurisdictional responsibilities. Another approach between local academic libraries or between nationally recognised centres of excellence might be the purchase of alternate editions of expensive works in a similar way to arrangements operated among some American law libraries.

The growth in the number of law firm librarians will increase the need to attract suitable staff and reinforce the need for specifically law library orientated training. However, law librarians will still only be a small sector of the library profession. Special courses at library school level will not be viable, but more courses at the continuing library education level will be provided, possibly by cooperation between BIALL and the Library Association and the library schools.

Nothing has been said about the impact of information technology, not because it will be insignificant, but because it will be all pervading. The age of communication by post and publication in book form (of bibliographical and reference material at least) is on the way out. During the next five years the transfer of information, be it union lists, requests to borrow or for photocopies, or referral of enquiries, will be through an electronic network also using e-mail and fax. The problem will be finding a network which all law librarians can use. Many will be tied into the network adopted by their parent body. In order that law libraries continue cross-sector cooperation, the networks used by different sectors must be mutually accessible. While this will speed communication and service to readers for those libraries which can install information technology, the disadvantage is that electronic communication could produce a new information poor in law library terms. Small firms, local law societies, and others, whose budget for books was small may not be able to diversify to information technology equipment, subscription and telecommunication charges.

REFERENCES

Anderson, M., Bloomfield, B., and Hamilton, G. (1986), Future cooperation in library provision for law. *The Law Librarian*, vol. 17, no. 3, (December), pp. 91–93

Bradford (1989), *Library and Information Plan for Bradford*. City of Bradford Metropolitan Council.

British and Irish Association of Law Librarians (1971), *Report of the Committee on Cooperation*. London, The Association.

British Library (1982), *Report of the British Library Working Party on Provision for Law*. British Library.

Duckett, J. (1987), Consortia: an American perspective. *The Law Librarian*, vol. 18, no. 2, (August), pp. 51–57.

Hammersmith and Fulham Public Libraries: law collection policy guidelines (1986), *The Law Librarian*, vol. 17, no. 1, (April), pp. 37–38.

Logan, R. (1987), Law libraries and their users, in Moys, E. M. (ed.) *Manual of law librarianship 2nd ed*. Aldershot: Gower. Chapter 1.

Moys, E. M. (ed). (1987), *Manual of Law Librarianship 2nd ed*. Aldershot: Gower.

University of London. Institute of Advanced Legal Studies (1986), *Report of the Policy Review Sub-Committee*. (The Megarry Report). London, The Institute. (Unpublished).

Medicine & health-care

Shane Godbolt

There are many different types of medical and health-care libraries ranging from educational, such as a medical school attached to a university; independent such as a Royal College or private Society; commercial such as a pharmaceutical company; government funded or sponsored such as the Department of Health and Social Security or Medical Research Council and charitable such as the King's Fund Centre and the Wellcome Institute for the History of Medicine. The libraries vary greatly in size. The most numerous type in the network of medical libraries covering the United Kingdom (UK) are those in the National Health Service (NHS) postgraduate centres and these libraries are also the smallest. The larger medical libraries are found in the university and private sectors.

Issues of funding, rationalisation, new technology, new formats of information, and the sheer pressure of the continuing proliferation of the literature affect all medical libraries. These changes are having profound influences on the way libraries operate and the nature of their future services. Cooperation here is essential to survival. Working together at the grass roots level is vital, but it is also just as vital to realise that each service is part of a larger whole and has to be plugged in to the decision making networks at the national level.

The UK is fortunate in having an infrastructure of professional associations invaluable for providing a network of professional information and support as Meadows shows in Chapter 6. This infrastructure has developed rapidly in recent years, to meet changing and new needs and circumstances. There are a wide range of organisations catering for medical and health-care librarians and these interlink to form a sophisticated and developing national network. The establishment and success of many new groups in recent years indicates the breadth of interests of today's medical librarian. User groups have spawned across traditional boundaries, for example the JANET User Group for Libraries (JUGL) inaugurated in 1986 and the UK Online User Group (UKOLUG) in 1978.

The emergence of important managerial groups such as the National Health Service Regional Librarians Group (NHSRLG) and the University

Medical School Librarians Group (UMSLG) has also been a feature of recent years.

Keen interest in the medical field has long existed across national boundaries and the most important new development in this area has been the setting up of the European Association of Health Information and Libraries (EAHIL) in 1987.

The latest trend in Britain, in the United States and elsewhere has been the development of library networks; approaches are varied but objectives are common. Standards of service to the user have been raised through coordination and cooperation, to make more effective use of local and regional resources. Increasing professionalism has been a hallmark of activity in our field and we have been fortunate in that the technology has thrown us tools to pursue the goals of increasing effectiveness and efficiency to users.

THE NATIONAL SCENE

Within the organisations for information professionals in the UK, there are many specialised groups which concentrate on specific aspects of information provision. An overview has been written by Forrest (1987) and in describing their value she wrote 'These groups foster cooperation and the exchange of expertise, thus ensuring the growth of professional techniques even in the present climate of financial constraint'.

LA Medical Health and Welfare Libraries Group (MHWLG)

The most important professional group for medical and health-care librarians is the MHWLG, which was formed in 1978 by a merger of the Medical Section (formed in 1947) and the former Hospital and Handicapped Readers Group (formed in 1962), making a membership total of almost 2000, a considerably larger membership than either of its predecessors and a total which is maintained currently. Forrest (1987) has written, 'This union reflects the current approach to medicine which sees the practitioner and patient as partners in the process of health-care, an attitude which has developed further with the introduction of patient information services. It is the leading professional association for librarians working in all aspects of health-care including those in universities, schools of nursing, health authorities, postgraduate medical centres, staff and patient libraries in hospitals and public library services to handicapped and disadvantaged readers'.

In 1989 the Group produced its first publicity leaflet with the help of the LA Publicity and Public Relations Group. The leaflet outlined the benefits which membership offers: a varied programme of meetings and study days, many of which are now organised in conjunction with other professional associations; an annual weekend Study Conference held in a different location each year, with an exhibition as a major feature and which attracts well over 200 delegates; and a quarterly newsletter with current literature listings.

The *Newsletter* is the main method of communication with members and it is also issued as part of the Group's journal *Health Libraries Review* (vol. 1, no. 1, 1984, Blackwell Scientific Publications). The journal is available to MHWLG members at a special reduced rate. The background to the growth of the *Newsletter* from 36 pages in 1978 to over 400 pages in 1983 and the creation of a professional journal has been described by Godbolt (1987). A *Directory of Medical and Health Care Libraries in the United Kingdom and Republic of Ireland* (7th edition 1990, recorded 675 libraries) is produced regularly. MHWLG also has several special interest sub-groups amongst which is the Nursing Information Sub-Group, which has opened its membership to include practising nurses and therapists and which also runs an active study-day programme and publishes a quarterly newsletter.

Representatives of the Group serve on a variety of other committees to keep in touch with developments and liaison is maintained with other bodies having related interests such as the NHSRLG. The Committee provides an official channel through which the views of the membership can be expressed in submissions and policy statements to other bodies. These documents, and others such as those emanating from the NHSRLG, are normally published in *Health Libraries Review,* making the corporate view widely known throughout the membership and strengthening the status of health-care librarians bringing enhanced confidence and morale to the developing professional role.

The Group's activities are summarised in its annual reports, which encapsulates its major coordinating role, for all contacts and information in this field. There is a companion Scottish group the Association of Scottish Health Sciences Librarians (ASHSL) which was set up in 1970 and formally constituted in 1974. The 1990 MHWLG Conference in Edinburgh was a joint venture with ASHSL. There is also a Welsh group.

Subject cooperation

The Aslib Biosciences Group and the Association of Information Officers in the Pharmaceutical Industry (AIOPI) are two other examples of smaller but important and active groups in the field.

UK Online User Group (UKOLUG)

Set up in 1978, this is one of the largest of the special interest groups of the IIS. Membership is not confined to members of IIS, the parent body. UKOLUG organises a regular programme of meetings, publishes a bi-monthly *Newsletter* and medical librarians are prominent amongst its members. A London Online Local User Group (LOLUG) was convened informally in 1985 (Farbey, 1986) and meetings continue to be held. Since 1984 UKOLUG has held biannual state-of-the-art conferences and has published proceedings of these.

CD-ROM User Forum

In 1988 UKOLUG formed this to provide information on all matters relating to CD-ROM technology. The Forum planned a stimulating year of meetings for 1990 run along workshop lines, whenever possible, so participants were able to gain practical experience. In cooperation with the Library and Information Technology Centre the group has published an excellent practical guide to CD-ROM (Gunn and Moore, 1990).

CD-ROM (Biomedical) User Network

This Group, formed in 1988, is a special interest group of UKOLUG. Membership is open to non-members of the IIS and UKOLUG but an essential qualification for membership is the actual possession and use of CD-ROM hardware and software in the member's library.

The network was formed to assist members with problems associated with software and hardware, and service administration and management (for example, workstations, booking, security and documentation). The Group has had some success in negotiating with suppliers concerning software modifications and pricing structures. Specimen user guides and a fault report form for general use are practical examples of cooperative initiatives by the Group which currently has around 70 members.

On the CD-ROM front an interesting initiative has been reported (Wentz and Whitsed, 1990) whereby the North West Thames Regional Information Technology Agency (RITA) has set up a scheme to assist medical libraries within the Region with the costs of implementing a CD-ROM service. RITA has purchased CD drives and paid the first year's subscription to MEDLINE on CD-ROM for eligible, participating libraries. Libraries in the scheme are all eligible for discounts thereafter. RITA has supported an experienced librarian in coordinating and distribution arrangements and as a result faster and easier information retrieval is benefiting many more health-care professionals across the Region. Some other NHS Regions are presently negotiating similar schemes and the advantages of moving together, thereby creating a network of knowledge and experience on which to draw within a Region are obvious, quite apart from the financial discounts involved.

Managerial Bodies

These are also of importance to medical librarians although they are not, strictly speaking, associations since membership is by invitation only. The origin of these groups, like many others, has been through a series of informal contacts.

The NHS Regional Librarians Group

An account of the origins, organisation and work of the NHS Regional Librarians Group (NHSRLG) has been written by Forrest and Carmel (1987). The Group is composed of librarians who are responsible for the organisation of a coordinated network of hospital and health libraries within a Region of the NHS. These networks, some of which are highly developed, provide training and cooperation schemes for the librarians within the geographical area they serve and so act as local associations. The Group provides a national focus in the representation of library services to the NHS and the representation of NHS libraries to the profession. It liaises with DHSS and other official bodies on matters of policy relating to librarianship in the health service. Its objectives include: the development of national policies; advice on library management; coordination of services and raising the awareness of the users and the policy makers of the potential contribution of library services to health-care.

The Group currently has 17 members representing Scotland, Northern Ireland, Wales and the 14 English Regions. Its importance is summed up by Forrest and Carmel (1987): 'the combined expertise, initiative and authority of the RLG has made a significant impact on NHS library provision; its continued growth and development is crucial to the survival of the information network it maintains'.

Librarians of London University Medical Schools (LLUMS) & UK University Medical School Librarians Group (UMSLG)

Informal contacts had long existed throughout the University of London but trends towards more formal activity were initiated in the late 1970s with the setting up of the Library Resources Coordinating Committee, whose main objective was to develop coordinating activities and cooperative initiatives throughout the libraries of the University of London. In 1978 the librarians of the then twelve undergraduate medical schools met and a medical group was formed with the aims of discussing matters of mutual interest, exchanging information and experience and designing questionnaires for the collection of comparable data in such areas as staffing, budgets and workloads. Within the Group several medical libraries have operated a successful photocopy supply service. The success of its meetings and the benefits gained later led to proposals for the formation of a larger group, the UK University Medical School Librarians Group (UMSLG).

The inaugural meeting of this Group was held in April 1983. One of its most important activities has been the collection and collation of statistics. UMSLG was constituted as an autonomous body which meets twice a year to consider and comment on issues relevant to its members' libraries. At its inaugural meeting the perceptive suggestion had been made by Tony King, Southampton University, that the Group should consider the possibility of formal liaison with the Standing Conference of National and University Libraries (SCONUL) through one of its advisory committees.

Following an approach from UMSLG to SCONUL this was implemented in 1985, when SCONUL, which conducts much of its work through a number of Advisory Committees, set up an Advisory Committee on Medical Materials (SCONUL-ACMM), whose work has been summarised since 1987 in the SCONUL Annual Reports. Elected representatives of UMSLG serve on SCONUL-ACMM. A number of important issues are under review including the perennial problem of the relationship between university medical school libraries and the NHS. There is no focus for research and development in medical information policy in the UK, comparable to that provided by the National Library of Medicine (NLM) in the USA, and following discussions with the British Library a paper has been prepared by SCONUL-ACMM in consultation with NHSRLG on the role of the British Library for medical and health information (SCONUL, 1990), which is intended to stimulate discussion and action on a wide range of issues.

The medical libraries represented by SCONUL are amongst the largest in the UK and several have additionally a 'regional' role, through acting as the regional library for their NHS region and through service on NHSRLG. SCONUL holds an Annual Meeting of Consultation with senior medical librarians from the national, university and medical research sectors and from the NHSRLG. The mechanisms are thus in place for gathering information from all senior managers on pertinent problems and issues facing the profession in this specialised field. Many members usefully wear more than one hat, having a university and a regional responsibility.

In 1986, following the setting up of revised pre-registration training procedures by the Library Association, NHSRLG and UMSLG formed a Joint Training Sub-Committee, which has done much useful work and has produced a core training programme for pre-registration candidates, which was accepted by the LA in April 1988, subject to information being given as to its implementation and adaptation on each occasion it is submitted (Hewlett, 1988a). Other useful tools developed under the auspices of the Committee are a Progress assessment checklist (Hewlett, 1988b) and Exercises for pre-registration trainees (Cooke *et al.*, 1989).

London Medical Librarians Group

In June 1986 a small group of London-based medical librarians meeting at the British Medical Association (BMA) agreed to form an informal forum of librarians working in organisations which lay outside the universities and the National Health Service. Its members are all invited to the SCONUL-ACMM Annual Meeting of Consultation and include the Librarian of the Royal Society of Medicine, Britain's premier medical library and a back-up library to the British Library, the Royal Colleges the Wellcome Institute for the History of Medicine, and the BMA itself.

Subject and other initiatives

It is worth recording the following also:

- *Psychiatric Libraries Cooperative Scheme (PLCS)* was set up in 1982 and is now a flourishing network with 101 members
- two successful national meetings of orthopaedic librarians held in 1988 and 1989 reported by Smith & Allen (1990)
- *National Library of Medicine Classification User Group (NLMC)*, where one of the many valuable activities has been to organise a series of 'subject specialist' meetings in fields of medicine where the literature causes particular problems of classification
- *Medical Information Working Party* formed in June 1984, following informal discussions between representatives of the LA MHWLG and the Publishers' Association Medical Group to provide a forum for the exchange of views between medical booksellers, librarians, publishers and subscription agents
- *Library & Information Plans (LIPs)* and the *Health Information Sector*: a national seminar on this topic organised by the British Library Research and Development Department at the King's Fund Centre, London was held in October 1989 (Shimmon, 1990)
- *Health Information Plan (HIP)* in the Northern Region whose developments to date have been reported by O'Donovan (1989, 1990)

THE INTERNATIONAL SCENE

Medical librarianship is a thriving international commodity. As well as bringing overseas medical librarians to the UK, the work of bodies such as the British Council has taken many British medical librarians to different parts of the globe, particularly to developing countries where there is much to receive as well as give in working with colleagues often coping in the face of overwhelming odds.

The World Health Organisation (WHO) has announced a world goal of 'Health for all by the year 2000', and managements at regional and local levels need to set objectives within national strategies. Carmel (1989) has talked about the development of 'National Focal Point libraries' (NFPs). Despite problems NFPs have already acted as a mechanism for addressing the problem of information poverty in healthcare in developing countries.

Five well attended international congresses on medical librarianship have been held since 1953, the sixth and first to be scheduled in a developing country being held in Delhi in 1990. The International Federation of Library Associations and Institutions (IFLA) set up a Biological and Medical Sciences Section in 1977 which is active and produces a quarterly newsletter. The National Library of Medicine produced its long range plan in 1987 (NLM long range plan, 1987) giving all medical librarians much food for thought (Tabor, 1988), and providing vital background on the likely direction of future developments. NLM research funding has given great impetus to the development of Integrated Academic Information Management Systems (IAIMS), suitable infrastructures for which have hardly begun to emerge in this country.

The implications of the ADONIS project have been discussed by David and Martin (1989) and Campbell and Stern (1990). How Europe will tackle its increasing dependence on the American information systems, notably MEDLINE, is another challenge we shall face in this decade (Franklin, 1990).

Perhaps most significant however, has been long overdue developments in channels of communication with our European neighbours. The first European Conference of Medical Libraries was held in 1986 (Forrest et al., 1987) and this set the scene for a new era of collaboration between European medical libraries, bridging also the gaps between East and West Europe. The European Association of Health Information and Libraries (EAHIL) was formally constituted in August 1987 at IFLA's Brighton Conference. Now with some 500 members in over 26 European countries, a regular newsletter and biannual conferences, and the possibility of EEC grants for collaborative projects between libraries, particularly in the field of data processing, there is an exciting future ahead if medical librarians can seize the opportunities offered.

REFERENCES

Campbell, R. and Stern, B. (1990), ADONIS – the next stage? *Health Libraries Review,* vol. 7, pp. 20–21.

Carmel, M. (1989), Health information in the Third World: initiatives and problems. *Health Libraries Review,* vol. 6, pp. 110–111.

Cooke, R., Gillespie, I. and Hartley, B. (1989), Training for L.A. chartering in health-care libraries. Part III. Exercises for pre-registration trainees. *Health Libraries Review,* vol. 6, pp. 25–28.

David, M. and Martin, G. (1989), The ADONIS experiment. *Health Libraries Review,* vol. 4, pp. 193–199.

Farbey, R. (1986), London online local user group (LOLUG) 19 March 1986. *Health Libraries Review,* vol. 3, p. 181.

Forrest, M. (1987), Professional associations for medical librarians in the UK, in: Deschamps, C. and Walckiers, M. eds. *Medical libraries: cooperation and new technologies. First European Conference of Medical Libraries*, Brussels, Belgium, 22–25 October 1986. Amsterdam: Elsevier (North-Holland).

Forrest, M. and Carmel, M. (1987), The NHS Regional Librarians Group. *Health Libraries Review,* vol. 4, pp. 160–163.

Forrest, M. *et al.* (1987), First European Meeting of Medical Libraries, 22–25 October 1986, Brussels. *Health Libraries Review,* vol. 4, pp. 43–46.

Franklin, J. (1990), Can European biomedical literature survive? The increasing dependence of Europe on American Information Systems, in Armstrong, C. J. and Hartley, R. J. editors, *Online information retrieval today and tomorrow.* UKOLUG. pp. 131–140.

Godbolt, S. (1987), Health Libraries Review: the need, the challenge and the future, in: Deschamps, C. and Walckiers, M. eds. *Medical libraries: cooperation and new technologies. First European Conference of Medical Libraries*, Brussels, Belgium, 22–25 October 1986. Amsterdam: Elsevier (North-Holland).

Gunn, A. and Moore, C. (1990), *CD-ROM a practical guide for information professionals.* London: UKOLUG and LITC.

Hewlett, J. (1988a), Training for Library Association chartering in health-care libraries. *Health Libraries Review*, vol. 5, pp. 181–188.

Hewlett, J. (1988b), Pre-registration training in health-care libraries. II Progress assessment check-list. *Health Libraries Review*, vol. 5, pp. 237–245.

NLM long range plan (1987). (Report of the Board of Regents) Panel Reports 1–5, Bethesda, Maryland, USA. National Library of Medicine.

O'Donovan, K. (1989), Progress towards a Health Information Plan in the Northern Region. *Health Libraries Review*, vol. 6, pp. 214–216.

O'Donovan, K. A. (1990), Health Information Plan for the Northern Region, regional seminar and open session, 17 November 1989, Newcastle upon Tyne. *Health Libraries Review*, vol. 7, pp. 88–89.

Saunders, W. L. (1989), *Towards a unified professional organisation for library and information science and services: a personal view.* (Viewpoints in LIS No. 3). The Library Association.

SCONUL (1990), The role of the British Library for medical and health information. *Health Libraries Review*, vol. 7, pp. 14–19.

Shimmon, R. (1990), Library and Information Plans and the health information sector: a national seminar organised by BLRDD October 1989. *Health Libraries Review*, vol. 7, pp. 86–88.

Smith, P. F. and Allen, L. C. (1990), The first two national meetings of orthopaedic and related librarians. London 18 November 1988 and Oxford 14 April 1989. *Health Libraries Review*, vol. 7, pp. 30–31.

Tabor, R. (1988), Planning for the future? National Library of Medicine long-range plan. *Health Libraries Review*, vol. 5, pp. 248–251.

Wentz, R. and Whitsed, N. (1990), Getting together with compact disc; a regional MEDLINE CD-ROM initiative for libraries. *Health Libraries Review*, vol. 7, pp. 204–207.

Audiovisual materials

Helen P Harrison

PROPERTIES OF AUDIOVISUAL MATERIALS

A brief introduction to the different audiovisual materials will indicate some of the impediments to widespread dissemination, access or cooperative lending or collection. Audiovisual materials come in many formats, but the major groupings which require coordination of collection and acquisition, selection, control and conservation are:

- moving images: film and videograms
- sound recordings: disc, compact disc, audiotape and cassette
- still images: photographs, slides

Other audiovisual materials can be a combination of these materials, or sets of slides, computer software, kits and packs, many of which can be packaged and treated as books.

Moving images

Film is a standard medium which can be used across national boundaries without transfer problems, but it is expensive, cannot be reused, unlike magnetic tape, and is vulnerable to permanent damage from careless handling and projection. A film collection needs inspection equipment to check the material and laboratory facilities to effect repairs. One film material – nitrate – is highly volatile, and unsuitable for interlending purposes or collection anywhere but an archive. Cooperation in collection and preservation between libraries and archives is important for film material.

Videograms – the generic term for video recordings – are normally magnetic recordings with rerecording capability. But this advantage can be a disadvantage if tape is erased accidentally, either by recording over or by bad storage and misuse. Videotape is not a universal medium, there are several systems in use in the world and one country's tape will not necessarily play effectively in another country. Colour systems provide the most obvious example. Although it is possible to play an NTSC (typically American) tape on a PAL (UK) set there is usually a loss of colour. Transferring from one system to another is possible, expensive, and beyond the means of most libraries. The different formats will influence a library's collection policy. Stock and machinery have to be matched, and as videotape systems are frequently updated obsolescence of stock and machinery may occur within a short time. A library with a collection of video material will need replay equipment for viewing and checking purposes.

Sound Recordings

Sound recordings include gramophone records, audiotape, audiocassettes and the compact disc (CD), as well as archival formats. Audiotape is a magnetic medium and shares the properties of the videotape, but it is much more standardised, especially in its cassette format – the compact cassette is universally accepted, making collection and exchange an easier task, although cassette tape is not a good storage medium. Records are more permanent but susceptible to irreparable damage in use. CDs are less vulnerable to damage than records, but even they are not the long-term solution. Nevertheless, the relatively inexpensive sound recordings make them a good candidate for collection and there is less need of extensive cooperative schemes.

Still images

Photographs and slides are relatively inexpensive to acquire, and again it is probable that most collections can acquire material for their own use. The sheer number of photographs and slides produced leads to selective collection, by subject area. Photographs come in negative and positive format, and the negatives are seldom lent or exchanged. Unless photographs are collected in a book or slides in a set they are not really suitable for interlending. Copying is a more frequent method of exchange.

Although the technology is converging there is no sign of a universally acceptable single carrier like the book, emerging in the audiovisual field.

COLLECTION

One obvious area for cooperation is that of collection, and although the materials are closely related it does not mean that it is advantageous to gather them all together in one massive collection, and a network of audiovisual collections has grown in the UK with varying degrees of cooperation between them.

Some archives and libraries specialise in format and others in subjects, for example, national archives specialising in sound (the National Sound Archive of the British Library), or film (the National Film Archive). Others combine sound and moving images such as the National Film and Sound Archive in Australia, or the National Archive of Canada's Moving Image and Sound Archive. Other archives specialise in audiovisual in a particular subject area for example, the Imperial War Museum, film/video, sound and photographic archives, or the Royal Institute of British Architects (RIBA) with its photographic archive on architecture. Other archives such as the broadcasting archives have several formats, and a wide range of subjects. Libraries on the other hand are very likely to have audiovisual collections comprising several formats. Public libraries have an increasing interest in audiovisual collections, lending material for home use according to demand.

There is another type of 'library' to consider for moving image materials in particular; the distribution library. This is a specialist type of collection which deals with the commercial hire of feature and documentary material to other libraries. Some audiovisual material is expensive to produce and purchase and may only be required for one or two showings. It is uneconomic for most libraries to acquire these materials outright for limited use and the distribution libraries exist to serve this demand. Distribution libraries are commercial, service centres rather than part of the network of the libraries we are considering here. Nevertheless they form a link in the chain of cooperation in considering audiovisual collections.

Cooperative collection

There have been one or two schemes for cooperative collection of which the most successful is GLASS (The Greater London Audio Specialisation Scheme) a scheme for the collection of sound recordings in London. It was based on the public libraries which already had a tradition of cooperative acquisition and collection in music librarianship. The British Universities Film and Video Council Audiovisual Reference Centre performs a similar role for higher or tertiary education allowing members to preview material at a central point without the necessity for an institution to make several copies for exhibition and preview purposes.

Other libraries which have tried cooperative schemes with audiovisual material include resource libraries and centres pooling resources and expertise, more than cooperation at the level of collection. This type of scheme found some success in regions, and SHEMROC (Sheffield Educational Media Resources Organising Committee) and NEMROC (Newcastle) were the two most noted examples. However cooperative schemes of collection were not so popular with audiovisual collections as it is not always feasible to lend or exchange.

Libraries often do not want to keep one of everything, as material goes out of fashion and older material becomes in need of preservation. We all know of collections kept long after their useful life, gathering dust on the shelves, and deteriorating rapidly. Multiple copies are not made of the more specialised materials which makes the few copies which exist very expensive.

Exchange/Interlending

Interlending is one of the most important areas of library cooperation, but does not happen often with audiovisual materials. It is much more likely that copies are provided. However this requires resources for blank cassettes, technical equipment and backup for transfer and machine time. Unless a library is geared to this activity it is not as easy as it sounds. The audiovisual departments of UK universities tried a scheme of providing copies of audiovisual materials, especially videocassettes, during the 1970s, but the scheme foundered as costs quickly outran the advantages, and there was little commercial interest. There was also the question of actual value of the productions. Production is expensive and if the market is limited the production costs can rarely be recovered, even at the sometimes exorbitant prices charged. Another possible way of acquiring video material is to record off-air, but again technical equipment and a certain amount of technical knowledge are required. This obviously only applies to material which is transmitted 'on-air' in the first place. Copyright regulations bring their own difficulties to bear on cooperation. Even with the new UK Copyright Act, where the situation has eased for recording off-air, there are still licensing schemes to contend with.

Resource Centres

Just as no one publisher can provide the entire stock of material required by a library, so no one source can supply all the needed audiovisual materials. A degree of 'cooperation' shows in the formation of national, regional or education authority viewing centres where prospective users of audiovisual material could sample the material before purchase. For example the Inner London Education Authority (ILEA) Media Resources Centre provided a viewing centre, where teachers could sample a wide and appropriate range of material and equipment. It provided a useful service but was overcome by events and also might not have been able to keep up with the mushrooming products of the audiovisual industry. The Centre later became the Learning Resources Centre and ceased to function on the abolition of the ILEA.

Such a scheme is now being suggested on an international scale. A Regional Resource Centre for Distance Education has been established in South Asia with its headquarters in Thailand at the Sukhotai Thammathirat Open University. Similar institutions in the area, including one at the Allama Iqbal Open University (AIOU) in Islamabad and the Indira Gandhi Open University in New Delhi will participate in sub-regional activities opening resource centres and collecting materials for their particular regions, as outliers for Thailand. These have been encouraged by Unesco and indicate an important advance in the concept of resource sharing for this region. This is an interesting development in cooperation and it is hoped and anticipated that other regions will set up similar collections and centres.

AREAS FOR COOPERATION

Between the two areas of libraries and archives, cooperation is best described as tacit rather than explicit: resource sharing rather than material sharing. There are three types of institution in which cooperation may be found.

Archives

Archives collect widely in their sphere of interest which in the case of a national archive includes material distributed in the country concerned, not just national production. There is a small network of cooperation among national, specialist and regional archives dependent once more on *ad hoc* agreements rather than firm and binding rules. The film archive of the BBC has arrangements with the National Film Archive and the Imperial War Museum, and the sound archive similar arrangements with the National Sound Archive to transfer relevant material – either allowing off-air recording or providing a fund for the production of copies and allowing for exchange or deposit. The National Film Archive and the Imperial War Museum exchange film materials by agreement and material may be exchanged between the national and regional archives.

International exchange between archives is also practised but here rules of protection of national cultural heritage and property make for more difficulties. Importation and exportation of moving image materials can become a costly business, subject to both legal and customs regulation. The Unesco Recommendation for the Safeguarding and Preservation of Moving Images (1980), underlines the necessity for archives to protect the cultural heritage of countries by acquiring and exchanging relevant material from abroad and being encouraged to do so rather than discouraged by the restrictions.

Cooperation between libraries and archives

Cooperation tends to be in the form of assistance from the archives in taking unique material for permanent preservation, as well as providing advice and expertise especially on the technical side. The archives have more to offer libraries than the converse in the way of technical assistance, but the libraries could be used more to ease the burden of access to the archival material for reference, viewing or listening copies. Access to archives is restricted for the good reason that the archives' major function is preservation of the cultural heritage. The preservation copy goes into the archive, but libraries could deal with the viewing and listening copies. The National Sound Archive has a free service for individuals and small groups by appointment. Outlier listening services have also been established in the British Library at Boston Spa and at the Devon Library Services Headquarters in Barnstaple. Although the NSA collections are primarily for reference, a commercial copy service is available subject to copyright clearance.

In some areas the local broadcasting station deposits material in a library radio collection, or an oral history collection.

Cooperation between Libraries

Exchange is not usually an option and interlending is difficult as many libraries have no facilities for copying. Traditionally one does not lend original or copy material for several reasons: loss of 'original' or copy material, damage in use and recently the wide availability of many audiovisual materials produced commercially.

COPYRIGHT

This cannot be forgotten in any dealings with audiovisual, and library cooperation is no exception. It has to be remembered in any use of audiovisual material, in any exchange or deposit of material, in showings, in exchange, and in recording and copying. The Open University scheme allows for off-air recording but has a clause whereby institutions recording the material are obliged to destroy it after a short period of one year for copyright reasons. Material which is used in the Open University and other education programmes has a short shelf life; the material is 'cleared' for use for perhaps eight years and then goes 'out of copyright'. Unless someone has the foresight and the resources to 'reclear' such material it is effectively lost for future use except as a reference copy in the Open University's own library. Now while some material may have such a short life, as it requires current and up-to-date material and facts, other material can arguably be said to have a much longer useful life. It happens also with a great deal of broadcast material. This is one problem which until now has not been solved but it might be the subject of research for the future – finding a way for reference and research libraries to acquire and maintain collections of useful material for a wider audience and future generations.

FUTURE DEVELOPMENTS

Existing collections are of many different types, some archives, some commercial, some reference (or last resort collections), some loan or hire collections. A national audiovisual collection would require unlimited funding and storage space, something we all know is neither practical nor viable, but a network of existing collections is more attainable.

A network of collections needs to consider:

- who keeps what
- who does what in the way of distribution and access

There is some coordination of effort in exchange schemes and schemes of selection or selective acquisition. No one collection can expect to collect everything. Audiovisual collections tend to sort out among themselves the most appropriate areas for housing certain materials. Regional archives of sound and moving images provide a second level of cooperation. Collections also exist in public and education libraries, and sometimes the master material is deposited in the regional archive and copies retained for reference.

The potential is there for a network, but probably for historical reasons connected with the different genesis, functions and purposes of the collections it has never been realised. There is much scope for development. The fact that no interlending scheme exists even today indicates that there are problems. With audiovisual materials it is less a question of lending as creating a network of cooperation for collection, the preparation of bibliographic tools of the available materials, and conservation; ensuring that the material exists somewhere and that those who need to know of its existence can do so in standard directories. In effect the network exists and it may already be in place in certain areas, but it is in need of rationalisation and drawing together to realise its potential.

REFERENCES

Cornish, G. P. (1983), Interlending of audiovisual materials in the United Kingdom: the present and the future. *Audiovisual Librarian*, vol. 9, no. 4, (Autumn), pp. 193–196.

IASA Technical Committee (1976), Towards a standard for exchange tapes between research sound archives. *Phonographic Bulletin,* vol. 16, pp. 36–37.

International Telecommunication Union (1985), *Sound tape recording, television tape recording and film techniques for the international exchange of programmes.* ITU. International Radio Consultative Committee, Geneva.

Pinion, C. F. (1980), *The interlending and availability of audiovisual materials in the UK: report of a survey in 1979.* British Library (BLRDD Report 5526).

Unesco (1975), *Multinational exchange mechanisms of educational audiovisual materials.* Unesco CEREP, Paris.

Unesco (1980), *Recommendation for the safeguarding and preservation of moving images (Belgrade).* Unesco, Paris.

Sport and recreation

CAROLYNN RANKIN

The Sport and Recreation Information Group (SPRIG) was formally launched at an inaugural meeting in May 1984. SPRIG is a non-profit making organisation financed through the annual subscriptions of its members. Its affairs are vested in an Executive Committee elected from the membership. SPRIG hopes to attract both information providers and information users and all members are encouraged to participate in the activities of the group. The aims of SPRIG are:

- to encourage the bibliographic control of the literature
- cooperative exploitation of resources
- to disseminate information to users in the field
- to improve the awareness of sport and recreation documentation throughout the information profession

SPRIG is a voluntary organisation and owes its origin in part to informal contact between librarians and information officers working within the world of sport and recreation. As in any specialised area of interest you soon get to know who else is involved in the same type of work. Informal networks build up as you find out who else can help with particular enquiries, and who may be experiencing similar problems! The formation of SPRIG enabled these contacts to take on a more formal footing – many ideas and 'why don't we try' projects then had a banner head under which to work. To ensure some financial resources an annual subscription is payable and to date there are 81 organisational members and 45 individual members. The bulk of membership is from the information profession, a mixture of further education and higher education, public and special libraries. It is encouraging that the register also includes local authority recreation officers, sports centre managers and lecturers from the education sector. Overseas membership hail from as far afield as Hong Kong and Australia.

THE WORK OF SPRIG

Publications

When SPRIG was formed, the inaugural committee felt it was vital to keep members up to date and well informed and so the *SPRIG Bulletin* was launched. Issued twice a year and available as part of the subscription, the *SPRIG Bulletin* now contains features and regular items such as the Information Technology corner.

SPRIG also publishes a 'How to find out about' series of free leaflets. These are on topics of particular interest and are a guide to resources. Each lists the main sources of literature such as bibliographies, abstracting and indexing journals and reference texts. Information is also given on relevant databases and organisations. Topics covered to date are dance, sports medicine, sports science, physical education and careers in sport. Committee members are usually 'volunteered' to prepare these – one of the burdens of office!

The *SPRIG Union Catalogue of Periodicals in Sport and Recreation*, published in November 1988 is a good example of the cooperative spirit of SPRIG. It was agreed that this would be a very worthwhile project, but unfortunately no member of the Committee could commit considerable work time to the project. An ideal compromise was reached. A post-graduate student from Leeds Polytechnic School of Librarianship began the programming aspect of the union catalogue as a class project. National Coaching Foundation (NCF) staff on the same campus provided the initial specification for the project design, sent out the questionnaire to participating libraries and hosted the database in its embryonic form on dBase III. The project then moved house to the Sports Documentation Centre computer at Birmingham University Library. There it was edited before moving to receive further programming at the London Sports Medicine Institute at the Medical College of St. Bartholomew's Hospital, London, finally emerging as a printed resource in November 1988. The Union Catalogue includes over 650 titles, and SPRIG hopes to publish an updated edition in due course.

Meetings

SPRIG meetings are usually held twice a year, with the autumn meeting usually coinciding with the AGM. Subjects covered to date are:

- online access
- sports statistics
- finding out about video in sport
- a question of sport – is coaching the key for the 90s?
- physical education

The meetings are intended to appeal to a wide target audience, aimed at both the librarians and information staff and other professionals working in the world of sport. It is important for the 'providers' and the 'users' to come together at these forums, particularly as we are trying to develop effective and efficient services for the future.

Travel Grant

The SPRIG Committee has instigated a travel grant to enable group members to take advantage of overseas visits. Although the award is small in financial terms, it displays a willingness to encourage professional development – and the resulting reports should provide valuable information on the sport information systems in other countries.

SPRIG Student Dissertation Prize

To encourage interest in information resources in sport and recreation an annual dissertation prize has been established. SPRIG offers a prize for the best original dissertation in the fields of sport, recreation and leisure undertaken as part of a student's normal work at under- or post-graduate level at a British educational institute. This may be a study of the management aspects of library/information services in the field, a bibliographical essay or guide to the literature. The response from the library schools so far has not been overwhelming but we hope some students may develop an interest in this area.

SPORTS INFORMATION PLAN

In January 1989 over 70 delegates attended a meeting convened by SPRIG to discuss a National Sports Information Strategy. Sport information in the UK is largely uncoordinated and served by an informal network of local authorities, commercial agencies, academic institutions and special libraries. SPRIG has done much to increase awareness but recognised the need for a coordinated National Strategy. Response to the meeting supported the feeling that a major examination of the current provision of sports information is necessary. A basic proposal for a National Sports Information Plan has been drawn up by the Sports Council in conjunction with other organisations (see Appendix below). This has been based on examples of local Information Plans. The proposal is now under consideration by the British Library and the Office of Arts and Libraries, and we hope funding may be forthcoming for preliminary research necessary in the development of such a plan.

The aims and objectives of the National Sports Information Plan are:

- to evaluate the current position in sports information provision and the services provided
- to identify the existing and potential user groups and evaluate their requirements
- to make the most effective use of resources to meet the user requirements, avoiding duplication of effort where possible
- to identify key issues which potential contributors wish to incorporate into the planning process

The Sports Council has identified funding to help in the development of the plan and is acting as the lead agency in its preparation. A sector plan for sports information would be the first such national plan.

APPENDIX

THE SPORTS COUNCIL

NATIONAL SERVICES DIVISION

PROPOSAL FOR A NATIONAL SPORTS INFORMATION PLAN

Introduction

> This paper outlines the problems affecting the coordination of sports information services in the UK and proposes an investigation into the feasibility of setting up a Library and Information Plan for sports information.

Background

1. The various services providing sports information in the UK have developed on an *ad hoc* basis. The majority began as services to discrete groups of users, e.g. for staff in particular organisations, or for people in a particular profession, but most of them now provide more general services. The Sports Council has worked with some of these services on an informal basis for many years and has developed a classification scheme and thesaurus which has been adopted by some libraries and extended at their request. The Council has also advised that services should have compatible hardware and software where possible and has occasionally provided grant-aid to this end.

2. However there is no formal mechanism for cooperation. The Sport and Recreation Information Group of which the Council is a founder member, was established in 1984 to provide a forum for discussion for users and providers of sports information, and since its foundation one of the main areas of concern has been the fragmentation of services and the perceived duplication of effort within those services. Enquirers are unsure which organisation to approach for information and consequently are contacting numerous bodies for help. This is an unsatisfactory position for the user, and is a process which can lead to further duplication of effort by the responding organisations.

3. It is considered by a number of organisations and individuals, as evidenced in the response to a SPRIG open meeting in January 1989, that a major examination of the current provision of sports information is necessary.

4. A review of the situation, without any mechanism for pursuing methods of cooperation would lead to few positive developments. It is therefore suggested that the providers of sports information seek to produce a national plan, (based on the examples of local information plans), for the subject area of sport on a UK basis.

5. The first step is to evaluate the existing sports library and information services and the demands made of them, and to examine the feasibility of producing a Library and Information Plan to enable resources to be coordinated.

Aims and objectives

6. The following are the main aims of the strategy in its final and planning stages:

   a. To evaluate the current position in sports information provision and the services provided. This will include the public, private and voluntary sectors.
   b. To identify the existing and potential user groups and evaluate their requirements.
   c. To make the most effective use of resources to meet the user requirements, avoiding duplication of effort where possible.
   d. To identify key issues which potential contributors wish to incorporate into the planning process.

Summary of organisations involved and commitment

7. The Sports Council has identified funding to help in the development of the plan and is willing to be the lead agency in its preparation. Support for the concept of the plan has been given by the Scottish Sports Council, Sports Council for Northern Ireland and the Sports Council for Wales.
8. SPRIG is willing to provide whatever help it can in the development and implementation of the plan. The majority of the organisations represented at the SPRIG meeting indicated a willingness to be involved in the production of such a plan, and many organisational members of SPRIG have since offered support and assistance with the development of the Plan.

Methodology

9. External consultants will be used to carry out data collection and analysis. Most of the information services we are dealing with have small staffs and therefore secondment for this work is not a viable option. The main element of the consultants work will be:

(a) Data collection – supply
- (i) The information services for sport will be identified.
  There are potentially a large number of organisations to be included in the survey. It could include the four national sports councils, ten regions, public library authorities, libraries in educational institutions, professional organisations, youth organisations, commercial information providers, voluntary organisations and disability organisations. It is therefore suggested that criteria for inclusion in the survey be established at an early stage.
- (ii) Postal questionnaires will be sent to all those identified to establish current and planned services.
- (iii) Main providers will be selected for semi-structured interview.

(b) Data collection – demand
- (i) Main user groups will be identified.
- (ii) Main organised groups will be selected for semi-structured interview.
- (iii) Where no usage data for services is available, the logging of enquiries (perhaps 3 weeks over 3 months) will be considered.

(c) Plan preparations
- (i) Analysis of findings. (consultants)
- (ii) Report writing. (consultants)
- (iii) Presentation to steering group. (consultants)
- (iv) Preparation of written statement (consultants & project leader)
- (v) Consultation process. (project leader)
- (vi) Preparation of final plan. (project leader)

Timescales

10. Data collection and analysis – 6 months.
    Production of written statement – 2 months.
    Consultation process – 3/4 months.
    Adoption by cooperating agencies – 6 months.
    Implementation – will be phased, according to priorities and available funding.

Steering Committee

11. A Steering Committee would be set up for the project comprising, where possible, representatives of the various interest groups up to a maximum of twelve. A chairman would be appointed who would play an active role in the formation of the Plan. General meetings and discussions open to all interested parties would also be held.

Wider applications

12. A sector plan for sports information would be the first such national plan. While able to draw on existing experience of the production of local plans, much will be learnt during the development of the plan, which will be of use to other subject areas considering such a step.

[The Sports Council wish to stress that this document is a proposal only, and that approval and funding have not yet been secured.]

10

Functional cooperation: an exercise in bridge building

DIANA EDMONDS

We librarians tend to be insular beings. So in the professional literature we read a great deal about cooperation between librarians who have something in common – cooperation between librarians working in the same geographical area, cooperation between librarians working in the same subject field, cooperation between librarians working in the same type of libraries. All very sensible and even laudable, but just a moment, in the course of their working lives, some librarians come into contact with people who (heaven forbid) aren't librarians ... and recognising that they have interests in common with these outsiders, whom they have observed with suspicion over the professional fence, some have even started to develop formal cooperative links with non-librarians.

Three cooperative organisations are considered within this Chapter, all of them concerned to develop functional cooperation with others who are involved in the same specialist area of activity. While some of the partners in this cooperative exercise are librarians, others are not. The United Kingdom Serials Group, the Library and Information Research Group and the National Acquisitions Group all break the traditional mould of interlibrary cooperation by taking cooperative activity beyond library walls.

THE UNITED KINGDOM SERIALS GROUP

The United Kingdom Serials Group (UKSG) aims 'to bridge the gap

Functional cooperation

between the producer and the end user of serials', and its objectives stress the potential for bridge building:

- to encourage and promote a continuing discussion concerning serials and associated areas, between all interested parties in the information industry, both nationally and internationally
- to develop and maintain links between all those concerned with the production, distribution and use of serials
- to encourage professional awareness in all those connected with serials
- to encourage and assist in the development of appropriate research in the field of serials management

The Group was formed, initially on an *ad hoc* basis, in 1975, following a conference on periodicals which was organised by Blackwells, a major serials agent and library supply company. The second Blackwells Periodicals Conference, held two years later, generated enthusiastic support for the formation of a national organisation, with a membership open to all parties who are interested in serials. So the United Kingdom Serials Group (UKSG) was formally established in 1978, to represent the common interests of a variety of parties who are interested in serials, including librarians and information scientists, booksellers, serials agents, publishers and individual users: all members are treated equally and pay the same membership rate. Management of the Group's affairs is carried out by a committee, elected annually, which works on a voluntary basis. UKSG now employs an administrator to undertake the day to day work of the Group.

Since 1978, UKSG has expanded, growing to a membership of some 500 by 1990. The academic sector represents the largest proportion of members with some 35% of the total coming from universities, polytechnics and colleges. 'Trade' membership accounts for around 22%, with the largest group, the publishers, accounting for more than half of that total. Membership is not passive, either – over 300 delegates attended the 1990 Annual Conference, a figure which rivals the attendance figures at some of the national information conferences organised within the UK. The Annual Conference is the highlight of the Group's activities, planned to allow in-depth discussion of major issues affecting the serials world. Topics covered in recent years include the automation of serials management, copyright, CD-ROM, binding, the services of subscription agents and research techniques and results.

In addition to the Annual Conference, UKSG organises an educational programme which operates throughout the year, providing a range of courses and seminars targeted at different levels of staff working with serials: subjects covered within the programme have included periodicals administration, finance and serials control, automation and CD-ROM. These seminars provide the opportunity for all levels of staff to discuss basic problems of serials management.

UKSG is now also an active publisher: since 1988, the Group has produced *Serials*, the Journal of the UK Serials Group, three times a year. *Serials* contains papers read at the Annual Conference together with other articles; it also has a newsletter function, including news items of interest to members. The publication of this high quality journal has proved beneficial in terms of membership growth, as it appears to have attracted a number of members to the organisation, several of whom live and work outside the UK. In addition to the regular publication of *Serials*, UKSG also cooperated with the British Library in the production of the fifth edition of *Current British Journals*: over 9,000 journals published in the UK are included.

The interest in serials is not confined to the United Kingdom and sister organisations now exist in the United States (NASIG, the North American Serials Interest Group), in Australia (ASIG, the Australian Serials Interest Group) and also in China. These organisations have adopted the same policy as UKSG, opening membership to all parties who are interested in serials. UKSG itself has a large number of overseas members: in February 1990, these overseas members amounted to 32% of the total. In recognition of the level of interest in European countries, UKSG organised the first European Serials Conference in the Netherlands in September 1990.

The UK Serials Group stresses that it is an autonomous body, and that it is not linked to any other existing organisation in the information industry, 'so that the best interests of all concerned may be achieved'. Nor does the organisation seek to act as a pressure group. Rather it allows contentious issues to be opened up to debate within the context of the membership.

THE NATIONAL ACQUISITIONS GROUP

Just as the UK Serials Group brings together librarians and the trade in the serials business, the National Acquisitions Group (NAG) brings together librarians and the book trade in a 'single, broadly-based organisation' which aims to stimulate, coordinate and publicise developments in acquisitions. The possibility of establishing an organisation concerned with the acquisition of materials for libraries was mooted at a Council of Polytechnic Librarians (COPOL) Conference, in 1985. Acquisitions librarians at that time suffered a sense of isolation from their colleagues in other libraries and from the book trade. Although there were opportunities to meet other acquisitions librarians and bibliographic services officers at national library conferences, where contacts with exhibiting suppliers and publishers could also be made, these opportunities were few and far between.

The suggestion for the development of an independent association concerned with the acquisition of materials for libraries was greeted with enthusiasm, and NAG was formally established in April 1986 at an inaugural conference in Oxford. In order to ensure the Group's independence from other bodies, commercial sponsorship was raised – 28 companies donated a total of almost £7,000 to provide a sound financial basis for NAG. This initial funding has since been built upon by membership subscriptions, seminar fees, advertising, publication sales and sponsorship for specific items or events (Morley, 1989).

Membership of the group is open to all parties concerned with library acquisitions – booksellers, librarians, library suppliers, library automated systems suppliers and publishers. In 1990, membership stood at about 380: 65% were librarians, 15% publishers and 20% suppliers.

NAG's constitution specifies that its purpose and overall aim is to bring together those publishers, booksellers and suppliers of books and other library materials, automated systems suppliers and librarians involved in the process of library acquisitions, to enable them better to exchange information and comment and by doing so promote understanding and good practice between them. Within this context, the term 'library acquisitions' is broadly defined as the production, selection, purchase, supply and exploitation of books and other materials, equipment and software for use in libraries and information units in the UK and abroad, together with the management of resources used in that process.

Within the overall aim, the Group has a number of objectives, including the following:

- to recruit and unite members in common discussion of acquisition policies and practices

- to provide opportunities for NAG members to bring forward acquisitions issues for discussion
- to initiate discussions of acquisitions issues beyond the membership of NAG, throughout the relevant media and without regard for profession or employment
- to cooperate with other organisations whose activities (in whole or in part) are relevant to the purpose of NAG
- to promote knowledge and understanding of technological developments in publishing, bookselling and library and information work, and their use in acquisitions
- to gather information about library acquisitions and disseminate it to members and non-members actually or potentially involved in acquisitions activity
- to improve the awareness of producers, suppliers and librarians of the state of art of acquisitions in libraries and information units and *vice versa*
- to influence other organisations and individuals to adopt its opinions and standards when promulgated

NAG, like UKSG is sensitive to the commercial interests of its trade members: the constitution specifies that 'NAG will in no way act against the interests of its commercial members, nor will it knowingly divulge information or stimulate discussion of matters likely to prejudice the business of any company'.

The Annual Conference of the National Acquisitions Group provides an opportunity for those concerned with acquisitions to meet and to discuss key issues. In addition to the Annual Conference, the Group organises about six seminars each year for both professional and non-professional staff: topics covered in the seminar series have included bibliographic services for public libraries, automated acquisitions and publishers' pricing policies. Several events have been organised in collaboration with other bodies, including the Library Association, the Publishers' Association and UKSG.

A *NAG Newsletter* is issued twice a year and is regarded as 'the main channel of communication' between the Executive Committee and its membership. The Newsletter includes news of Committee and Group activities, and those of other book trade bodies, together with articles on topics of interest and details of recent publications relating to library acquisitions. Another communications tool produced by NAG is the

Directory of Acquisitions Librarians, which lists the names of librarians working in the field, and also provides details of acquisitions systems in use in their libraries. The Group is now planning to publish an authoritative journal dealing with the subject of library acquisitions, as soon as it is practicable to do so.

THE LIBRARY AND INFORMATION RESEARCH GROUP

UKSG and NAG bring together the librarian and the 'trade': the third group considered in this Chapter crosses the divide between the researcher and the practitioner. These two groups are often interested in the same areas of librarianship or information work, but approach the situation in a different way. Practitioners are sometimes suspicious of researchers, and concerned about their lack of practical experience – I well recall visiting one librarian during the course of a project relating to the complexities of cataloguing procedures only to be asked 'Have you ever worked in a library?'

The Library and Information Research Group (LIRG) aims 'to bridge the gap between research and practice' by bringing together all parties with an interest in library and information research and investigation, whether they operate within the profession or elsewhere. Formed in 1977, the membership of the Group included a large number of people who were employed as information science researchers: since that time, membership has broadened, perhaps reflecting the broadening interest in information related research in this area. The current membership is not large – some 130 members in the UK and 30 overseas members – but is broadly-based including researchers, practitioners and managers. In addition to the personal members, there are also around 100 institutional members which subscribe to the journal *Library and Information News* which is published by the Group.

LIRG is one of the small number of independent professional associations which work 'in association' with the Library Association, and, each year, receive a small grant from the LA. Its activities are coordinated by an elected committee of members from all types of libraries, research centres and teaching departments. The aims of the Group are to provide:

- contact between researchers for exchange of experience and ideas; and between researchers, practitioners and managers for information, feedback and input

- information on current research and related activities
- education and training through courses, meetings and seminars
- encouragement to individuals, especially inexperienced and part-time researchers
- a forum for discussion and development of research methodologies and techniques
- a pressure group capable of influencing national research policy

In practical terms, LIRG is concerned primarily with the organisation of meetings throughout the UK: one major meeting is held each year, often over a weekend. Topics covered in recent years include research in public libraries, management information systems, performance measurement and collection development. Recently LIRG has organised a number of one day workshops on a specific aspect of research methods, including interviewing techniques, the analysis of data and the dissemination of results: these workshops have proved extremely popular, attracting many librarians who are interested in undertaking some research in the particular area in which they are working. In addition to these national meetings, a number of local groups organise meetings: a group in the south east organises monthly meetings in London, and there are also active groups in the north east, based in Newcastle, and in the north west.

In addition to its programme of meetings, LIRG is an active publisher, producing a periodical, *Library and Information Research News*, and a number of monographs, published in cooperation with a commercial publishing house. The standing of the organisation is reflected both in the high quality of these publications and in the frequency with which it is asked to comment on key issues affecting the profession.

THE BENEFITS OF FUNCTIONAL COOPERATION

The three cooperative organisations discussed in this Chapter, UKSG, NAG and LIRG, each promote cooperative links in a specialist area of the information industry. A great deal of interlibrary cooperation is concerned with the high-level development of policies: although, in the long-term, these policies have an impact on librarians working at the grass roots, these librarians might be forgiven the assumption that cooperation is an erudite pursuit indulged in by senior management over extended lunches. In contrast, UKSG, NAG and LIRG are practical organisations which provide their members with practical benefits. The three organisations operate in a very similar way, organising meetings, workshops and seminars, producing newsletters and other journals to disseminate information, and in general giving members an opportunity to meet others with similar interests: because members sometimes approach these issues from different sides of the fence, there may be an opportunity to make fundamental changes which will benefit all parties.

UKSG, NAG and LIRG all exist to bring together individuals who are involved in a specialist area of the library and information profession. They are successful simply because these individuals recognise the practical benefits of belonging to the organisation – and in consequence are willing to give their time and energy to assist its development. Because membership is open to all who are interested in the topic, these organisations can bridge the gap between librarians and the non-library world. Communication between the two sides certainly helps to improve everyone's knowledge: often this improvement in knowledge leads on to practical developments, which are of benefit to all parties.

INFORMATION CONSULTANTS AND BROKERS

Functional cooperatives bring together those who are concerned with a particular function or activity – and typically bring together librarians and the 'trade'. But increasingly librarians themselves are active in trade. The private sector within the information profession has expanded considerably in recent years, and these professionals feel the need to meet together and to learn from each other's experience just as traditional librarians have done.

The largest group of freelance librarians and information professionals are those who call themselves 'consultants'. There are now an increasing number of library and information consultants operating in the UK, and there have been a number of attempts to develop a cooperative grouping for them. In 1986, some 30 consultants working in various areas of information met in the Rembrandt Hotel in London: this so-called 'Rembrandt Group' discussed a number of issues including the increasing number of part-time or semi-retired people entering consultancy, and their failure to charge appropriate rates; the failure of some major public bodies to pay adequate daily rates for consultancy was also highlighted.

Following the initial meeting, the Rembrandt Group set up a small working party to discuss the possibility of establishing an association for consultants, and a feasibility report was produced. The functions of the proposed association were very different from traditional library and information cooperatives, and had commercial implications. They included:

- developing a more positive image of information consultancy
- producing a joint brochure to promote the sector
- group insurance negotiations
- credit checking of clients
- joint advertising
- advice on taxation and VAT matters
- a skills database of sub-contractors
- joint lobbying of major clients to secure appropriate fee rates

As Gurnsey and White (1989) comment, the emphasis of the Group was on marketing, rather than on quality control – and they suggest that the issue of registration would need to be tackled by the membership. However, the Rembrandt Group did not go on to formally establish itself as a consultants' cooperative or as a trade association. Consultants still continue to cooperate informally, often passing on work to others if they are too busy to do it themselves, or if they feel that another consultant's skills are more appropriate. But to date, there is no organisation specifically for information consultants, other than the general professional associations which encompass all information specialists. The reason for this is probably quite simple – pressure on time. Consultants often work alone, running relatively small businesses: like many small business owners, they are often too busy doing the job to spend time on anything which does not increase profits. I suspect that the Rembrandt Group suffered from a lack of the energetic support which is so apparent in UKSG, NAG and LIRG. As information consultancies grow larger, who knows? In future years, we may need to add a consultants cooperative to the list of functional cooperatives.

Towards the end of the 1980s, the ranks of the library and information consultants were augmented by a new breed – the information brokers, providing packaged information for their clients. While consultants are essentially an isolated breed, a brokerage typically has a number of staff, in order to ensure that clients can rely upon a rapid response to their enquiries. In December 1989, during the 13th International Online Information Meeting in London, the inaugural meeting of the European Information Researchers Network (EIRENE) was held. This first meeting was organised by two UK-based information brokers, Pauline Duckitt of Vital Information Ltd and Jill Cousins of First Contact Ltd, and was attended by more than 40 information brokers from eight European countries. The success of this meeting and subsequent comments encouraged the organisers to establish a formal network of information brokers.

The organisational structure is merely a means to an end: the founders stress that 'our aim is not to create an organisation but to promote contacts between information brokers'. The issue of affiliation to other larger groups within the information profession was discussed at a meeting of information brokers in Frankfurt. Brokers debated whether their interests needed to be represented by another organisation. Should they affiliate with EIIA, EUSIDIC or FID? 'The answer was clear – NO'. One broker summarised their requirements as 'the opportunity to meet each other over a good lunch and cocktails, to gather relevant information and to have access to an informative list of other brokers' (Editorial, 1990).

The aim of EIRENE is to 'promote contacts between European information brokers, thereby increasing access to information and promoting the development of information brokerage as a commercial activity'. The group exercises some control over membership: full membership of the organisation is restricted to bona fide brokers. There are now over 40 members based in countries throughout Europe.

In order to keep members in touch with each other, a twice-yearly newsletter is produced. The newsletter, appropriately named *Contact* provides information on developments in information brokerage throughout Europe, giving news, profiles of information brokers and product reviews. A directory of members is produced with the first issue of the newsletter published each year, and details of amendments and deletions are produced with the second issue. The directory is also available to non-members for a fee.

In addition to the publication of the newsletter and the directory, an annual meeting is organised by EIRENE: two such meetings have been held so far, both timed to coincide with the International Online Information Meeting, which attracts so many international delegates. The Second Annual EIRENE Meeting held in December 1990 was an extended half-day programme, with a buffet lunch followed by papers on topics of relevance to the assembled information brokers, topics such as liability, the impact of European legislation on information brokers, and brokers from the client's viewpoint. Papers given at this meeting are to be printed in the journal *Infomediary* which is published in the Netherlands. At the Annual Meeting, EIRENE members have an opportunity to meet each other – and to find out about the services provided by other brokerage firms. The emphasis is on doing business, and members can display promotional literature during the meeting.

EIRENE has many of the attributes of the functional cooperatives discussed earlier in this Chapter – it gives members an opportunity to meet each other, to hear papers on subjects of interest and to exchange information; it publishes a directory, so that members can identify and locate each other, and it produces a newsletter to keep members in contact with each other. The difference between them is the element of trade: EIRENE is a trade association in embryo. At the last meeting, however, it was suggested that a broker's user group should be established, to bring together trade interests and those of the users. Now where have we heard that before?

REFERENCES

Editorial (1990), *Contact*, no. 1, (June).
Gurnsey, J. and White, M. (1989) *Information consultancy*. London: Bingley.
Morley, M. (1989), Librarians and the book trade in the United Kingdom: the development of the National Acquisitions Group. *Library Acquisitions: Practice and Theory,* vol. 13, pp. 65 – 71.

11

Bibliographic cooperation: an overview

Peter Stubley

Unlike cooperation that takes place between specific types of library or within well defined subject areas, the term bibliographic cooperation can be interpreted in a wide variety of ways. It can be used to describe the national and international work being undertaken to facilitate the transfer of bibliographic information between countries and different computer systems; for an examination of the hardware, software and services provided by integrated library system suppliers, particularly cooperatives such as BLCMP; for a discussion of the increasingly important transmission of information between libraries and the book trade; and even a consideration of the factors surrounding access to the union catalogues (manual or online) of other libraries or systems. In the space of a Chapter it is only possible to provide an overview of the many aspects of this subject and this is what the author sets out to do. By providing a substantial bibliography it is hoped that the interested reader will be able to pursue the major topics of individual interest in more detail.

Bibliographic cooperation has for years been acknowledged as a factor underpinning much of modern-day librarianship. In spite of this, it has tended to be related areas such as the development of integrated library systems that have attracted most attention and only with contentious statements such as the British Library's *Currency with coverage* paper (1987) have bibliographic matters been brought to the forefront. This lack of 'glamour' attached to the bibliographic record detracts from the importance, necessity and high level of work involved if local, national and international library systems are to continue to improve. Bibliographic cooperation centres on the bibliographic record and the available databases of such records and, accordingly, the Chapter begins with a description of the extensive cooperative work to facilitate local and international bibliographic transfer.

CODES, DESCRIPTIONS AND FORMATS

Most librarians would appear to be as concerned about the format of bibliographic records as they are about telecommunications settings for online searching: it is incidental detail that interferes with the important issues of service delivery. For those libraries that insist on creating all their catalogue records internally for running solely on their own hardware – fewer as time goes by – the matter has no relevance, but for those that want to communicate bibliographically with the outside world it is an important factor. It could be argued that, in one respect, format is unimportant because to convert from one to another only necessitates a conversion utility (with or without Open Systems Interconnection). This begs the question of the cost of such a utility, its availability at the right time, and whether the library's bibliographic information will be compatible with any data added from external sources. In the microcomputer world it is becoming increasingly possible to transfer different file types, retaining format, between what has formerly been incompatible hardware (for example, from IBM PC to Macintosh). Because of the increasing availability of bibliographic data from a variety of sources – outlined in this Chapter – it would appear that library systems have to move quickly in a similar direction. This is achievable to some extent at present, but there are two main differences between PC and library systems. Firstly, the economics of writing file converters very much favours the enormous market of the personal computer world. Secondly, and more importantly, while there are standards for bibliographic control, these are not universally applied and the present section reviews some of the inconsistencies that need to be resolved before the unfettered international exchange of records can take place.

The mainstays of any system for the cooperative exchange of bibliographic records are standards for bibliographic description and the format for the exchange of data in machine-readable form. It could be argued that these standards have been the true instigators of cooperation world-wide and that most other forms of library cooperation have sprung from these beginnings. (From the perspective of cooperative staff training, this proposition becomes less easy to justify, but such is the trouble with generalisations.). However, the main issue is that cataloguing codes such as the Anglo-American Cataloguing Rules (AACR) and exchange formats such as MARC (machine readable cataloguing), however well known and used nationally, are actually 'pseudo-standards' when considered from the international viewpoint.

Cataloguing codes and bibliographic description

The present version of AACR, AACR2 1988 revision, is the result of over 80 years of Anglo-American cooperation. Stemming from the 1908 Joint Code, work initiated by Melvil Dewey to establish a uniform cataloguing practice in the English speaking world, it is not surprising that it has maintained a stranglehold on British and American librarianship for so long. This is especially so when one recalls the furore over the changes wrought by the introduction of AACR2, centring primarily on the high cost of changeover from AACR1. Who, having put significant resources into such large-scale changes in the early 1980's, would be willing to surrender to the putative benefits of a new code? Anyone wishing to remind themselves of some of the debate over AACR2 should consult Ayres' (1980) provocative and extremely entertaining paper on the subject. Much of the concern has now died down but, in an area where cooperation would appear paramount to ensure success, it is interesting to return to comments written by Massil (1982): 'What has been disappointing is the uncoordinated nature of these developments, the lack of an agreed network scheme for comprehensive upgrading of files and the (initial) atmosphere of disagreement in which the practical changes were proposed'.

In the current context it is not the lack of cooperation in changeovers to major revisions that is important but the fact that AACR2 is not a truly international standard, in spite of following the ISBD(G) (General International Standard Bibliographic Description) for descriptive cataloguing. Any cataloguing code such as AACR2 comprises two sections: the bibliographic description and the means of access to the records – main entry, headings and such like. The ISBD is a family of recommendations – there are at present eight ISBDs for dealing with different categories of material such as monographs, serials and maps –

for creating the bibliographic description of items in a fixed sequence. It is an attempt to move away from what was the traditional approach of transcribing details as they appeared on the title page, but has as its ultimate intention the production of interchangeable records 'so that records produced in one country could be easily accepted in library catalogues or other bibliographic lists in any other country' (IFLA, 1978). ISBD(G) was drawn up by IFLA and the Joint Steering Committee for Revision of AACR and 'dozens of national bibliographies now use ISBD as the basis for their bibliographic description, including those of all the major English-speaking countries' (Hagler and Simmons, 1982).

One of the main disadvantages of the ISBD is the complex punctuation that is used to separate the discrete areas of bibliographic description. Unfortunately for the library user, the intention of using this for computer manipulation has been carried through to the presentation of records, potentially giving rise to international confusion rather than harmony. The IFLA Section on Cataloguing is considering the simplification of this aspect.

Attempts at agreement on a truly international cataloguing code are also around 80 years old but in many respects the profession is still a long way from the desired result. This is probably due to the preeminence and universal implementation of AACR1 and AACR2 in the English-speaking world for, as Sule (1990) trenchantly says 'the internationality of the headings had to give way to the expectations of the local clientele, which did not wish to be confronted with exotic names if there was – for example – a nice English one instead'. Jeffreys (1990) makes a similar point in commenting that the non Anglo-American content of AACR2 is basically for the benefit of cataloguers in Anglo-American libraries rather than for direct application in the countries to which reference is made. Sule goes on to provide a fascinating account of the different treatment of headings, with examples, from a comparative survey of the cataloguing codes of France (AFNOR – Association Française de Normalisation), Germany (RAK – Regeln für die alphabetische Katalogisierung), Holland (FOBID – Federatie van organisaties op het gebied van het bibliotheek–, informatie– en dokumentatiewezen) and Italy (RICA – Regole Italiane di Catalogazione per Autori), in addition to a consideration of AACR2. From this it is clear that the greatest inconsistency among different national cataloguing codes, and therefore the biggest drawback to the international exchange of records, arises from differences in the formulation and choice of headings. The inconsistencies arise primarily from the method of formulation of these codes because the Paris Principles on which they were based permitted different degrees of interpretation. As a result the headings for several individual and corporate authors vary by virtue of the differing languages in use.

The achievement of the aim of international exchange of bibliographic records would therefore seem not to lie in imposing an international cataloguing code or in compromising national approaches, but, some would say, through the implementation of automatic name authority control. In discussing work related to the British Library's name authority list, Oddy (1986) defines the authority record as containing 'the established form of heading, various notes helpful to the cataloguer or user, and the variant and related headings from which references have been made'. It is generally recognised that creating name authority files in this way is not cheap and so the prospect of generating international versions would appear to be particularly daunting. At the same time it is difficult to see how these might be used. If it is accepted that national cataloguing codes with their implicit differences are to remain, then name authority files will presumably be used at the national level so that all the foreign language variants of names are converted to the recognised national heading on receipt. As each country has its own rules for headings, it follows that separately created name authority files will be utilised for each country (or countries with a common language) and that a single international name authority file would be impractical. What international cooperation would do is make it easier to recognise the headings of concern, and presumably the transfer from one national authority list to another could be automated to reduce the overall workload. Though an ideal, it is by no means agreed that international authority control is something we should be working towards. Smethurst (1990) covers this issue in an excellent paper on European cooperation: 'We will not easily achieve a European standard for each of the forms of personal names, let alone institutional and corporate names. To construct a common European thesaurus to deal with the languages of names and the language of subject descriptors would immediately involve us in political questions which even the European Community would seek to avoid'.

Issues of international (and, for that matter, local) bibliographic cooperation cannot ignore the fact that online public access catalogues (OPACs) are becoming increasingly important as sources of access to records, for both users and library staff. In those libraries that have installed them, OPACs have also become the preferred means of access. In this context, where serial access to records is replaced by database search techniques, some observers maintain that the traditional concept of main entry ceases to have any meaning. There are arguments for saying that in an age of OPACs the need for careful control over bibliographic description is even greater than before, and anyone who has been presented with displays of numerous variants of the same author's name will sympathize with this view. However, chaos in OPACs is not simply caused by the disappearance of main entries but by the careless application of cataloguing rules (or by the rigid application of different codes). One way around this is to utilise *automatic* authority control as described by Ayres (1983): 'We should not try to set up an elaborate mechanism of rules which establish preferred headings. What we should be doing and what the computer will enable us to do is to select the approach that any reader is likely to make and ensure that it is linked to all other likely approaches. There is no future at all for cataloguers if we do not get away from the attitude which sets out to tell the library user what we consider is best for him.' In particular, it must be remembered that OPACs are in an extremely early stage of development and that the possibilities offered by them, and the way in which they are used, are liable to change significantly in the years ahead. Any discussion of the future of cataloguing codes must take account of this fact.

Exchange formats for bibliographic records

The format in general use for the exchange of bibliographic records is, of course, MARC. The core of the format is now almost 25 years old and there is certainly a feeling that its longevity owes nothing to the elegance or efficiency of its design. MARC could thus be said to have *imposed* cooperation or coordination on librarians, instead of encouraging it, by being the major format at the time it was required. In this way it is perhaps its own era's version of the IBM PC – a machine which has flourished through sheer weight of numbers purchased (and which, through its very name, appears to inspire security and confidence) in spite of the intractability of the hardware. Perhaps MARC was only likewise acceptable because it was initiated by all the solidity of the Library of Congress (LC). But this does not tell the whole story for it is significant that it was a national library and not a commercial enterprise that instigated MARC. At the time of its introduction there was little money to be made in a machine readable format for library records (there is probably precious little to be made still) and the idea (or ideal) of integrated library systems was some years in the future. Throughout its life there have been complaints that MARC is not an easy format to get to grips with and it is apparently disliked by most systems people. In spite of this, most libraries with nationally or internationally important collections insist on supporting the format for the benefits it offers. As Moon (1989) says: 'the cost of adhering not simply to institutional standards but to the somewhat irksome AACR2 and UKMARC formulae is high, but the Library (of Edinburgh University) firmly believes that the cost of not doing so will be higher in the long run'. Useful background reading to a history of MARC and the use of conversion programs between the UK and US version can be found in Long (1984).

In spite of *nominally* being a standard, MARC suffers from the drawback of having different interpretations for each national implementation. There are a veritable babel of variants – in 1984, Long reported 20 national or regional formats – and, perhaps as would be expected, even the US version (LCMARC) differs from the UK version. The outcome is that MARC tapes in these different national formats are not directly interchangeable and cannot be loaded indiscriminately on the same computer. Hopkinson (1984) points out that '... as early as 1971 it was clear that the assignment of tags, indicators and subfield identifiers was so varied between national formats that tailor-made programs would have to be written by any national agency that wished to use records from another'.

Attempts to surmount these difficulties have taken different forms, depending on need, perceived use, and perspective. Thus, a company like BLCMP, in supporting its own database, transfers all incoming data into a single format closely based on UKMARC. Member libraries then have no compatibility problems when adding data to their local systems. National libraries, on the other hand, have different priorities and many are actively working towards the interchange of bibliographic data across international boundaries. While this is possible with individual national MARC formats, it presupposes that each national library uses a translation utility to convert each non-standard format into its own version i.e. 20 or more different MARC formats require the same number of conversion programs. How much better if all nations could agree on a standard for the international exchange of bibliographic data in machine-readable form. Even if individual countries did not use this standard internally, a single conversion utility would ensure that they had access to all other nations' records and that their own could be easily translated for use elsewhere.

This generally agreed communication format exists as UNIMARC, the result of many years work on the part of IFLA. Not only has UNIMARC been specifically designed as an international exchange format, it has also been created for use in conjunction with the various ISBDs so that the content descriptors of tags and indicators match the order of elements from the ISBDs. Sule (1990) points out that several national bibliographic agencies such as the Library of Congress, the National Library of Canada, the Bibliothèque Nationale and the Deutsche Bibliothek are already able to convert their records into UNIMARC and that the British Library has progressed some way towards a conversion utility. However, some countries have gone further and adopted a variant of UNIMARC as their national format or provided the ability to directly use UNIMARC data in their systems. In spite of this, the format is still not widely used for the exchange purposes for which it was designed but present economic pressures, particularly the opportunities outlined in the *Plan of action for libraries in the EC* (1987) (see below) *may* see renewed (cooperative) efforts to endorse and utilise this format. The fact that many national, academic and research libraries have substantial holdings of foreign language materials – Romance and Germanic languages, but increasingly non-Roman scripts – for which machine-readable records are not easily available should provide at least some incentive to proceed.

The Common Communication Format (CCF) was developed by Unesco to enable the international exchange of bibliographic information for materials in any format and type. As such it is hospitable to records of both books and individual papers from journals and it can therefore integrate information from online database hosts and national bibliographies. It was developed at the request of member states who could then create the necessary databases for access within their country rather than at the expense of telecommunications costs. By incorporating elements from both UNIMARC and the UNISIST Reference Manual for abstracting and indexing services it forms a useful bridge between the two types of record, and ensures that some of the national data in UNIMARC format will be available to users of the CCF. Hopkinson

(1985) provides an extensive review of the work in creating the format together with examples of its use.

European initiatives

The problems associated with the international transfer and exchange of bibliographic records, together with a recognition of 'the importance of libraries and their role as intermediaries to knowledge and culture' have been addressed, at least at policy level, in the *Plan of action for libraries in the EC* (1987). One of the prime motives in establishing the plan appears to have been the recognition that libraries in the European Community have not responded to (or had the resources to respond to) the 'information revolution' as actively as their counterparts in North America. Further useful commentary can be found in the paper by Iljon and Manson (1990). The *Plan* is outlined more fully in Chapter 3.

With a view to improving access to the holdings of libraries across Europe and with a particular emphasis on the application of information technology, the *Plan of Action* proposes five (recently reduced to four) Action Lines by which its broad objectives may be achieved. The first two of these relate directly to bibliographic cooperation, though proposals for the other Action Lines may also have relevance to this area. Action Line 1 – library source data projects – emphasises the creation and/or enhancement of machine readable national bibliographies and the standardisation issues associated with these, together with the retrospective conversion of catalogues of internationally important collections. Particular stress is placed on helping those EC countries without a national bibliography or with incomplete records for a national bibliography. The support for enhancements to national databases has already begun in the form of a pilot/demonstration project being undertaken by a Consortium of seven national libraries (Denmark, France, Federal Republic of Germany, Italy, the Netherlands, Portugal, and the UK) coordinated by the British Library. The aim of the project is to improve the interchange of bibliographic records, and CD-ROM has been chosen as a cost effective delivery medium and a means of ensuring widespread distribution of cataloguing data. The overall proposal comprises nine sub-projects and, in relation to what was written at the start of this paper, one of these will aim to develop MARC conversion routines from the CD-ROM exchange formats. Action Line 2 – the international linking of systems – indicates a particular interest in OSI

(Open Systems Interconnection) and has likewise given rise to a pilot/ demonstration project, in this case the identification and supply of material for interlibrary loan across libraries in the UK, the Netherlands and France. Consideration is to be given to interlibrary messaging in an OSI environment, and thereafter testing of the search and retrieval protocol in conjunction with the identification of items in union catalogues.

DATABASES FOR BIBLIOGRAPHIC COOPERATION

Before the ready availability of machine readable bibliographic records, when cataloguers were a plentiful breed and catalogues were created wholly internally, the union catalogue had limited utility compared to the ways in which present cooperative bibliographic databases are used. The early union catalogues and the British National Bibliography (BNB), though the forerunners of cooperation, were primarily utilised as standard tools for bibliographic and location checking rather than as bases for internal catalogue records; though, of course, both LC and BNB provided subscription catalogue card services. Due to a lack of any form of automated cooperative cataloguing, and probably as a result of the amount of work involved in its production, the card catalogue was seen as one of the primary products of the library, a monolithic shrine at which all users and most library staff must worship.

Nowadays, the utilisation of imported bibliographic records is so all pervasive that most librarians accept them as a fact of life. Computerised databases – international, national or at the local library level – are one of the primary reference tools of the librarian rather than a novel alternative to printed sources. For example, in addition to the provision of catalogue records, cooperative databases are utilised for acquisitions, for interlibrary loans as an alternative to the British Library Document Supply Centre, and for answers to reference and bibliographic enquiries. They are also useful vehicles for collection development, forming the base for creating local or regional subject collections. Though, in general, they do not yet have the utility of journal databases used in online searching – the number of access points and the possible search strategies are presently severely limited – bibliographic databases are now being used for similar purposes, and this utility can be expected to increase in the coming years if the economics prove favourable. If the records in cooperative databases are enhanced with subject or publishers information, as outlined at the end of this Chapter, it will also be possible to carry out book selection on screen, feeding information directly into the acquisitions process as required. In spite of this, and returning to the cataloguing perspective, it is surprising that some libraries with integrated systems still create the majority of their records internally. The reasons for this are various but probably include: lack of access to a cooperative database that could be used for generating catalogue records directly; an emphasis on particular standards of catalogue creation – either of higher or lower standard than those used by others; or a belief that cooperative record generation and access offers no cost benefits compared to in-house creation.

Resource implications

As the early research projects into computerised library systems began to attract attention and the full potential of automation became apparent, so work practices in technical services departments began to alter. In some instances, these changes coincided with institutional pressures to reduce staffing costs, with the consequence that many vacant posts remained unfilled and in some cases were lost from establishments. These frozen posts would not on their own have forced libraries to encompass cooperative cataloguing, but they may have acted as an impetus. Prior to automation a number of academic libraries – and probably others – used non-professional staff in the cataloguing process but computerised cataloguing enabled this change to be adopted in a larger number of institutions. The use or non-use of classification in an imported record will also have an effect on the staffing position. The net result is that many libraries who import machine readable records have cataloguing departments that are both considerably trimmer and of a different constitution – in terms of professional to assistant ratios – than they were at the start of the 1970s.

However, the staff savings made as a result of the introduction of automated cooperative cataloguing must be counterbalanced by the need for staff in new areas, notably on the systems side. For as integrated systems have increased in complexity, with the need for maintenance, customisation, backup and overall management to reap the full benefits for users and staff alike, so has the need grown for a 'systems section' in the library in place of the single, isolated – or even part-time – systems librarian of the early 1980s.

The other key resource issue, the cost of bibliographic records, is one in which no recent independent results have been published. Such comparisons that are spread by word of mouth do not always have a strong basis in fact and tend to represent the views of interested parties: librarians proving their own internal cost efficiencies or system suppliers emphasising lower costs than their competitors. The main reason is the difficulty, if not the impossibility, of establishing a meaningful and universal unit cataloguing cost in the face of all the variables: non-professional versus professional staff costs; short records versus full records; quality checking at various stages of the cataloguing process; the different pricing mechanisms – together with the difficulty of separating the cataloguing component from all other elements – imposed on libraries by the system suppliers; and the perceived needs of the users of different library types. This is a complex area that requires a considerable amount of research before the issues can be clarified. This fact was recognised at the Newbury seminar described below and was one of topics included in the list of potential research areas.

Databases for cooperative operation

With the increasing demand for machine readable bibliographic records, libraries are investigating a variety of supply options. Some of these are obvious, particularly where libraries are members of cooperatives. For example, a member of BLCMP will carry out the bulk (if not all) of its search for records on the BLCMP database and any not found will be created locally and added for use by all other libraries. The database totals 8.5 million bibliographic records comprising UK and LC MARC tapes, Whitaker's Books in Print, the British Library Document Supply Centre database, and the BLCMP Union file. Many members find the vast majority of their needs on the database, having to create records for less than 10% of new acquisitions (the largest gaps are in the areas of foreign language publications, audiovisual materials and ephemera). Because of its size it also acts as a useful resource for retrospective conversion. Full details of the database and the range of services offered by BLCMP – it is no longer a cataloguing-centred cooperative as many librarians still seem to think – are provided by Stubley (1988). Other libraries will primarily use the services of OCLC. However, less well known databases are starting to come to prominence, and may form a real challenge to the traditional record suppliers. Two of these are described briefly below. Though the Book Data database, being a commercial undertaking, is not cooperative in the manner of BLCMP, it does indicate the increasing availability of bibliographic information among a user community looking for different sources of data. Thus, for the purposes of this Chapter it has been construed as cooperative in the broadest sense.

CURL

CURL (the Consortium of University Research Libraries) comprises seven university libraries with especially strong research collections: Cambridge, Edinburgh, Glasgow, Leeds, London, Manchester and Oxford. Since December 1987 the Consortium has been working on a UGC-funded pilot project to establish a cooperative database of holdings at Manchester University, the steps taken to arrive at this point and covering some of the later work being described by Ratcliffe and Foskett (1989). The database currently being created from these seven major collections would appear to have one major advantage: size, though it may be some time before the full benefit of this becomes apparent. Thus, though the overall size of the joint collections is in excess of 20 million volumes, Perry (1990) reports that the present database consists of approximately two million records, and this includes duplicates which have not been (deliberately) systematically excluded in addition to BNB tapes from 1986. She points out that 'around 40% of the records are from the 1980's, with 15% from each of the two previous decades, leaving only 30% of material being pre-1960'. The advantages of CURL for large scale retrospective conversion of older material has thus yet to be realised. Records are transferred to libraries either by downloading into PCs and then uploading into local databases, or by tape supply. Though transfer across JANET (the Joint Academic Network) is desirable for this purpose it is not yet possible until binary transfer facilities across the network are improved. Further technical details on the setting up of the database, methods of access and the transfer of records will be found in Perry (1988). The cooperative nature of CURL is emphasised in the non-charging policy for records among members and in the intention of permitting, ultimately, other university libraries to have free access to the database across JANET. With further development, CURL appears to have the potential to become one of the major suppliers of bibliographic records to university libraries in the UK.

Book Data

Book Data is an independent UK company that was established in 1987 to coordinate information from publishers on current and forthcoming titles and make this available to end users such as booksellers and library suppliers. All services are subscription based. An overview of the work involved in setting up the Book Data database, the information contained in the records and the services offered is provided by Martin and Vernon (1990). The advantages of such a database are that it provides enhanced bibliographic data (with 'a considerable level of UKMARC compatibility') and non-bibliographic information which could be of use at the selection stage and for enriching search terms within OPACs: author information; book abstract; an edited contents list; price and availability. 'The principal purpose of Book Data services is to improve the effectiveness of promotion and sales at all levels of the book trade, nationally and internationally. But once a record of this kind becomes available, backed up by a clearinghouse which takes responsibility for its consistency, its regular updating, and its distribution to the user community, it can be used as source material for many other purposes. In Book Data's case, the record is being used as a source for British Library CIP and for *British Book News* entries.' A CD-ROM version of the database, BookFind–CD, was launched in January 1991. The increasing importance to librarians of linking with machine readable data from publishers is dealt with in the following section on bibliographic requirements.

Access to OPACs

The spread of OPACs further offers opportunities for any library catalogue to be treated as a bibliographic utility. The possibility of one library downloading records from another's OPAC and using these as bases of catalogue records is unlikely, but for libraries in a particular region, OPACs offer opportunities for improving services through the remote checking of availability of material, both by users and library staff. Safeguards to prevent unauthorised borrowing, or agreements widening library membership or charging for services may arise directly from this improved access to catalogues, but each library or group of libraries will have their own response to this initiative.

Access to the OPACs of UK university libraries and some polytechnic libraries over JANET is already widespread, but in Scotland the SALBIN

(Scottish Academic Libraries Bibliographic Information Network) project has coordinated this approach on behalf of academic libraries, in particular with the view to providing search facilities for library users. The system comprises a user-friendly communications package – menu driven – working on an IBM PC or compatible to enable users to search, and download or print from, the OPACs of a large number of libraries at will. Ralls (1989) reports that 'this remote use is the acid test of user-friendliness, and we are already seeing improvements in the Scottish OPACs as shortcomings, bugs and ambiguities are uncovered by users with no friendly guidance notice or leaflet to hand'.

It should be possible to expand significantly the usefulness of this approach once OSI is established. Kruiniger (1990) gives a fascinating indication of how this could operate in practice for a library user contemplating to search the catalogues of four libraries with three different systems (for example, URICA, BLCMP (at two libraries) and Geac). 'If the searches are complex and iterative, the task becomes daunting. A Library Directory system would be capable of resolving this to provide a *single* logical view of all four databases *and could execute searches on all four simultaneously*, if appropriate. In addition, the researcher would be able to specify the profile of the result set he wanted – perhaps full author and title information but with corporate authors abbreviated and publication date but no other fields.' Based on the current operation of networked OPACs, this ideal is some way off. In any case, as Kruiniger further points out, the hardware on which OSI-based library systems run will differ from those currently installed.

BIBLIOGRAPHIC REQUIREMENTS

Considerable efforts have been made in the last few years to question and investigate in depth the bibliographic needs of UK librarians. No doubt one of the instigators of this was the British Library with their Consultative Paper *Currency with coverage* but other forces have also been at work. The automation programmes of most libraries, and in particular the growth of OPACs, have increased demands from both library staff and users for methods of access to data that differ from the traditional. This has also raised a serious questioning about the use of bibliographic data and an awareness that a bibliographic record fulfils different criteria at the various stages of selection, acquisition, cataloguing, issue and online public access. This is hardly a new acknowledgment, for debate on these topics has taken place amongst librarians for many years. The difference in the current discussions is twofold. Firstly, there is common agreement at high level that *something must be done* to bring record access into the machine age and secondly, there is a realisation that others in the book chain share a reliance on bibliographic data, though the scope and purpose of these needs may differ in some instances from those of the librarian. Accordingly, a variety of discussion channels have been established between librarians, publishers, booksellers, and suppliers of bibliographic data and it looks as if some of these deliberations are now beginning to bear fruit. Like the work on codes, descriptions and formats described above, these further examples of bibliographic cooperation have the potential for granting long term benefits to librarians at all levels in, and even beyond, the profession.

Enhancement of bibliographic data

Much recent work has centred on the deficiencies of cataloguing codes and bibliographic descriptions to provide the information really needed by users in an automated environment. A key seminar (Bibliographic records in the book world, 1988) was organised by the British National Bibliography Research Fund in Newbury in November 1987 to discuss these issues. The requirements of users from a range of backgrounds – reader services librarians, acquisitions librarians, booksellers, and the British Council – were presented at the opening session. From these it was possible to a draw up a list of desirable enhancements to bibliographic records that included timeliness, accurate price, intellectual level, author information, reviews, word counts, contents pages, and book abstracts. At the same time, Bryant (1988) warned delegates not to forget the experimental reduced subset of the UKMARC record which satisfied 97% of needs. In the other sessions it became clear that much of the data required by librarians was available elsewhere – from publishers, library suppliers, Whitaker, Book Data, and the CURL database – though sometimes in uncoordinated forms and in data structures not always compatible with library norms. Ways were discussed of coordinating record creation so that publishers could feed into the national library process, and a programme for future research was drawn up.

Since that time cooperative bibliographic initiatives have continued apace. In particular, the Centre for Bibliographic Management at Bath

Bibliographic cooperation

University, and City University are engaged on a joint research project to examine the design and use of subject-enriched catalogues using Bath University Library catalogue, records from Book Data, and the OKAPI retrieval software. The research is scheduled for completion in October 1991. Also, relying on information presented at Newbury and combining it with additional findings, Dempsey (1989) has systematically researched the needs of publishers, booksellers and librarians and drawn up a list of the data element requirements of each faction. Emphasising the points made at the Newbury seminar, one of his conclusions is that 'there already exists within the book world the resources to meet those needs. However, the apparatus (technological, commercial and political) does not yet exist for the dissemination of data into an 'all through' system'. On the related theme, one of the working groups of BEDIS (Book Trade Electronic Data Interchange Standards Committee) has identified those data elements that should be included in publishers bibliographic databases to enable publishers' information to be used throughout the library and book trade community. One of the terms of reference of the working party was to make recommendations on how these data elements might be accommodated into the existing UKMARC format and these have appeared in their recent report (BEDIS, 1989). Some of the elements directly address the requirements identified at Newbury i.e. short title; author details; target readership; and contents information. Among the recommendations of the report are that consideration be given to the establishment of a clearing house to manage and monitor the transmission of bibliographic information between the suppliers of data, and that the British Library be asked to consider the extension of the UKMARC format to accommodate the additional data elements. If these recommendations are accepted, they will provide a boost for the attainment of an all-through exchange standard for bibliographic data in the book world in its widest context.

The work of BEDIS is more wide ranging than a consideration of the transfer of bibliographic information, as reported by Hall (1989). In addition, it was set up to report on standards for the transmission of commercial messages such as orders and invoices, work that has resulted in a recommendation to adopt TRADACOMS, a format widely used in the UK commercial sector. The commercial and bibliographic aspects of the work of BEDIS, together with the reports of the other working parties – on a standard for short titles, sales data, and standard address numbers – were presented at the recent BABEL II conference (BABEL

II, 1989). With the setting up of BTECC (Book Trade Electronics Communication Committee), BEDIS has become, in effect, the standards arm of the new committee which comprises members from the Booksellers Association, the Publishers Association and the Library Association. The work of this committee lies outside the remit of the present Chapter but those interested should consult the paper by Greenwood (1989) who refers to the committee as 'a rare animal in the British book community: a truly cooperative venture. ... The linking of BTECC and BEDIS brings together two separate strands that have been developing in the UK. With one body coordinating a strategic approach to the 'wiring-up' of the book world, and the other looking at the common standards that might be required, there would seem to be a real chance of progress in this area'.

REFERENCES

Ayres, F. (1980), The code, the catalogue and the computer: an assessment of AACR2, *Vine*, no. 32, (February), pp. 3–13.

Ayres, F. (1983), Is there a future for cataloguers? *Catalogue and Index*, no. 70, (Autumn), pp. 1–4.

BABEL II: an account of the second conference on data standards for electronic data interchange in the book world, (1989), *VINE*, no. 75, (October), pp. 10–12.

BEDIS (1989), *Publishers bibliographic databases: final report of BEDIS working party 1.* BEDIS.

Bibliographic records in the book world: needs and capabilities (1988), *Proceedings of a seminar held on 27–28 November 1987, at Newbury.* British National Bibliography Research Fund.

British Library (1987), *Currency with coverage.* Consultative paper.

Bryant, P. (1988), End user requirements of bibliographic records, in *Bibliographic records in the book world: needs and capabilities. Proceedings of a seminar held on 27–28 November 1987, at Newbury.* British National Bibliography Research Fund. pp. 14–19.

Dempsey, L. (1989), *Bibliographic records: use of data elements in the book world.* Bath University Library.

Greenwood, D. (1989), Books and electronic data transmission, *British Book News*, (January), pp. 16–17.

Hagler, R. and Simmons, P. (1982), *The bibliographic record and information technology.* Chicago: American Library Association. p. 116.

Hall, A. (1989), The work of BEDIS, *Outlook on Research Libraries*, vol. 11, no. 10, (October), pp. 3–5.

Hopkinson, A. (1984), International access to bibliographic data: MARC and MARC-related activities, *Journal of Documentation*, vol. 40, no. 1, (March), pp. 13–24.

Hopkinson, A. (1985), Standardizing data exchange: the Unesco common communication format, in *9th international online information meeting 3–5 December, London,* Oxford: Learned Information. pp. 295–304.

IFLA. (1978), *ISBD(M): International standard bibliographic description for monographic publications.* London: IFLA International Office for UBC.

Iljon, A. and Manson, P. (1990), The plan of action for libraries in the European Community: new partnerships, in L. Dempsey, *Bibliographic access in Europe.* Aldershot: Gower. pp. 39–46.

Jeffreys, A. (1990), The Anglo-American Cataloguing Rules, 2nd edition, (AACR2): now and in Europe, in L. Dempsey, *Bibliographic access in Europe.* Aldershot: Gower. pp. 262–268.

Kruiniger, H. (1990), Applications of emerging OSI standards in libraries, in L. Dempsey, *Bibliographic access in Europe.* Aldershot: Gower. pp. 139–149.

Long, A. (1984), UK MARC and US/MARC: a brief history and comparison, *Journal of Documentation*, vol. 40, no. 1, (March), pp. 1–12.

Martin, D. and Vernon, M. (1990), Book Data: the design and development of a new kind of bibliographic database, in L. Dempsey, *Bibliographic access in Europe.* Aldershot: Gower. pp. 225–231.

Massil, S. W. (1982), Standards for sharing in bibliographic systems, *Catalogue and Index*, no. 65, (Summer), pp. 1–6.

Moon, B. (1989), Case study: Edinburgh University, in L. Brindley, *The electronic campus: an information strategy.* London: British Library. pp. 98–103.

Oddy, P. (1986), Name authority files, *Catalogue and Index*, no. 82, (Autumn), pp. 1–4.

Perry, S. (1988), The CURL database project, *VINE*, no. 73, (December), pp. 4–8.

Perry, S. (1990), The CURL bibliographic database, *ITs news*, no. 21, (February), pp. 12–15.

Plan of action for libraries in the EC (1987), European Commission (unpublished discussion paper).

Ralls, M. (1989), SALBIN: freedom of access for users unlimited, *VINE*, no. 75, (October), pp. 28–31.

Ratcliffe, F. W. and Foskett, D. J. (1989), The consortium of university research libraries (CURL): a new cooperative venture in the United Kingdom, *British Journal of Academic Librarianship*, vol. 4, no. 1, pp. 1–18.

Smethurst, M. (1990), Towards a Golden Age?, in L. Dempsey, *Bibliographic access in Europe*. Aldershot: Gower. pp. 30–38.

Stubley, P. (1988), *BLCMP: a guide for librarians and systems managers*. Aldershot: Gower.

Sule, G. (1990), Bibliographic standards, in L. Dempsey, *Bibliographic access in Europe*. Aldershot: Gower. pp. 248–255.

12

Regional library cooperation:

LASER

Jean Plaister

The objects for which LASER, or to give it its full title London and South Eastern Library Region (Limited), is established are: '...to improve library facilities available to the public by the promotion of cooperation between Library Authority Members and Subscribers and between such other libraries within or outside the Region having functions in relation to libraries or which store, create or manage any form of information'. This is a wide brief and although in the early days, the Region concentrated on the maintenance of a union catalogue and interlibrary lending, it is to the credit of our predecessors that they had the vision to see beyond them into other areas of cooperation.

Born out of the need to supplement the services of the government-financed National Central Library in the late 1920s and early 1930s, LASER has tried to react to changes in circumstances and to be proactive in anticipating the needs of its members.

An important factor in its development is that LASER has always been a 'cooperative'. Although it now has a corporate legal status as company limited by guarantee it still belongs to its members – its shareholders as they are now called. There may not always have been total unanimity but there has always been a pride in being a member of LASER and the organisation has attracted librarians of note to be its chairmen and members of its Management Committee.

A strength and yet a weakness has been the dominance of LASER by public libraries. Because the National Central Library was already closely involved with the University, learned societies and colleges in London, the membership of the London Union Catalogue organisation (LUC) set up by the Metropolitan Boroughs in 1928 was limited to public libraries. The LUC was not initially involved in interlibrary lending, but following the establishment of the South Eastern Regional Library System (SERLS) in 1932 to provide interlending services for public libraries outside the London area the LUC also developed an interlending role. LUC and SERLS were housed in the National Central Library premises and there was common use of the union catalogues until 1973 when the NCL became part of the British Library and moved to Boston Spa.

When LASER was established by the amalgamation of LUC and SERLS in 1969 provision was made for non-public libraries to become members of the Region in order to bring it into line with the other Regions and to make it easier for the Minister to implement Section 3 of the Public Libraries and Museums Act 1964. Alas, the Minister has not designated the Regions under the 1964 Act, but since 1973 when LASER was physically separated from the NCL by the establishment of the British Library Lending Division at Boston Spa, the involvement of non-public libraries within LASER has become increasingly important.

Recent developments, which will be touched upon later in this Chapter, envisage closer links between the public library and academic library sectors to improve access and to exploit the riches which exist in London and the south east.

'No library is an island' and in the relatively small, largely urban area of London and the Home Counties, regional self-sufficiency has been another strand of development. Starting in the 1940s, self-sufficiency or subject specialisation schemes for fiction in English, non-fiction, popular foreign language material and more recently, audiovisual materials, have been developed. In the early days these were totally public library based but in recent years non-public libraries have participated in the non-fiction subject specialisation schemes.

With the advent of the British Library Lending Division in 1973 and its enhanced resources for the purchase of books, the national non-fiction subject specialisation scheme was abandoned. LASER, however, felt that its self-sufficiency schemes still had a part to play, not only as collections for interlibrary lending but as centres of excellence to which the public had right of access. Inevitably, the importance attached to these collections by individual libraries has varied, but the City of Westminster Medical Library and the Greenwich collection on sports and pastimes have a national reputation for example.

For many years LASER has seen itself as a catalyst for library cooperation and interlibrary lending. This is not in any way to denigrate the achievements of the other Regional Library Systems which have developed services to meet the needs of their particular area and clientele. Rather it is the size of the population served by LASER and the demands of its users which have provided the impetus for change. The number of notifications to the LASER union catalogue in the 1960s stimulated research into the use of library automation. Then, as in later years, LASER has been successful in obtaining research grants which have provided resources for research and development (East & Plaister, 1971).

These early automation experiments with ISBN and BNB numbers led to further expectations by LASER members and ever eager to oblige, LASER began work on the conversion of the regional union catalogue into machine-readable form and its use as a basis for local catalogue conversion (Plaister *et al.*, 1973). This work provided the basis not only for the establishment of an online minicomputer system at LASER headquarters but for the provision of machine-readable catalogue entries in MARC format to member libraries and a SRS (Selected Record Service). In line with its objectives, LASER was developing new services on a cooperative basis.

Hardly had the minicomputer system been installed at LASER headquarters than member libraries asked for dial-up access. A limited service was set up in 1982 and this inevitably led to demands for a more sophisticated system which would incorporate a messaging system as well as access to a bibliographical database and library locations. The VISCOUNT Project (Viewdata and Interlibrary Systems Communication Network) successfully proved that a computerised network for interlibrary loans could link together not only libraries within LASER and the British Library Document Supply Centre but other Regional Library headquarters and test-site libraries, which with the benefit of a PLDIS (Public Library Development Incentive Scheme) grant can extend the VISCOUNT service to other Regional headquarters in 1990–91.

Because of its involvement in interlibrary loans networks and automation, LASER has been invited to participate in the development of application standards for OSI (Open Systems Interconnection) and has recently been successful in obtaining a large grant from the European

Commission to undertake an 'OSI Pilot/Demonstration Project between Library Networks in Europe for Interlending Services' working in cooperation with organisations in France and The Netherlands.

Where do these developments leave LASER and the other Regional Library Systems of the UK? Throughout its existence, LASER has recognised the importance of the Regional structure. It is more than just an interlending system. Each Region is a cooperative of libraries engaged in a range of library and information services. The English Regions and to a lesser extent those in Wales have been controlled and financed by their members.

The advantages of this system, certainly as far as LASER is concerned is that the Region can quickly respond to requests for the development of services, i.e. transport scheme for interlibrary loans, Cooperative of Indic Language LASER Authorities (CILLA), Prestel and LASER-Viewdata Information Service (L-VIS) services. The disadvantages have been for many years, the lack of a satisfactory legal status and the paucity of capital to develop sophisticated systems to meet the needs of increasingly sophisticated library services.

Section 3 of the Public Libraries and Museums Act 1964 appeared to provide the means for the English Regions to achieve a satisfactory legal status but successive governments have failed to implement this Section of the Act and on the advice of the Office of Arts and Libraries LASER and the North Western Regions became companies limited by guarantee. The provisions of the Local Government and Housing Act 1989 relating to Local Authorities interests in companies will now make it extremely difficult for LASER to operate efficiently and the Region is looking at ways of escaping from local authority control. Closer liaison with the academic library sector is one of the options being investigated. This liaison was under discussion before the Local Government and Housing Act appeared and has just added impetus to the proceedings.

In these days of economic stringency the need for more efficient and effective use of resources is increasingly important. The areas which have been identified include:

- the development of closer links between the higher education and public library sectors in south east England
- the future of book and journal resources in the south east and the storage and exploitation of these resources

- development of closer links between JANET and LASER's VISCOUNT communications network, and through them to the European networks
- the joint exploration of bibliographic projects
- cooperation in training librarians and in the use of techniques available in the private sector (an area in which LASER is already involved)
- more effective use of LASER transport scheme

Useful in themselves, these initiatives, however, beg the question of the future role of library cooperation. We know very little in statistical terms of the inter-relationships and inter-action between libraries in the United Kingdom. Although Britain has a world-wide reputation for document supply and interlibrary lending there has been no coordinated national plan with the relationships between the parties clearly defined. The reports on *The future development of libraries and information services* (Future development..., 1982; and Future development..., 1986) proposed:

- the organisational and policy framework
- working together within a national framework
- progress through planning and partnership

Although the recommendations in these reports have led to the establishment of LINC (Library and Information Cooperation Council) and to the development of LIPs (Library and Information Plans) as far as LASER is concerned the situation is still fragmented and piecemeal.

LASER is currently addressing as an essential part of its European Community OSI Project, the processes, supply and delivery mechanisms of interlending. But this is only part of the equation. What is also needed is an agreed list of service objectives which look both at the service user and the service provider. The modelling exercise also needs an analysis of stocks so that centralized document supply and de-centralised interlibrary lending can be set against demand. This also involves an investigation of current purchasing abilities, choice of acquisitions, duplication factors of stock provision, lending policy and access.

Advances in technology and telecommunications can inter-connect disparate systems and lead to the development of successful technical infrastructures for interlending and other cooperative library services. The technical infrastructure is, however, the means and not the end. It is the service and functions of interlibrary lending and other forms of cooperation which need to be defined, and this poses the following questions:

- how and by whom should appropriate service objectives be formulated?
- should there be a coordinated national plan, with relationships between all parties clearly defined?
- how many functions should be addressed initially?
- if research is required who should fund it?

These questions relate to library cooperation throughout the United Kingdom and to wider links with Europe. They are also of vital importance to LASER and its future development so no apology is made for including them in this Chapter. The time for talking is over. Action is needed before new systems are set in place. LASER is anxious to participate as it believes that no library or information unit can operate in isolation.

REFERENCES

East, H. and Plaister, J. M. (1971), *The South Eastern Regional Library System: design and development of a computer-assisted method for book location recording.* (OSTI Report No. 5117). London, LASER.

The future development of libraries and information services: 1 the organisational and policy framework; 2 working together within a national framework. (1982). (Office of Arts and Libraries, Library and Information Series No. 12). HMSO.

The future development of libraries and information services: progress through planning and partnership. Report by the Library and Information Services Council. (1986). (Office of Arts and Libraries, Library and Information Series No. 14). HMSO.

Plaister, J. M. *et al.* (1973), *Conversion of a regional union catalogue into machine-readable form and its use as a basis for local catalogue conversion.* (OSTI Report No. 5164). London, LASER.

Regional library cooperation:

Regional roller coaster: the accelerating progress of the Regional Library Systems

Diana Edmonds

For many librarians, the practical face of interlibrary cooperation in this country is the Regional Library System. First established in the 1920s and '30s, the Regional Library Systems were designed to enable libraries within the same geographical area to borrow material – normally books – from each other. In order to facilitate this interlending process it was usually felt necessary to develop a union catalogue of the stock held by member libraries. The Regional Library Systems were at the hub of local interlending: the union catalogue could not easily be copied so request forms were sent to the Regional Headquarters – and the forms were then circulated to libraries which held copies of the item required. Later, of course, technology provided the means of distributing at least part of the catalogue to the members – so the union catalogues were transferred to machine-readable form and a computer-generated microfiche version was provided for members. In addition to providing the key to interlending by developing the union catalogue, many Regional Library Systems also become involved in the transportation of stock – true document delivery services! These transport systems offered – and continue to offer – rates lower than the Post Office, and they have saved their users a considerable amount of money over the years.

There are now seven Regional Library Systems in England, whose history and activities are detailed in *Interlending and library cooperation in the United Kingdom and Republic of Ireland* (Jones, 1986). In the 1990s, however, these Regional Library Systems appear to be at a crossroads. Many feel that the services which they have traditionally provided are rapidly becoming outmoded. In a recent paper, Michael Long, the Manager of the Northern Regional Library System (NRLS), commented that interlending, which has historically been the *raison d'etre* of the Regional Library Systems, 'is now a marginal activity for most libraries' (Long, 1990). While facing marginalisation, they also face competition as the British Library Document Supply Centre (BLDSC) is now the preferred source of interlending for many libraries, certainly in the area of journal articles. A greater threat lurks around the corner. All traditional document delivery services are threatened by new technology which could allow data to be downloaded from a central electronic source rather than being produced in hard copy, photocopied and posted to a library.

Regional Library Systems have responded in different ways to the challenges of the '90s. The recent developments in LASER, the London and South Eastern Regional Library System, have been detailed earlier in this Chapter. In what follows, I should like to highlight the differing developments taking place in two other Regional Library Systems, the Northern Regional Library System and the West Midlands Regional Library System.

THE NORTHERN REGIONAL LIBRARY SYSTEM

The Northern Regional Library System was the first truly regional scheme to be established in the United Kingdom. The Report of *Regional Libraries in England*, issued in 1928 by the Committee of the County Libraries Section of the Library Association had suggested the establishment of 'regional grouping' to alleviate pressure on the resources of the National Central Library. Following the formation of a small but successful scheme in Cornwall in 1928, the Northern Regional Library System was established as the first fully organised regional system in the country. At that time, the major concern of NRLS was the compilation of a union catalogue for the area covered by the Regional System, the counties of Cumberland, Durham, Northumberland and Westmorland. Because of the 'high cost of book transportation using the Post Office', NRLS also developed a transport scheme, using Trutime Deliveries, a commercial contractor, to deliver books from one library to another: the service offered was felt to be 'considerably cheaper and frequently more speedy than that available from the Post Office', with a same day delivery service provided at a bargain rate of six pence per book. The service began in 1932 and probably continued until wartime rationing limited the use of petrol for non-essential journeys.

If this historic saga sounds familiar, it is because a number of the Regional Library Systems are still primarily concerned with the maintenance of union catalogues and the administration of transport schemes designed to deliver documents from one library to another. Until 1988 NRLS followed the same pattern. Certainly, it did rather more than maintaining the union catalogue of monographs, by producing and publishing catalogues of local history material, of vocal scores and of play sets: it also published a regular diary of meetings held in the Northern Region for librarians and information specialists. A latter day transport scheme established in 1977 proved to be highly successful, saving the members thousands of pounds each year. Indeed, a review of cooperation in Newcastle upon Tyne noted that, despite its relatively small funding levels, NRLS was 'relevant to the needs of its members' (Edmonds, 1986).

In 1986, however, NRLS, in association with three of the four county councils within the Region, Cleveland, Durham and Northumberland, submitted a proposal to the Office of Arts and Libraries for the development of a Library and Information Plan (LIP). The proposal was successful, and individual LIPs were accordingly prepared for the individual county authorities, and for the Northern Region. The Northern Regional LIP was highly innovative – no other LIP had tackled this planning process from the Regional perspective.

Within the context of the Regional Library and Information Plan, 150 organisations provided details of the library and information services which they control; they also gave their views on information provision throughout the Region, and suggested new developments which would improve facilities and services for themselves and for their clients. In-depth studies were also made of the provision for information for innovation, the provision for health information and the transport needs and systems of information providers.

Many issues highlighted within the local LIP documents were raised by interviewees in all three counties; these issues included:

- the need for directories of information resources
- the need for more union lists of holdings, such as serials and local studies material

- the need for training for information workers
- the need for support to improve information technology applications
- the need for an increase in the shared use of premises

The Regional Plan highlighted similar issues, and also focussed on the need to raise the profile of information at a Regional level. Although there are many libraries and information centres within the area, it was felt that there was no organisation which represented 'the totality of information within the Region' (Northern Regional Library System, 1988). Overall, there was a general consensus that many issues could be tackled more effectively at a Regional level than the local level – and that there was a need for a facilitating or development agency to address these issues.

The Northern Regional Library System with its broadly-based membership of libraries throughout the Region seemed ideally situated for this facilitating role, and in 1988 the British Library Research and Development Department funded a supplementary study to look at the practicalities of transforming a Regional Library System into an information development agency (Edmonds, 1988). Such a transformation required money: following the review, NRLS applied for funding under the Public Library Development Incentive Scheme, and was awarded the maximum grant of £40,000. In the same year, the Northern Region Councils Association allocated an additional £22,500 to the organisation.

It was felt that a new function needed a new name and a new image – and so Information North, the information development agency was launched with the aim of 'coordinating information provision in support of economic and social development' (Brewer *et al.*, 1988). The same services which members have traditionally expected of the Regional Library Systems continue to be provided by Information North/NRLS – but in addition, the new agency has developed into a number of other areas.

One of the most obvious developments has been the professional image presented by the organisation. Information North now produces a regular newsletter, *IN*, which is well written and produced, and which is circulated to some 2,500 individuals and organisations. Information North has also produced a range of other publications including *A Directory of Information Resources in the Northern Region*, a series of publications relating to the provision of health information within the area and a series of *Information Guides* produced by the north east cooperative, Network. Information North has recently assembled the data for a regional skills register and this, too, is to be produced in the near future.

Information North has also become involved in research and consultancy, not necessarily using in-house staff, but employing external staff with appropriate skills. Information North has now managed a number of research studies, including a feasibility study on the cooperative marketing of small press promotions. Information North has an R&D Fund, and has earmarked money in 1990/91 for the PANDA project, designed to provide 'public access to a newspaper database and archive' by producing CD-ROM disks giving the full-text of the *Northern Echo*, the major north east newspaper.

One of the areas highlighted in the Northern Region LIP was the issue of health information: a separate Health Information Plan is currently being prepared under the *aegis* of Information North. On an initial practical level, Information North purchased Helpbox, the database of national self-help groups, which has been augmented with local information. Helpbox North already contains details of some 1,100 organisations in the north and is still expanding: it is now a unique resource within the Region. Information North staff provide information on demand to subscribers of the service; non-subscribers can also use the service, paying a fee for each search undertaken.

As an organisation highly involved in LIPs, Information North has coordinated the work of Information North and the three County LIPs in the area; it is now taking on a national role in this area by managing the promotion, development, monitoring and evaluation of LIPs in the UK on behalf of LINC (Library and Information Cooperation Council). Information North is also moving into the field of training, an area which was highlighted in the Library and Information Plan: a recent seminar and exhibition was held on the theme of *Automation and the Management of Interlibrary Loans*. Information North intends to develop further in the areas of consultancy and training in the near future. A Projects Officer has recently been appointed to take forward projects in which Information North wishes to become involved, while a Training Officer is shortly to be appointed to develop activities in the area of training.

Amidst all this activity, the routine of interlending work has not been forgotten. Because of its proximity to BLDSC at Boston Spa, NRLS has always handled loans rather differently to the other Regional Library

Systems, by sending interloan requests directly to Boston Spa, rather than circulating them within the Region; any material which cannot be satisfied by BLDSC is then obtained via the Regional Interlending network. Information North has however decided not to participate in the VISCOUNT Project undertaken by LASER, initially in cooperation with the South Western Regional Library System (SWRLS), North Western Regional Library System (NWRLS) and the National Library of Scotland, and in which East Midlands Regional Library System (EMRLS), Yorkshire and Humberside Regional Library System (YHRLS) and the West Midlands Regional Library System (WMRLS) are now active. It has, however, allocated funds to review its union catalogue within the next year.

WEST MIDLANDS REGIONAL LIBRARY SYSTEM

The West Midlands Regional Library System was established in 1931 covering the five counties of Hereford, Shropshire, Stafford, Warwick and Worcester. The Headquarters of the Regional System was housed within Birmingham Public Library which, almost 60 years later, is still its location. There are currently some 37 members, including eleven public library authorities which represent four counties and seven metropolitan boroughs, seven institutions of higher education, four college libraries and fifteen special libraries. Until recently, WMRLS concentrated almost exclusively on the task of facilitating Regional interlending, collecting data for its union catalogue, providing details of holdings on request from member libraries and undertaking a significant proportion of the practical activities relating to interlending within the Region. In addition, it has for a number of years operated a transport scheme which ensures the cheap and efficient transfer of material between members.

Unlike the Northern Region, the West Midlands has not had the catalyst of a Library and Information Plan to stimulate development. In 1989, however, the Regional Library System employed a consultant to review the organisational structure and effectiveness of WMRLS, and to consider the potential benefits of recent developments in automation. The report on this project presented WMRLS with a *Strategy for the '90s* (Edmonds, 1989). It highlighted the unique position occupied by WMRLS in bringing together public, academic and special libraries within the West Midlands into one organisation, and urged WMRLS

Regional cooperation

staff to seek new opportunities in initiating cooperative ventures within the Region. While looking outwards, it was also suggested that WMRLS should improve its structure and effectiveness by introducing the use of information technology to speed up interlending procedures. This recommendation was implemented almost immediately by providing access to the BLCMP database which contains bibliographic and location data: BLCMP is based in Birmingham, and a number of its membership also belong to WMRLS.

A supplementary review considered the costs and the benefits of VISCOUNT, the online union catalogue developed by LASER, SWRLS, NWRLS and the National Library of Scotland. It was felt that access to VISCOUNT would allow WMRLS members to locate and to borrow more items from Regional libraries and from the Inter-regional network, rather than depending increasingly on BLDSC, a more expensive source of interloans. While the members would make direct savings, it was also expected that VISCOUNT would enable WMRLS to operate more efficiently by allowing staff to check locations more quickly online than they could using manual sources. WMRLS is now an active participant in VISCOUNT and has found that access to the database has speeded up their interlending activities considerably. Access to bibliographic data has also improved because VISCOUNT now contains millions of records, providing a source of information far superior to those used previously within the Regional Headquarters.

WMRLS is concerned to develop still further however, and is continuing to analyse its activities, its strengths and its weaknesses. Interlending is however still regarded as central to the organisation – and staff are concentrating on making the interlending process as fast and as effective as possible. There is concern about the quality of the union catalogue which is at the core of the interlending function – and WMRLS staff are currently assessing the best way to improve that central resource. It may be that the traditional method of developing the union catalogue – by collecting new entries and deletions from members – is no longer valid; the possibility of applying new technology to the problem of developing a union catalogue may be considered.

In addition to the union catalogue of monographs, WMRLS also holds a collection of catalogues which provide information on serials held within the Region: at the present time, consideration is being given to the best method of amalgamating and improving these catalogues, and of transferring them as a single file to a computer-based system which will be easy to update. WMRLS has also commissioned a Regional catalogue of vocal sets which is shortly to be published on microfiche; this will complement the hard copy catalogue of play sets which is held in WMRLS Headquarters.

WMRLS is becoming increasingly involved with cooperative activities outside the direct sphere of interlending and union catalogues. For a number of years, the Region has organised and hosted meetings of the Ethnic Minorities Librarians Group whose members meet to discuss matters of common concern. WMRLS now also acts as an umbrella organisation for a Training Officers Group (TOG), a Regional forum for training officers in public, academic and special libraries throughout the West Midlands; the Group organises and runs courses, exchanges information and supports training projects in individual libraries. WMRLS provides administrative support for TOG, and both underwrites and monitors its activities.

WMRLS, in common with a number of Regional Library Systems, has sponsored a NEWSPLAN project in its area: the NEWSPLAN Project Officer considered the availability of newspaper resources within the Region with a view to the microfilming of collections, in order to protect and preserve unique and vulnerable titles. And, like Information North, WMRLS is now becoming involved in the area of health information, initially gathering data on the existing provision within the West Midlands.

There are a number of organisations within the West Midlands which aim to develop cooperation between library and information units. WMRLS has recently compiled a directory of these cooperative schemes, in an attempt to draw together the various cooperative strengths, to improve overall awareness of activities, to avoid duplication and thus to improve services.

While expanding the scope of their activities, Regional staff are also concentrating on improving contacts with their members. Regular meetings are now held of interlending staff from member libraries throughout the Region; it is hoped to develop these meetings into a full training programme to inform and update staff directly involved with interlending procedures. In an attempt to spread its message still further, WMRLS issued its first newsletter in Summer 1990. On the title page, WMRLS is described as 'the enabling body for library and information initiatives': we look forward to hearing more of these initiatives in the future!

THE FUTURE OF THE REGIONAL LIBRARY SYSTEMS

The Northern Regional Library System/Information North and the West Midlands Regional System are both active and developing organisations, although their recent development has followed different paths. Is there then a correct migration path which all Regions should follow?

Studies of interlibrary cooperation in the United Kingdom demonstrate that, although libraries throughout the country profess similar cooperative principles, the tangible outcome of cooperative activity varies considerably from area to area. Within each locality, the pattern of cooperation is prescribed by the range of libraries and information units present within the area, and is also affected by external factors such as geographical location and economic forces. The Regional Library Systems are all dedicated to the development of cooperation between libraries within their Region – but they are all different, and each one has developed in a different way. A development path which is appropriate within the Northern Region, an area which is geographically isolated and which has a tremendous sense of Regional cohesion, may not be appropriate within the vast conurbation of the sprawling West Midlands, where the links between library authorities and library services outside the Region are just as important as those existing within the Regional boundaries.

Perhaps most important, the Regional Library Systems are themselves the tools of the regional libraries which support them: the priorities of the Regional Library Systems must, therefore, reflect the priorities of the member libraries. Otherwise, in an age of market forces, the public libraries which are the mainstay of the Regional Library Systems and which contribute many thousands of pounds to ensure their continued existence, may vote with their feet – and spend their subscriptions on more books, more shelves or more staff for their own library services.

There is no doubt that many members of the Regional Library Systems regard the primary purpose of those organisations as the maintenance of the interlending process, and the provision of cheap loans. Within the Regional Library Systems, borrowing is normally free: loans are provided without charge, on a reciprocal basis – I won't charge you if you don't charge me. This economic factor is still undoubtedly extremely important in ensuring the continued existence of many Regional Library Systems. So, if interlending is still important to the members of the Regional Library Systems, the Regions should approach the issue of interlending with initiative and imagination. This is easy to say – but not always easy to do – in a technology-dependent age – for Regional Library Systems have traditionally been operated on low funding levels, while technology is usually expensive.

In the area of interlending, the major issue which confronts the Regions is the problem of the union catalogue – as many of these are now inaccurate and incomplete. The quality of the catalogues varies from Region to Region. Although some member libraries have meticulously provided details of additions and deletions to Regional Headquarters, others have not. This problem has been exacerbated in recent years as some automated catalogue and circulation systems provided no mechanism for identifying and listing the additions and deletions which are essential data for the Regional System. Even if the additions and deletions are provided by the member libraries, Regional Library staff may not have time to amend the union catalogue, a process which still has to be undertaken manually in some Regions. In these circumstances, it is perhaps not surprising that libraries which are members of cataloguing cooperatives such as BLCMP find the locations which they obtain from their database rather more reliable than those available via the Inter-regional network.

The Regional catalogues are now elderly and unreliable – and the Regions need to address the issue before it is too late. If union catalogues continue to be maintained in the traditional way, by adding additions to stock and removing deletions, the system must be more effectively controlled to ensure that the catalogue reflects current holdings within the member libraries. Otherwise, alternative methods of gathering details of locations should be considered. An attempt to tackle the problem of the union catalogues has been made very recently by the VISCOUNT Technical Working Party which has prepared a draft policy statement relating to regional union catalogues: if the proposed policy is adopted nationally, it could provide a standard for quality control to be applied within all Regions. The Working Party is also hoping to develop a closer relationship with library automation software suppliers, to ensure that in the future the suppliers have a better understanding of the needs of the Regional Library Systems, as well as the requirements of individual clients. These developments are long overdue – but should be encouraged, nonetheless.

If union catalogues present such problems, should we perhaps forget about them altogether? It is, of course, already possible to interrogate remotely the catalogues of some major libraries either by direct telecommunications links or via a network such as JANET. Although this is undoubtedly a valuable facility, reliance upon direct access to individual catalogues in order to locate interloans could result in the larger libraries, as the obvious source of material, being swamped by requests – and then being required to protect themselves from this onslaught by imposing charges. If it were necessary to consult a number of catalogues in search of an elusive item, the process could prove lengthy and costly both in terms of staff time and telecommunications charges.

An alternative option to accessing the catalogues of individual libraries would be a radical review of the method of creating the Regional catalogues. Rather than recording additions and deletions to the central listing, it might be possible to make more effective use of the computer-based catalogues of individual library systems, which should, hopefully reflect an accurate position of the library's stock. Consideration should be given to merging the machine-readable catalogue files created by individual libraries – or at least enabling the end user to search the catalogue files generated by a number of individual libraries as if they were a single database. Of course, the union catalogues shared by those libraries which participate in cataloguing cooperatives, such as BLCMP, already present an alternative to the catalogues developed by the Regional Systems – and it may be possible in the future to widen access to these resources, or to incorporate them within Inter-regional union catalogues.

Inaccurate although the Regional catalogues may be, they provide the most complete listing of locations currently available to us – and the VISCOUNT project has drawn together, in a single database, the locations of stock held by an increasing number of Regional Library Systems. The holdings of the original participants, LASER, SWRLS, NWRLS and the National Library of Scotland have recently been augmented by data provided by WMRLS, YHRLS and EMRLS: financial support for the expansion of the database was obtained from the Public Library Development Incentive Scheme. The VISCOUNT database allows the searcher to retrieve locations using a variety of access points, including author, title, publisher and date of publication, and provides a considerable improvement on the retrieval facilities offered by the Combined Regions microfiche catalogue which limits access to ISBN. It is planned that end-users from all Regions will eventually be allowed to access the VISCOUNT database directly. It is to be hoped that this project will secure funding to enable its computer facilities to support this large database – and even to allow consideration of the production of CD-ROM versions of the catalogue, which would allow end-users to search for locations in the comfort of their own workstations rather than at the end of a telecommunications line.

Surely this end-user access sounds a little worrying for the Regional Library Systems – could they simply fade away, leaving the development of the union catalogue to a data processing bureau which incorporates amendment tapes from member libraries into a global database, while the end-users access the database without any reference to the Regional Library System? In a technology dream world, yes they could. But it takes considerably longer to fund and implement technological developments than it does to describe them – and in the here and now, Regional Library Systems are providing practical interlending facilities which their members still require, and are still prepared to pay for.

Do Regional Library Systems have a future beyond interlending? Certainly, they have an excellent user base from which to operate, and which they have used on many occasions in the development of cooperative activities. More than any other organisation, they bring together libraries and information services throughout the Region – some which are members, others which use the transport scheme. If the Regional Library Systems can begin to represent their users in discussions with external agencies, and in raising the profile of information, there is a potential for considerable development in the future. As Information North's recent history has shown, the Regional Library System can be transformed into an information development agency, initiating and responding to a wide range of information-related activities. Michael Long's paper stressed that it is essential for those Regional Library Systems which wish to develop to prepare an action plan – and indeed it is important that this should be a realistic business plan, taking into account the additional costs which will be incurred in this developmental role. The public libraries have traditionally provided the majority of the subscription income received by the Regions – and it may be necessary to review this subscription structure if the advantages of membership are to be more equitably distributed.

There are many issues to be considered by the Regional Library Systems in this development process: they may need a different staff structure, they may need a different image. But the basis for development exists – and can be exploited. The Regional roller coaster could yet break free from the track!

REFERENCES

Brewer, S., Long, M. T. and Winkworth, I. (1988), Information North: Library and Information Plans and the transformation of a regional library system. *Library Association Record,* vol. 90, no. 7, (July), pp. 392–395.

Edmonds, D. J. (1986), *Current library cooperation and coordination: an investigation.* (Office of Arts and Libraries, Library and Information Series, No. 15). HMSO.

Edmonds, D. J. (1988), *Information North: the transformation of a Regional Library System.* Prepared for the British Library Research and Development Department.

Edmonds, D. J. (1989), *The West Midlands Regional Library System: a Strategy for the '90s.* (Unpublished report).

Jones, C. (ed) (1986), *Interlending and library cooperation in the United Kingdom and the Republic of Ireland.* Circle of Officers of National and Regional Library Systems.

Long, M. (1990), The Regions: which way now? Unpublished paper given at a workshop during the *Forum for Interlending 3rd Annual Conference, Edinburgh*, 28–30 June.

Northern Regional Library System (1988), *A Library and Information Plan for the Northern Region 1988–1993.* NRLS.

13

Who wins? Some issues concerning 'compound' library cooperatives at the local level

PETER STUBLEY

Even a trivial review of the literature indicates that local library cooperation is long established. On closer inspection, one finds that the term *local* is invariably used to be synonymous with *public* but while the majority of cases described do not unremittingly follow a single model they can broadly be viewed as consisting of a central information unit – or series of units – which provides services to, in general, less well resourced members. As pointed out by Kennington (1985), superimposed on this can be a whole network of contact points and service provision influenced by environmental, organisational, technological and human factors. A full description of public library cooperation is provided in Chapter 7 by Stuart Brewer.

In contrast to this traditional view of local library cooperation, the present Chapter deals primarily with what Sewell (1979, 1982), referred to as 'modular' schemes whereby modules or special interest groups were established which members could participate in or not, depending on their priorities and strengths. The idea was taken from early practice in Newcastle upon Tyne and though subsequently used to describe other schemes in Sheffield and Birmingham the term does not sit comfortably with developments there. What is under discussion here is an aggregation of major or significant resource centres working across different library types within an area to provide agreed combined services to a wider clientele. As no suitable term has so far been used for such an aggregation, the word *compound* has been coined for the purpose of this Chapter. Thus, compound library cooperation is cooperation between academic, public and special libraries in a region, generally a city, which also acknowledges the contribution in each case from the local Department of Librarianship. These compound cooperatives further differ from the public library-based schemes in one other important point: they came together from the standpoint of mutual strength rather than as a result of weakness on the part of some members. As Harris (1980) expressed it: 'all libraries taking part should have sufficient resources to be able to contribute effectively – there should be no passengers'.

The cooperative schemes in Birmingham, Newcastle upon Tyne, and Sheffield have been chosen because of their established nature, their presence in the professional literature, and their success in a number of areas of activity. As such, an overview of the organisation and activities of these schemes forms the background material but the main thrust of the Chapter is a discussion of a number of issues relating to the current position of compound library cooperatives. Most particularly the question needs to be asked: in the present financial climate can anyone – library user; librarian; information worker; institutional head – really benefit from library cooperation? Hence the title. Unfortunately there is no easy answer. And though the points raised come from an experience of working in academic libraries associated with compound systems, several of them will have relevance to other cooperative associations.

COOPERATIVE ORGANISATIONAL STRUCTURES

At a time when the Library and Information Plans (LIPs) initiatives are beginning to show effects (see Chapter 4) and the nature of some schemes may change, it may be considered irrelevant to dwell on the historical origins of the schemes. However, it is interesting to note that in both Birmingham and Newcastle this was due to the foresight and enthusiasm of individual librarians or groups of librarians. In Birmingham, where BCOP (Birmingham Libraries in Cooperation) was formed in 1977, 'it was helped by new appointments at top level where the new chiefs wanted to gain a clearer understanding of how their own library fitted into the city picture and, crucially, were disposed to cooperate' (Hadcroft,

1985). In a similar way Harris (1973) pointed out that in Newcastle 'the vision of cooperation was blurred until rivalry was dissipated by changes of heart, staff and situation'. In contrast, Sheffield, though not lacking the leadership required, started the SLCC (Sheffield Libraries Coordinating Committee) from a different base. Although SINTO – the Sheffield Interchange Organisation – was well established, its emphasis was on public and special library provision and there was a perception of an untapped potential for cooperation among higher education libraries. Accordingly, in the early 1970s the Department of Education and Science funded a research project to ascertain the scope for local cooperation in this sector – Wilson and Marsterson (1974) – from which it was recognised that, in spite of the strong historical base and the high level of unplanned coordination, opportunities for further cooperation existed. It was for this reason that the SLCC was established early in 1975.

The compound cooperatives from these three cities all have a broadly common composition incorporating the local university library, the local polytechnic library, the local public library and the local library school. In spite of this common base there are, paradoxically, divergences in membership. Thus, BCOP has two university members, one from the University of Birmingham, the other from Aston University, and the Newcastle upon Tyne Libraries Joint Working Party includes the library of the Literary and Philosophical Society. Further, the individual working groups of the Newcastle cooperative encouraged and included membership from as far afield as Sunderland Polytechnic and North Tyneside Public Library. In Sheffield, the participation of the City Libraries in the SLCC created a strong link with SINTO and as time progressed a number of other local libraries and information services were invited to join. That the SLCC and the Newcastle upon Tyne Libraries Joint Working Party established a management committee of the chief librarians is (virtually) clear from their titles; BCOP has a similar top-tier grouping known as the Policy Committee.

When planning the organisational structure of local cooperative library ventures, several schemes created as their second tier – below the committee of chief librarians – working groups that, understandably, were related to specific library services or readily identifiable working sections within the members. Structurally this is a sensible solution for it easily identifies the staff who will be involved as coordinators and instigators in their own libraries. BCOP has formed three working groups of this type: technical services, reader services and staff training; and the SLCC created groups to consider reference and information services, government and official publications, automation, and training and education. At the same time groups are needed to investigate and undertake specific tasks on behalf of the cooperative as a single unit. To this end, the SLCC formed groups to create a union periodicals list for Sheffield and a published list of joint resources, and BCOP established a Fax Working Group to carry out research into the use of facsimile transmission for urgent interlibrary loans.

In all cases the keyword has been flexibility, new groups being established as necessary and older non-essential groups being disbanded (by and large) on completion of their briefs. All the systems have adopted this approach but Newcastle, in particular, is proud of having pioneered this flexibility virtually from the start. McDonald (1989) reports that 'a lack of proliferation of working groups is seen as a positive virtue. They are regarded as important only in securing objectives which could not otherwise be achieved in other ways. The real risk, as with other library groups, is that they could become ends in themselves rather than a means to an end. It can often be more appropriate to stimulate existing library organisations to cooperate more effectively or to encourage specialist staff in individual institutions to work together informally than to create new working groups'. In spite of this attempt to streamline the organisational process, dead weight has tended to accumulate in all three cooperatives where, through lack of initiative or commitment, some groups have managed to remain in existence long after their active contributions have been made, if indeed any ever were made. While this lack of achievement can be a function of the personalities involved, it also relates to the perceived importance of the group among its individual members, together with the responsibility invested in it by the management committee. The success of groups is also, to some extent, a reflection of the importance and significance shown by each of the chief librarians in the cooperative as a whole. If staff are not given the lead and encouraged to participate in cooperative activities, they are unlikely to do it for themselves. The strength of the management group and the encouragement given to each of the working groups are equally important in this matter and some members of working groups feel that when ideas and suggestions have been made upwards, too frequently are these thrown aside as unrealistic or as not pertinent at the current time. The perception of the goals and work of the cooperative are perhaps inevitably different between top management and those below but where this is so the chiefs must both point the way and give a certain amount of free rein. Without this, even the most enthusiastic working groups will lose heart and cease to care.

The importance of staff with an open attitude towards cooperation cannot be stressed enough, in terms of both initiating and maintaining compound schemes. The danger of the individual-led cooperative is that new staff with different priorities will not bring the same degree of commitment when enthusiasts move on. What is required is the cult of the individual fused with a sound rationale for maintaining cooperation that can be accepted and followed by all staff in each institution and it may be that the LIPs go some way to providing the basis for this. It is too early to say whether or not the LIP-based cooperatives will be carried along with the same air of enthusiasm and encouragement as their more informal predecessors but it could well be that the camel, – the 'horse designed by a committee' – will be far more appropriate for the increasingly dry spell ahead.

One interesting difference between the philosophy of the Birmingham, Sheffield and Newcastle initiatives is the way they saw themselves responding to outside stimuli such as government and professional pronouncements. In the early stages of cooperation, when the emphasis was on forging an identity and encouraging staff to create a joint approach to services, there appears to have been little difference, but with greater development came the need to embrace a wider perspective, at least in Sheffield. When the terms of reference of all working groups were reviewed in 1982, one significant phrase found its way into all: 'to consider developments at local, regional, national and international level in (name of relevant working group for example, government and official publications), and to advise the Sheffield Libraries Coordinating Committee accordingly'. The SLCC would then take up the baton, and responded to such documents as *Making a business of information* from the Cabinet Office Information Technology Advisory Panel, the Library Association's Futures Working Party report, as well as various LISC papers. Newcastle appear to have taken a centre line, maintaining a finger on the national pulse while actually responding in writing to fewer initiatives, for example *Currency with coverage* and the British Library's strategic plan to 1994, *Gateway to knowledge*. Many of these nationally produced reports were also considered by the BCOP Policy Committee, particularly where there was likely to be direct local impact, but the necessity of making a national response was not felt as strongly as it obviously was in Sheffield. Even within the SLCC a re-thinking of this role was discussed with a view to reducing its importance, ironically coming at a time when the committee was recognising that it would have to change if it was to encompass a Sheffield LIP.

COOPERATIVE ACTIVITIES

Sewell (1979) states that 'cooperation is the reciprocally beneficial sharing of resources, developed or pre-existing, by two or more bodies'. As reported by Yelland (1980) he goes on to say that 'the total range of resources, not just books and other media but staff expertise and technology, needed to be built upon for the benefit of the community'. It is clear that this has happened with varying degrees of success in the compound cooperatives but here is not the place to provide a comprehensive or comparative discussion of the services available. Instead, in the section on document delivery, some suggestions are outlined for possible improvements in service in general. The sections on collection development and staff training which follow are intended to provide only a flavour of the advantages and disadvantages of these activities.

Document delivery

MacDougall, *et al.* (1988), in an investigation into cooperation among academic libraries in the East Midlands, looked in detail at two distinct aspects of document delivery: 'user to material' and 'material to user'. The conclusions of the material to user survey indicated that a regional interlibrary loan scheme would not be cost effective and that 'to establish such a scheme would appear to be reinventing the wheel; it could not compete with a more cost effective and efficient British Library'. Although local factors would influence the scale of results of similar surveys in other regions, the conclusions are likely to be the same. This was *felt* to be the case in Birmingham and the vast majority of interlibrary loans are likewise channelled directly to the British Library Document Supply Centre. However, an experimental fax service for the supply of urgently required journal articles to library users was begun in 1984 between the four BCOP libraries (Stubley, 1986) and has proved a popular and enduring service. This BCOP initiative, stemming from

British Library-funded research, is an example of a service which could only have been achieved within a cooperative environment, though all the individual libraries have subsequently utilised fax for more general document provision within their organisations.

But material to user is very much a library problem: it is basically the responsibility of librarians, individually or in concert, to determine how best to provide an interlibrary loans service. In contrast, one of the prime advantages of local cooperation for many users is the ability to gain access to collections from which they would otherwise be barred from borrowing. For researchers in particular, this factor may prove to be far more important in the longer term than the satisfying of immediate information needs. Furthermore, the planned influx of 'external' users can be a means by which members of compound library cooperatives critically review their service provision, and the results would provide benefits to even their more regular customers. For once the displaced user has crossed the previously unattainable threshold he or she is in a new world of library staff, layout, photocopiers, issue systems, rules and regulations and must be guided and assisted accordingly.

Some of these aspects are already handled, to lesser or greater extent, by the cooperative schemes described in this Chapter. For example, to help users in negotiating their way from one side of Birmingham to the other, BCOP provides location maps of each of its libraries together with bus route numbers; Sheffield and Newcastle provide something similar. On a mere directional level perhaps this is all the user needs but how much more accommodating would be an information pack created by each host library incorporating all relevant information. The pack need not be comprehensive, but it should at least acknowledge the fact that users from other organisations come with different criteria and backgrounds from the majority of library users within the parent institution. The fact that these externals are library literate might indicate, for example, that the information pack should preferably not consist of a standard library guide aimed at undergraduates, but should be specially written for the visitor.

Cooperation must not only function at the highest level of an organisation, its importance must be communicated to all staff involved with face-to-face contact with library users so that the welcoming and induction of visitors is carried out with the same second nature offered to 'official' borrowers. It should be unnecessary to say that this can only be achieved with comprehensive staff training, though it is an area that could particularly benefit from a cooperative provision so that all staff appreciate the differences (in philosophy, layout etc.) between libraries. (This also helps in other ways. In Birmingham, visits to all BCOP libraries by the fax operators encouraged an understanding of the internal pressures faced by each organisation and how these might occasionally adversely affect the response to fax requests.)

Once the visitor has entered the unfamiliar territory there are two areas of interest that will prove particularly important: photocopying and borrowing. This is on the understanding that factors such as layout and signposting are adequately handled for the day-to-day clientele. It may be argued that photocopying is the full responsibility of the user and that it is unnecessary for the library to make special arrangements. However, the problem is complicated by the fact that many of the users who are willing to travel between libraries are academic staff with research interests. Indeed, these are sometimes the only category of borrower permitted to have reciprocal rights between cooperative libraries. As academics they may have free photocopying in their parent institution – even if the money is subsequently recovered from departments – and it would seem not unreasonable to offer the same facility in all libraries of the cooperative. By using a simple method of recording it should be possible for each participating library to submit information on cooperative photocopying back to the parent library for agreed reimbursement. It could be argued that the administrative cost of such a system would be too great but in fact the numbers taking advantage of such interborrowing schemes is small, and possibly one of the reasons for this is that libraries are not providing the services that users really need. Even with increased take-up it should be possible to devise a time-efficient scheme. And none of the above takes into account the fact that visitors will have to familiarise themselves with different and increasingly complex photocopying machines. For external users not associated with an institution, such as public library users, the suggested scheme would not be possible and means of direct charging would no doubt have to be retained.

Similar points relate to the borrowing of material. Thus, if two or more of the libraries have the same issue system, there would appear to be no real reason why borrowers should not use their library ticket at all of these. However, it is truly ironic, and not a little depressing, that the four BCOP libraries, being the initiating libraries of BLCMP and all retaining membership of this cooperative, use three different issue systems among them. So if, as appears likely, local cooperative libraries cannot agree on one of the ultimate cooperative acts – that of purchasing the same integrated system – the least that can be done is to issue *bone fide* visitors with registration/borrower tickets before they leave their home site rather than wait for this to be an ordeal in the new library. When credit card companies have admitted new members to their ranks they hand out their piece of plastic immediately instead of delaying until the first purchase is made. In a similar way, once we are satisfied with their integrity we should trust our larger community of users. An alternative would be to issue these borrowers with a single ticket – the Birmingham/Newcastle/Sheffield library card – that would permit borrowing in all agreed libraries, no questions asked (and space for four or more bar codes permitting). When OSI (Open Systems Interconnection) actually arrives, perhaps this possibility will become a reality.

One argument against streamlining services in this fashion is lack of demand, but users with low expectations probably perceive libraries as bureaucratic bodies incapable of putting into effect simple solutions. The response to this is that we should be in the vanguard, providing the user-friendly services that we feel people would appreciate, rather than waiting, until eternity, for someone else to advance the good idea.

Collection development

Cooperative acquisitions is an area that appears to be admirably sensible to undertake locally until the various ramifications and effects of policy are investigated. As Line (1986) says: 'this attractive concept is not easy to put into effective practice, for several reasons: such schemes have to be planned, managed and monitored, libraries involved have to accept a continuing obligation to acquire and retain the material in question, and so on'. He goes on to say that the economics may prove favourable in the case of local major collections, but again it depends on the level and type of use. Academic libraries are unlikely to forego the purchase of multiple copies of standard texts, background course material or urgently needed research monographs just because they are available down the road: while some librarians would see the value of this, their academic colleagues will not be as understanding. Similarly, the other library would not take kindly to being used in this way. In fact, to prevent the erosion of core collections between geographically close academic libraries, most cooperatives do not allow undergraduate students to have reciprocal borrowing rights and however strongly librarians emphasise *access* it may be borrowing that many users want.

The only reason for cooperative purchasing would appear to be the creation of regionally important subject collections but most libraries can no longer afford to play these acquisitions games with the current state of their reduced book budgets. In the study by MacDougall, *et al.* (1988) the possibilities of Conspectus were investigated for assessing collection levels across the East Midlands. After careful consideration, and discussions with staff at the British Library and the National Library of Scotland, it was 'concluded that carrying out a Conspectus of library collections in the East Midlands would probably not be useful unless the libraries were intending to participate in planned resource sharing in an attempt to eradicate duplicate titles and extend the resources held between them. Indeed, Conspectus and cooperative programmes would make little sense unless academic and research rationalisation were to take place'. This last point is the crux of the matter and emphasises the fact that cooperative acquisition is no longer an issue for the librarian to decide in isolation: it intimately involves organisational collection development based on teaching and research programmes and the future directions of the individual institutions themselves.

In spite of this unpromising background, work that could aid cooperative collection development – in the form of union catalogues – has been a feature of two of the systems while the third has taken positive steps to directly confront the issue. The BCOP libraries are fortunate in being able to make use of their membership of BLCMP so that their complete holdings are readily available from the BLCMP Union Catalogue. The Sheffield libraries, not belonging to a single cooperative or automated system, started from a different base and consequently there is no union catalogue of monographs in the City. However, they have established SULOS, the Sheffield Union List of Serials, which is maintained by Sheffield University Library. Newcastle is the only system to attempt to get to grips with the cooperative stock issue, at least on paper, and their *Newcastle Libraries Agreement 1989* is an impressive document (it is included as an Appendix to Chapter 7). Some cynics might say it represents no more than practices they have been developing informally for years – logically concentrating stock in the academic libraries where teaching and research are based. In spite of this, it is to be hoped that the agreement bears fruit over time and that the benefits arising from it find their way into the librarianship literature.

Staff training

MacDougall and Prytherch (1989) have recently edited a set of papers on cooperative staff training and there is little need to duplicate this work, for each of the schemes covered here have a Chapter devoted to their staff training activities (McDonald, 1989; Stubley, 1989; and Usherwood, 1989). However, it is worth repeating that the benefits accruing to staff through cooperative training are significant: a knowledge of collection strengths of other libraries; an understanding of their problems on a macro level (with users, buildings, collection layout etc.); an insight into the operation of particular functional and subject areas; and a strengthening of links between local libraries through personal knowledge and contact. This latter is one of the most cogent arguments for cooperation, for a knowledge of the right person to contact at the right time can save endless wasted telephone calls and false leads when hunting for information in what would otherwise be a foreign library. No amount of formal arrangements imposed by chief librarians can compare to the benefits bestowed on users, and the satisfaction felt by library staff, when information is provided through links with personal friends and acquaintances.

WHO WINS?

One of the built-in assumptions concerning cooperation, particularly from those who have no direct involvement with such schemes, is that it enables a more efficient deployment of resources. This misapprehension is rarely held by librarians, and the literature on library cooperation, both published and committee papers, contains frequent caveats on ignoring this essential point. In discussing the role of the Coordinating Committee, particularly with regard to the planned LIP, the SLCC emphasised that 'concern was shown by some members of the group that cooperation should not be seen as a way of alleviating the financial contraction which all libraries are undergoing at the moment. It was felt that cooperation should give a heightened awareness of how cuts will effect libraries in the area as a whole.' (Sheffield Libraries Coordinating Committee, 1986). At a time when all libraries have been forced to become inured to working with reduced materials and staffing budgets, cooperation must be subject to the same reviews as all other areas of library service. Appearing at around the same time as the SLCC comments, Line (1986) remarked: 'what is essential is a radical and ruthless scrutiny of every activity for cost effectiveness – including sacred cows such as participation in minor (and perhaps major) cooperative schemes', and, 'withdrawal from unnecessary cooperation seems one simple and obvious way of saving money'.

When looked at from the resource viewpoint one could cynically argue that cooperation can only be successful if take-up is low. If cooperation is successful in conventional terms – with large numbers of borrowers and increased demand on services – this could impose an unacceptable strain on already pressurised resources leaving two real alternatives: either the internal service must be cut to provide for external users or else the benefits that are being touted for these users will be much reduced. (Public libraries will not necessarily see these additional bodies as external users but they will still represent an additional client load) Few librarians will be willing to expand facilities to externals at a time when economic stringencies are forcing reduced internal services, and fewer still will be prepared to justify these types of cut-back to their management committees. Either way there do not appear to be any winners – on the library staff side or the library user side – with current resource levels. If this analysis is correct, one of the corollaries is that local cooperation has for years been provided by that narrow but discernible strip of extra flesh on the bone of library resource.

Judging by the activities of the systems described, the thinness of this cooperative strip has varied over time, influenced, no doubt, by the energy and workload of the individuals concerned. Certainly all the working groups of both the SLCC and BCOP have been through periods of high activity and virtual inertia. However, the tendency must be, because of the resource limitations mentioned above, for local cooperation now to be close to the bottom of all librarians' agendas. This may not be the case for chief librarians who understandably will continue to see local cooperative initiatives as one way of keeping in touch with wider political issues. For senior library managers – section heads and branch librarians – it is quite another matter, and it is they in particular who will increasingly begin to question, if they are not already doing so, whether cooperation should continue to lead the kind of charmed life that has kept it going in the past.

It could be argued – in the true spirit of the enterprise culture – that the relevant staff time is not available because the member libraries themselves are run ineptly and need to re-assess (or even assess!) their aims, objectives and priorities: so that they are run more efficiently and come to be in tune with users' needs! In so doing it may be discovered that some services can indeed be provided in a more cost-effective way, thus freeing time for other things. Whether this liberated time should be devoted to cooperative services or directed towards all those jobs that will continue to build up internally is another question. With economic factors having been the prime re-structuring force for several years now, it is extremely unlikely that libraries would discover the necessary slack for cooperation by this method. Present-day mores suggest that one base element will come to the aid of compound cooperative schemes and prevent them from sinking ungracefully into the sunset. However, money itself is not the complete answer and raises a number of ramifications for consideration.

Discussion in most libraries and information centres has now moved (somewhat sadly) from the philosophical to the pragmatic as far as income generation is concerned. Whereas in many institutions charging has yet to be introduced, the basic principle has been agreed, and it is only a matter of time before policies are implemented. However, charging for extant services is one thing – there is little or no staffing implication if the user base remains unchanged – but charging for *extra* services without increasing the staffing resource leaves the librarian in no better a situation. In fact, his integrity could be seriously undermined if he starts charging for services which ultimately cannot be delivered. Line (1989), again: 'Payment not only sets the system on a much firmer basis, it puts the suppliers under some obligation to provide a decent service'. In a wide ranging document on the development of external services in academic libraries White (1987) makes the point that 'only where a special unit exists, with designated staff whose time is principally devoted to external services, can a full range of options be satisfactorily accomplished.' From this viewpoint, there would appear to be little reason for not charging locally cooperating libraries for services. However, as the present take-up of cooperative services is low, these would not on their own justify separate staffing. Consequently, it would prove an unwise move to charge for this provision in isolation, without relating it in some way to charging for external services in the wider sense. Furthermore, White points out that there must be the recognition among library staff that external services are different, to avoid confusion, competition and, presumably, resentment, between the two. One corollary, if this occurs in the area of cooperation, is that the whole ethos of the cooperative spirit could be jeopardised.

These arguments assume that a pricing structure could be agreed within the compound cooperative and that, ideally, to foster the early cooperative spirit, the price would be the same for the same service irrespective of member visited. At this point a further enticing layer needs consideration: will not the pressures of the market economy and the overwhelming desire to generate as much income as possible set as direct competitors those libraries that formerly acted in cooperation? It is to be hoped that librarians are far too sensible to let the supermarket mentality drive their services in this way and a sense of balance must surely prevail. But once libraries and their institutions begin to rely on generated income, pressure will be exerted to maximise this income and the outlook for cooperation could be decidedly bleak. One way of approaching this conundrum is working in partnership, a method arising out of the LIPs and already adopted by one of the schemes, as described below.

(S)LIPPING INTO THE FUTURE

The implementation of LIPs had the potential for turning the type of provision described in this Chapter on its head, supplanting it with a much broader concept of compound cooperation and, more importantly, incorporating the ideas of strategic planning. If the examples described here are any indication this is happening in practice, but it is certainly not the only available option. Thus, though one of these cooperatives has recently embarked on rites of passage to be metamorphosed into a LIP resource, another is associated with, but separate from, its local LIP. As if to prove that there is no standard pattern for compound cooperatives, the third local scheme made an early decision not to apply for a City-based LIP.

From the start, and well before the introduction of LIPs, BCOP steadfastly refused to include members from the smaller libraries in the city and region on the basis that agreement between a mere five members was sometimes difficult, let alone within a more broadly-based committee. This is not to say that informal cooperation did not take place between BCOP members and others in the region, but the others were never allowed into hallowed BCOP committees or working groups. With similar thinking, when the possibility of a Birmingham LIP was raised a definite decision was taken not to press ahead with an application, partly because the perceived low resource base of the libraries would not stretch to such a venture. The subsequent strong support for the LIP idea by many cities, counties and regions has tended to leave Birmingham isolated in this respect. However, the present position of BCOP is not dissimilar to that at the time of its beginnings – new chiefs at three of the libraries and a new head of the library school – and accordingly one will watch with interest to see how cooperative services develop over the next few years.

At Newcastle the progress towards the LIP was carried out independently but with the knowledge of the Joint Working Party and both share some common membership. The LIP has been based on the NRLS (Northern Regional Library System) in association with the county councils of Cleveland, Durham and Northumberland, the whole being named Information North. The transformation of the NRLS into the new agency, which incorporates the roles and functions of the NRLS but at the same time offers fee-based services, is described in some detail by Brewer, *et al.* (1988). From their statement that 'Information North will plan on a cooperative and a modular basis the development of public and private sector information services' there is the implicit recognition that the Joint Working Party, being comprised of a large proportion of academic libraries, is engaged in somewhat different activities. At the same time, with the interest in income generation across all sectors of the library profession, the two will to some extent be pursuing similar but parallel objectives. This state of affairs should ensure an active pooling of ideas for some time to come and already Information North has acknowledged the importance of the *Newcastle Libraries Agreement 1989* as 'a model for the development of common standards in information provision and practice in the region'. Information North is covered in more detail by Edmonds in the Chapter 12.

A transformation of a different sort has taken place in Sheffield where the LIP has been created using the SLCC and SINTO as the recognised core of established and cooperative information provision in the City. The large number and wide range of information providers consulted in establishing the LIP came from the public, private and voluntary sectors and included the fields of business, arts, education, community and voluntary groups, health, local government and national agencies. The work was coordinated by Capital Planning Information (1989) with the overall goal of supporting 'Sheffield's development as an industrial and commercial centre, improving the educational, leisure and cultural facilities provided for its citizens and those who visit or are educated in the City and developing communication with all information users particularly those with special needs'.

The method of achieving this in the market economy is dealt with in detail in the report and acts in some way as a response to the concerns voiced earlier in this Chapter. The options for Sheffield had already been examined prior to the decision to prepare a plan and it had been agreed that to prevent a breakdown of cooperative arrangements which could result from unrestricted marketing of information services, a partnership – one of the key concepts from the original LIP papers – was the only real alternative. 'Better marketing is seen as essential within the chosen strategy of partnership. This recommended strategy can, and needs to, accommodate major changes in the approach to cooperative working. It can provide for reciprocal use of facilities and services under bi-lateral or multi-lateral agreements or for the setting up of contract arrangements involving payment for the needed service provision. The framework for partnership is seen as a flexible instrument which fits in to the local political ethos, provides for a range of options designed to provide better service for information users and is most acceptable to professional and other workers in this field.'

The Sheffield LIP will be progressed through three centres of energy. The executive body responsible for pursuing the aims of *Sheffield Information 2000* is the Board for Library and Information Services in Sheffield (BLISS). This executive includes the members of the SLCC but, as would be expected, incorporates members from outside traditional libraries, such as the Head of Radio Sheffield. Secondly, a number of Standing Committees have been formed in subject and key interest areas and, though these would appear to mirror the working groups of the SLCC, one important difference is that each Committee is chaired by a Board member. Finally, to ensure that the planning process maintains its present strong momentum and that liaison takes place between all appropriate agencies, the key coordinating post of Executive Director was filled in the summer of 1990.

Much work, of course, remains to be done. One aspect requiring careful consideration is the relationship of SINTO to BLISS, one suggestion from the report being that SINTO 'could retain those functions which are cost effective and valued by its members and take on the much wider role of "representing" the growing information sector in

Sheffield, as Information North is hoping to do in the Northern Region'. Whether this happens remains to be seen. What is clear is that there are exciting and challenging times ahead in Sheffield, the only dark spot on the horizon being the unfortunate acronym chosen for the group invested with management responsibility for the plan. We can only hope that BLISS does not go the same way as its namesake of a classification scheme. But perhaps the name is simply a recognition of the indisputable fact that the LIP was the foundation of BLISS.

REFERENCES

Brewer, S., Long, M. T. and Winkworth, I. (1988), Information North: Library and Information Plans and the transformation of a regional library system, *Library Association Record*, vol. 90, no. 7, (July), pp. 392–395.

Capital Planning Information (1989), *Sheffield Information 2000: the Sheffield Library and Information Plan 1989–1993*. Sheffield City Polytechnic.

Hadcroft, M. M. (1985), Library cooperation within a city, in J. Cowley, *The management of polytechnic libraries*. Gower in association with COPOL. pp. 213–235.

Harris, K. G. E. (1973), Cooperation: the Newcastle experience, *Library Association Record*, vol. 75, no. 8, (August), pp. 147–149.

Harris, K. G. E. (1980), Modular cooperation schemes, in M. Yelland, *Local library cooperation: its current state and future development*. British Library Research and Development Report No. 5578. pp. 3–4.

Kennington, D. (1985), *Local library cooperation in the United Kingdom*. British Library Research and Development Department Research Review 6.

Line, M. B. (1986), The survival of academic libraries in hard times: reactions to pressures, rational and irrational, *British Journal of Academic Librarianship*, vol. 1, no. 1, (Spring), pp. 1–12.

Line, M. B. (1989), Beyond networks – national and international resources, *IATUL Quarterly*, vol. 3, no. 2, pp. 107–112.

MacDougall, A. and Prytherch, R. (1989), *Cooperative training in libraries*. Aldershot: Gower.

MacDougall, A. F., Wheelhouse, H. and Wilson, J. M. (1988), *A study of various aspects of cooperation between the East Midlands University and Polytechnic libraries*. Report to the British Library Research and Development Department, Report No. 5989.

McDonald, A. (1989), Newcastle upon Tyne Libraries Joint Working Party: staff development group, in A. MacDougall and R. Prytherch, *Cooperative training in libraries*. Aldershot: Gower. pp. 216–250.

Sewell, P. H. (1979), *Library cooperation in the United Kingdom: existing arrangements, gaps in provision and research which may be needed*. British Library Research and Development Department Report No. 5479.

Sewell, P. H. (1982), Library cooperation in the United Kingdom, *Journal of Librarianship*, vol. 14, no. 1, pp. 1–8.

Sheffield Libraries Coordinating Committee (1986), *Minutes of meeting held on 23 January*. SLCC.

Stubley, P. (1986), Experience with facsimile transmission in Birmingham libraries. *Program*, vol. 20, no. 4, (October), pp. 415–419.

Stubley, P. (1989), BCOP: staff training within Birmingham, in A. MacDougall and R. Prytherch, *Cooperative training in libraries*. Aldershot: Gower. pp. 165–189.

Usherwood, R. (1989), SLCC: Sheffield's experience in cooperative training, in A. MacDougall and R. Prytherch, *Cooperative training in libraries*. Aldershot: Gower. pp. 190–215.

White, B. (1987), *Striking a balance: external services in academic libraries*. British Library Research and Development Department, British Library Research Paper 30.

Wilson, T. D. and Marsterson, W. A. J. (1974), *Local library cooperation: final report on a project funded by the Department of Education and Science*. (Occasional Publication Series No. 4). University of Sheffield School of Librarianship and Information Science.

Yelland, M. (1980), *Local library cooperation: its current state and future development*. British Library Research and Development Department Report No. 5578.

14

Conclusion

Norman Higham

In his Introduction to this volume Royston Brown quoted from George Jefferson (1977) on library cooperation, in particular his vision of the 1980s as a decade offering the opportunity to reassess the old and capitalise on innovations in library techniques and communications technology. 'This book', says Brown, 'will explore the extent to which that has happened...'. At the end of the book we are in a position to see if Jefferson's hopes were realised. Innovations there have certainly been, and examples of these have emerged in Chapter after Chapter. Not all have been within the field of automation technology, though the information technology (IT) elements have figured prominently. When Jefferson was writing the second edition of his book, online library management systems were emerging, based on mainframes and minicomputers. They offered an exciting glimpse into the future. But Jefferson was not in a position to see or even predict what are for library services probably the three most significant IT developments of the 1980s: CD-ROM, Integrated Services Digital Network (ISDN) and Open Systems Interconnection (OSI).

In the international field ADONIS is another development of considerable implications for document delivery; and the extension of MARC applications throughout more than thirty countries was a phenomenon of the 1980s. The creation of the *Plan of action for libraries in the EC* was an event of major importance for librarians and one which took some of us by surprise, especially when the level of funding was revealed. That there have been some disappointments here over delays and the complexities involved in working with the European Commission, is in itself a comment on the ramifications of cooperating

Conclusion

outside the circle of one's like-minded friends and immediate neighbours. But the awareness in Europe of the importance of information to a community whose aim is economic and industrial world power, is in contrast to the uncertainty with which this country approaches information.

Peter Beauchamp's review of government involvement in cooperation is full of new creations and developments. Indeed the Library and Information Services Council (LISC) (England) sprang with new strength out of the Library Advisory Council (England) at the beginning of the decade. What Alan MacDougall referred to as the 'good books' (page 9) were the *Future development of libraries* reports, the first (Future development..., 1982) of which preceded LISC(E) and recommended its creation, the second (Future development..., 1982) of which promoted 'working together' (Anglo-Saxon for cooperation), a more formal approach to cooperation and the reform of the National Committee on Regional Library Cooperation (NCRLC), and the third (Future development..., 1986) of which substituted 'partnership' for cooperation and proposed the concept of the Library and Information Plan (LIP).

These were milestones along the road of greater government intervention in library matters than ever before. They pointed the way towards Joint Enterprise (1987), the Public Library Development Incentive Schemes (PLDIS), and pump-priming grants to set up LIPs. LISC even examined the role of government in relation to libraries and information, and though the ensuing report which was circulated in confidence (see Beauchamp page 92) was in the view of those bodies which were consulted an unsatisfactory product, it provided an opportunity to press for further examination of the concept of coordination of services at a national level. Stimulating government interest in libraries is likely to lead to a questioning of the librarians' own assumptions, and we should not have been shocked or even surprised at the appearance of the Green Paper on charges in public libraries (Financing our public library service..., 1988). That the dialogue that followed proved effective was shown by the modifications introduced into the Draft Statutory Instruments (1990) which were circulated for comment in the summer of 1990 before being presented to Parliament.

The Chapter devoted to the British Library (BL) is a story of constant innovation, one of development in services and in technology and of increasingly heavy financial constraints and necessary adaptations to them. Its two strategic plans, in 1985 and 1989, *Advancing with knowledge* (British Library, 1985) and *Gateway to knowledge* (British Library, 1989), illustrate the changes in thinking that the years of difficulty imposed. One key theme set out in the introduction to *Gateway to knowledge* is significant coming as it does from a great library which is also a central services agency: 'In straitened circumstances cooperation with others, whether libraries or private sector institutions, is vital if we are to derive maximum value from our combined resources.' (British Library, 1989). The impact of technology is demonstrated in the account of the Research and Development Department's activities – support for VISCOUNT, Project Quartet, the Centre for Bibliographic Management and the UK Office for Library Networking, along with many other current projects.

In the public library field, as Stuart Brewer explains, the major elements in the decade are the difficult financial climate and the movement for greater and more formal cooperation, not only among libraries but also and increasingly with the private sector and with Government. The adoption of automated management systems proceeded on the whole by direct acquisition of packages from suppliers rather than within cooperatives. This arose partly because local authorities were large enough to contemplate a sizeable investment and partly because by the time most authorities took the decision to automate there were a number of commercial systems from which to choose.

The diversity of systems, though good for competition, has created a problem, common to other types of library, that the opportunities for cooperation with other authorities are reduced by the incompatibility of machine-readable catalogues and lending systems, even in neighbouring libraries. However, the development of VISCOUNT by LASER, now extended beyond the regions which participated in the original project, will mean that libraries have, through their Regional Bureaux, access to the catalogues of other libraries throughout the country.

In academic libraries the major development in library techniques has been the extension of automated management systems to virtually all higher education libraries and, in an increasing number of cases, the availability of these systems and their catalogues on college, polytechnic and university local networks. The major cooperative development in IT in universities, the Joint Academic Network (JANET), extended to include polytechnics, means that libraries (and in many cases their users) can consult the catalogues of other institutions. However, the merging of such catalogues to produce union catalogues is blocked, as in the public

Conclusion

libraries, by the diversity of incompatible systems. Only within cooperatives are there common databases for the exploitation of resources. I referred earlier to OSI as a development of the 1980s, but we are likely to be well into the 1990s before it has its full effect on library cooperation.

Peter Stubley's Chapter on bibliographic cooperation and Jean Plaister's on LASER provide clear examples of the innovative use of technology. At an international and European level the resources exist to exploit information technology for the benefit of cataloguing and the creation of national bibliographies. MARC is now old and UNIMARC underused, but the European initiative in particular is making possible renewed work on an efficient international format for the transfer of bibliographic information appropriate for the technological environment of the 1990s. Two major projects have been mentioned: the seven nations' national bibliographies project coordinated by the BL, and the OSI related project involving LASER and the Dutch and French, linking three national interlending systems. Both authors refer to the desirability of some form of coordination; Peter Stubley cites the BEDIS proposal for a clearing house to manage and monitor the transmission of bibliographic information between the suppliers of data, and Jean Plaister stresses the importance to LASER of action to define the service and functions of interlibrary lending and other forms of cooperation, raising questions concerning national coordination to overcome a fragmented and piecemeal situation.

The concept of Conspectus has during the decade crossed the Atlantic and aroused most interest among academic research libraries. That interest is variable; the British Library has adopted Conspectus, as have the Scottish academic libraries and the National Library of Scotland. But many librarians have remained sceptical of the cost-effectiveness of the exercise. It is to be hoped its cost-effectiveness can be tested, because if the practicability of assessing and communicating the strengths and weaknesses of cooperating libraries can be established, it may well represent an important aid in achieving national coverage in an environment of diminished resources. It has to be remembered that apart from technological developments the outstanding feature of the decade has been the drastic reduction in library funding in real terms in almost every year.

In this environment, public and academic libraries have adopted a form of cooperation archly labelled 'coalition'. Alan MacDougall in his Chapter on the conceptual framework uses the term to denote joint enterprises, development and training, but Stuart Brewer extends its meaning to cover campaigning on behalf of libraries. This took its most visible form in the creation in 1984 of the Library Campaign on behalf of public libraries, while in the academic library field bodies like SCONUL, COPOL and the Library Association itself lobbied and provided evidence and arguments against the cuts in funding. The difficult financial situation is likely to continue, in public and academic libraries as well as in the British Library (on whose behalf all library associations and similar bodies have campaigned), and the lobbying will continue. In the meantime libraries have had to come to terms with the situation and find means of ensuring standards and indeed survival. Cooperation is one of the measures, and throughout this book there are examples of such attempts, offset by doubts that cooperation will even help, let alone be the saviour of libraries.

It is not surprising that there should be scepticism. Cooperation has a long history in this century, is firmly entrenched and has become an institution. It is worth recalling something of its beginnings in interlending. They can be traced in records of meetings of librarians in the early years of the century; they emerged, not as a cooperative, but as a central agency for adult education, the Central Library for Students (CLS) in 1916. A number of public libraries subscribed to it after the 1914–18 War in order to borrow from its modest stock which was enhanced by the use of a number of outlier libraries. It was the Kenyon Report (Board of Education, 1927) that moved interlending from provision by a central agency to a system of voluntary cooperation between neighbouring libraries grouped around regional centres, themselves grouped round CLS. In 1931 this became the National Central Library (NCL), which continued until its incorporation in the British Library in 1973. From 1929 to 1938 Regional Library Systems (RLSs) were formed throughout the country, based on the recommendations of the Kenyon Report.

In universities a cooperative scheme of interlending had begun in 1925. This arose out of an initiative of the Association of University Teachers, and a Joint Standing Committee of academics and librarians was formed for its administration. Until shortly after the formation of the National Lending Library for Science and Technology (NLLST) in 1957 this scheme, backed up by the Science Museum Library was the main channel by which university libraries obtained material from other libraries. At its height over two-thirds of interlending in universities

Conclusion

used this means rather than other national or regional schemes. While most universities have been members of regional schemes, they have on the whole acted as 'net lenders', using the scheme as a means of enabling the public to have controlled access to their stocks.

Over the years there have been criticisms of the regional schemes. These began in the 1930s and received greatest publicity in the influential McColvin Report (1942), which pointed to low usage of RLSs against high costs and complexity, and the fact that they dealt only with interlending and not the other aspects of cooperation, such as cooperative acquisitions and subject specialisation. Significantly the report appeared at the same time as a meeting in the USA which led to the Farmington Plan, a cooperative acquisition scheme allocating subject responsibilities for foreign material among a number of major US libraries.

The equally influential Vollans Report (1951), also critical of RLSs, made a series of recommendations which, after extensive discussions at national and regional levels, resulted in the establishment of a cooperative acquisition scheme, an agreed level of self-sufficiency in each region and a sharing of the responsibility for cataloguing between regions and the NCL. The subject specialisation scheme survived until 1973, when it was felt that the existence of the British Library Lending Division rendered it no longer cost-effective.

The Royal Society Scientific Information Conference (Royal Society of London, 1948) made it clear that more attention should be paid to the problem of supporting scientific research. The cooperative schemes for providing scientific literature, incorporating the universities' interlending scheme and the central services of the Science Museum Library were neither speedy nor reliable enough to meet the needs of post-war research. The ensuing examination of this problem led to the establishment in 1957 of the National Lending Library for Science and Technology, under the unconventional and highly successful administration of Dr Donald Urquhart. Within a short space of time a revolutionary change had come upon the support for research, particularly among the science and engineering faculties of universities. The case for a central collection with a staff and methods dedicated to the rapid supply of journal articles was triumphantly established.

Criticisms of Regional Library Schemes and other forms of voluntary interlibrary cooperation were now strengthened. It was asked why could not the NLLST approach be applied to literature in the humanities and social sciences, using funds which were being wasted on cumbersome

RLSs and their increasingly out-of-date union catalogues. It was not appreciated by those critics that Urquhart's brilliant methods were admirably tuned to the needs of science and technology, which rested mainly on periodical literature – an identifiable collection of titles and an overwhelming emphasis on recent publications. An equally comprehensive collection of material in the humanities, providing for expressed and potential needs at many levels around the country, could not have been built up at the same speed as NLLST, if at all. However, the National Central Library was incorporated into NLLST when it became the British Library Lending Division – latterly the British Library Document Supply Centre (BLDSC). It could not be as comprehensive nor as self-sufficient in humanities and social sciences as it was in the sciences and technologies, and at an early stage made use of outlier libraries. It also found it appropriate to exclude certain levels of literature, the 'sub-academic', from its lending service. Regions have therefore continued to carry the responsibility for providing that level of material.

This potted history, crude and selective as it is, has elements which are worth taking into account in any discussion of cooperation today. The interlending aspect of the story began with a central service which found it did not have the stock to cope with demand, extended its scope by the use of outlier libraries without success, developed into a series of cooperative services based on regions aiming at a significant level of self-sufficiency. University libraries used their own cooperative scheme supplemented by the Science Museum Library and the NCL, which scientific researchers found slow and inadequate. A Government-funded centralised service was provided, whose success led to its extension outside science and technology. It could not meet all demands in the new fields from its own stock even though it made use of outlier libraries; it excluded certain categories which regions had to continue to handle and maintain a level of self-sufficiency. For most of the period there has been a mixture of centralised and decentralised arrangements with emphasis shifting with an almost tidal effect and a constant accompaniment of criticism of both elements of the mixture.

Does the survey of library cooperation presented in the preceding Chapters, displaying a wide variety of cooperative arrangements and new ventures, amount to genuine and productive cooperation, or is it a wasteful sham? If voluntary cooperation is doomed, was it doomed from the start, or is it doomed today simply because of the changed economic environment in which we operate? Is it effective diversity or

Conclusion

ineffective fragmentation? Accepting the examples of effective cooperation, to what extent are they cost-effective?

It is not just a linguistic point to ask what is meant by the word cooperation. Is the BLDSC's use of outlier libraries an example of cooperation, or simply of one organisation employing another to provide a service? The concept of the LIP includes the idea of contracts between member libraries for services – cooperation or commerce? A LIP is seen as a partnership in which members should benefit from what they do for each other, either in reciprocal facilities or by some kind of payment; formalisation and the ability to contract for services is a basic feature. Cooperation has traditionally meant a working together for mutual benefit, in which it is understood that burdens would be shared, though not necessarily equally, that in material terms those with most would contribute most and those with least would have most to gain. The inequality of burden is tolerated by the better-endowed who feel an urge to be altruistic, knowing at the same time that this will enhance or at least preserve reputation and goodwill.

A theme that has run through this book is that today the financial climate and the pressures from Government and other paymasters militate against the traditional form of cooperation and impose a more commercial approach. At the same time libraries are exhorted to cooperate in order to make the most efficient use of resources available nationally.

Among public library authorities there are different levels of library provision, as different priorities are allocated to various public services. Yet regional library cooperation depends on those authorities sharing common attitudes and assigning similar priorities to library services generally and the acquisition of books and periodicals in particular. Reciprocal facilities across authority boundaries are similarly based on the concept of equitable provision. Universities are today expected to compete both for students and for research grants. If this is taken seriously it is bound to affect their readiness to cooperate. A university with a well-endowed library is reducing its competitive edge if it shares its library with a less well-endowed university.

Public and university libraries, however, do still cooperate and share facilities. Either the competitive and commercial spirit does not rule, or those in charge do not know what is going on and what it is costing. Stuart Brewer, among other contributors, has commented that too little costing has been carried out of cooperative activities. Given the limited opportunities for income generation, one obvious method is to charge other authorities and institutions for services. That would certainly prompt libraries to know their costs more clearly, but it would probably itself not be cost-effective in view of the clerical and financial controls involved. But do we refrain from cross-charging for this reason, or because we favour the present system of voluntary cooperation, somehow absorbing and hiding the costs?

The BL is under pressure to reduce its costs and increase its income from libraries under similar financial difficulties. It has had to reduce its acquisitions at a time when libraries throughout the country are reducing their own acquisitions. Unfortunately for interlibrary lending they may well be cutting the same titles. It appears to add up to a picture of cooperation struggling to survive among libraries cutting resources in isolation, while central holdings are being weakened and central services made more expensive. The 'access rather than holdings' policy recommended in LISC's second report (Future development..., 1982) cannot succeed if holdings are being reduced in an uncoordinated way.

Until now we appear to have had in the country an effective (though not costed) interlending structure combining centralised services, supported by outliers, with regional cooperation plus informal arrangements, by which means a document supply rate of around 95% has been achieved. While the BLDSC restricts its holdings to 'academic-type' books the regions are able to supply around 75% of their members' requirements from within their regions. It is true that the numbers of items supplied in this way is a small fraction of the number supplied by BLDSC but they are none the less important for their readers. It is also true that interlending in general is a small part of overall lending, but the facility is a necessary part of library services, and certainly essential to research support.

The financial realities of the 1980s have served to weaken the resource base. This process of weakening needs to be reversed but, if major resources are not to be made available to individual libraries, they need to work together, to share resources. While it is true that shared poverty does not create wealth, a shared strategy is more likely to stave off its worst effects. We have seen so many cooperative acquisition schemes, set up with the aim of more efficient use of resources, die or languish. It is not surprising therefore that so often in this book doubts have been expressed about any form of voluntary cooperation which requires libraries to devote funds and staff to schemes not clearly beneficial directly to themselves.

Conclusion

The third LISC report (Future development..., 1986) on partnership attempted to grapple with this problem, and produced the concept of the Library and Information Plan. Peter Beauchamp explains the concept in Chapter 4, and describes how it was applied in a number of areas with pump-priming grants provided by the Office of Arts and Libraries (OAL). LISC considered such a cooperative scheme (generally referred to as a partnership) more likely to succeed because participants would enter into commitments and, for some purposes, legal agreements and contracts. The first issue (Spring 1990) of the bulletin published by LIPLINC, the LIP panel of the Library and Information Cooperation Council (LINC), introduces LIPs as follows:

> 'Library and Information Plans are three to five-year plans designed to create a framework within which organisations can make the best use of available resources. Through coordination, both providers and users can benefit.
> Cooperation between library and information services of all kinds is well established. However, advocates of LIPs believe that a more formal framework provides the best solution within which the coordinated planning of services can take place.'

It goes on to list the four stages generally adopted in the creation of LIPs (LIPLINC 1990):

- survey: auditing of resources
- analysis: identifying the issues
- plan: recommending action and determining the mechanisms
- strategic endorsement: the allocation or reallocation of resources

and finally *action*.

At a time when the library community was lobbying Government to intervene in the coordination of libraries, LISC's promotion of the bottom-up approach – local institutions are better placed to know their users' needs than central government and therefore it is at the local level that those needs are best met – looked to the suspicious like a shifting of the problem from 'them' to 'us', and in meetings up and down the country this criticism was made. Nevertheless, the proposal aroused great interest and a large number of applications for the first pump priming grants.

Now that over twenty LIPs are either established or being formed, the extension of the concept to cover subject-based groups of libraries and librarians (the 'sectoral' LIPs mentioned by Peter Beauchamp, and by Carolynn Rankin from the point of view of sport), the question has been raised whether this new dimension could distort the application of a concept which originated in a local approach. If it were to spread across a large number of subjects there could certainly be confusion at the very least. But at this stage the subject areas under consideration are highly specialised and form identifiable groups with particular problems, and it is not likely that many more subjects will require similar treatment.

The bottom-up development of LIPs has not, or not yet, covered the United Kingdom. So far we are little farther than the fragmented picture of cooperation painted in so many previous Chapters. And even a United Kingdom covered by LIPs would still be a collection of separate ventures only touching at the edges. This might be acceptable to the well-endowed networks of information, but because of unavoidable local circumstances not all will be well-endowed. Should we not be looking for a national system of libraries within which all users are served as well as possible, with no areas or groups of users disadvantaged? This would involve a strategy at higher than local level. LISC's proposal was intended to achieve firstly coordination at local level, in the hope that it would form the basis for collaboration between neighbouring LIPs. LISC was aware that the government was not in favour of itself undertaking the national coordination of local and regional services, and it therefore suggested that the one body which had something approaching a coordinating role for library cooperation in the UK, the National Committee on Regional Library Cooperation (NCRLC), should consider a wider and more active role.

Peter Beauchamp has explained LISC's proposals and the discussions which followed, culminating in the translation of NCRLC into the Library and Information Cooperation Council (LINC) in May 1989. NCRLC had for more than 50 years acted in a facilitating capacity for regional library cooperation. It provided the opportunity for liaison and collaboration among Regional Library Systems, and initiated a number of cooperative schemes at a national level. It was however hampered by a lack of resources and the need to rely entirely on the voluntary services of busy librarians at senior levels.

It was therefore unanimously agreed by all parties to the discussions that LINC must have funding, modest but sufficient to finance a secretariat and to set necessary reforms in motion. One of its major commitments at the outset was to monitor LIPs on behalf of OAL. The contract for Information North to carry this out on LINC's behalf was the first use of its facilitating funds, which ensured that expertise and relevant experience would be fully committed on a legal basis to the task, something which could not have been demanded under the previous voluntary arrangements. An important part of the monitoring is an evaluation of LIPs for which an independent consultant has been appointed.

LINC is being looked to by an increasing number of bodies to act as a focus for cooperative activities of all kinds. This is understandable in view of its representational nature, with membership from every branch of the library and information community and its unique position, embracing all Regional Library Systems across the whole of the United Kingdom and the Republic of Ireland.

The bottom-up approach implies a top-down response, and LISC suggested that LINC (or at least a reformed NCRLC) could be a spokesman at national level on multi-authority matters, working along with professional associations and the four LISCs to look at the nationwide provision of library and information services. If a national system of libraries is to provide a service adequate for the population of the 1990s it is important for resources marshalled at a local level to be coordinated at a national level.

In library terms coordination implies a facilitating, promoting and persuading rather than a directing role. There is no way such a body can tell autonomous institutions what to do with their resources. It would be concerned with working towards a national strategy for development, acting as a focus, a centre of information and body of consultation, monitoring and measuring, assessing, supporting joint exploitation of resources, acquisition, retention and preservation policies, technical and bibliographic standards, provision, education, training and status of personnel, promoting LIPs and cooperation generally and increasing public understanding and support for library and information services.

Even if for no other reason, our increasing involvement in Europe and the challenge it presents for European cooperation requires a national viewpoint which at present we are unable to assemble for lack, not only of appropriate organisations but also and mainly of information about our services and ourselves. The fact that Dr Phil Holmes of Jordan and Sons Ltd is chairing a working party of LISC engaged on a mapping and modelling exercise, attempting to establish the relationships among libraries and between them and other centres of information, is an indication that there is a lack of knowledge and that it is cause for alarm. France has set up a Conseil Supérieur des Bibliothèques under the *aegis* of the three ministers for education, culture and research, to be concerned with library matters at a national level, to devise a concerted policy on library techniques and on the provision and status of staff, and to speak for France in the European Communities *Plan of action for libraries*.

Michael Hopkins urges in Chapter 3 that there should similarly be a national voice for the United Kingdom in the *Plan of action for libraries in the EC*, from a body representative of the library and information community, acting as a focal point for cooperation and coordination in relation to the EC. He spells out clearly the outstanding importance for librarians in this country of developments within Europe. The movement towards the pooling of resources within the EC has considerable implications for the future of library services in a technology-based community. But he also warns that the *Plan of action* covers only certain aspects of library services, and that therefore we need to be closely involved in European librarianship generally.

The three major developments in IT of the 1980s, mentioned early in this Chapter, CD-ROM, OSI and ISDN, are likely to dominate much of the 1990s. They will enable librarians and increasingly individuals to have access to more information from a greater number of sources. Systems will be more open, and less under the control of local librarians, whether in public or academic libraries. Information and services will increasingly be bought in and budgetary skills will be increasingly important. National boundaries will no longer form barriers to the communication of information. In an unfamiliar situation the role of librarians is not easy to predict. But whatever they are doing (and whatever they are called) what they are handling will be even less confined within their own libraries than now, and much more with those outside – working together nationwide, Europe-wide, worldwide. In the world of the 1990s the resources of the United Kingdom will be a key element. Only by cooperating within an agreed national strategy can we hope to see them efficiently exploited for the benefit of the population of this country and for the general good throughout the world.

REFERENCES

Board of Education: Public Libraries Committee (1927), *Report on public libraries in England and Wales.* (The Kenyon Report). HMSO. (Cmd. 2860).
British Library (1985), *Advancing with knowledge.* British Library.
British Library (1989), *Gateway to knowledge: the British Library strategic plan 1989–1994.* British Library.
Draft Statutory Instruments. The Library Charges (England and Wales Regulations 1990). Reprinted in, Draft regulations laid before Parliament under 8(5A) of the Public Libraries and Museums Act 1964 for approval by a resolution of House of Parliament. *Library Association Record*, vol. 92, no. 10, (October), pp. 710–711.
Financing our public library service: four subjects for debate (1988). HMSO. (Cmnd. 324).
The future development of libraries and information services: 1 the organisational and policy framework; 2 working together within a national framework. (1982). (Office of Arts and Libraries, Library and Information Series No. 12). HMSO.
The future development of libraries and information services: progress through planning and partnership. Report by the Library and Information Services Council. (1986). (Office of Arts and Libraries, Library and Information Series No. 14). HMSO.
Jefferson, G. (1977), *Library cooperation, 2nd rev. ed.* Deutsch.
Joint enterprise: roles and relationships of the public and private sectors in the provision of library and information services. Report by the Library and Information Services Council and British Library Research and Development Department Working Party (1987). (Office of Arts and Libraries, Library and Information Series No. 16). HMSO.
LIPLINC (1990), *LIPLINC Bulletin*, no. 1, (Spring).
McColvin, L. R. (1942), *The public library system of Great Britain: a report on its present condition with prospects for pool war reorganisation.* The Library Association.
Royal Society of London (1948), Royal Society Scientific Information Conference 21 June–2 July. Report and papers submitted. Royal Society.
Vollans, R. F. (1951), *Library cooperation in Great Britain.* NCL.

Appendix A

Select list of organisations

Aslib (The Association for Information Management)
20-24 Old Street
LONDON EC1V 9AP

Association of European Documentation Centre Librarians
EDC University Of Wales
P O Box 430
CARDIFF CFl 3XT

BLCMP
Institute of Research and Development
Vincent Drive
BIRMINGHAM B15 2SQ

Board for Library and Information Services in Sheffield (BLISS)
Information House
67 Surrey Street
SHEFFIELD Sl 2LH

British and Irish Association of Law Librarians
Pinsent & Co.
26 Colmore Circus
BIRMINGHAM B4 6BH

British Council
10 Spring Gardens
LONDON SW1A 2BN

British Library
2 Sheraton Street
LONDON W1V 4BH

- BLISS (British Library Information Sciences Service)
  7 Ridgmount Street
  LONDON WC1E 7AE

- Document Supply Centre
  Boston Spa
  WETHERBY LS23 7BQ

- National Preservation Office
  British Library, Humanities And Social Sciences
  Great Russell Street
  LONDON WC1B 3DG

- Research and Development Department
  2 Sheraton Street
  LONDON W1V 4BH

- Science Reference and Information Service
  25 Southampton Buildings
  LONDON WC2A 1AW

British Standards Institution
Linford Wood
MILTON KEYNES MK14 6LE

Centre for Bibliographic Management
University Of Bath
BATH BA2 7AY

Select list of organisations

CICI (Confederation of Information Communication Industries)
19 Bedford Square
LONDON WC1B 3HJ

COPOL (Council of Polytechnic Librarians)
Brighton Polytechnic
BRIGHTON BN2 2NA

Department of Education and Science
Elizabeth House
York Road
LONDON SE1 7PH

European Foundation for Library Cooperation
BP 237
B-1040 BRUSSELS
Belgium

F I D (Fédération Internationale d'Information et de Documentation)
PO BOX 90402
2509 LK THE HAGUE
Netherlands

HERTIS
Hatfield Polytechnic
College Lane
HATFIELD AL10 9AD

Information North
Quaker Meeting House
1 Archbold Terrace
JESMOND NE2 1DB

Institute of Advanced Legal Studies
Charles Clore House
17 Russell Square
LONDON WC1B 5DR

Handbook of Library Cooperation

Institute of Information Scientists
44-45 Museum Street
LONDON WC1A 1LY

IFLA (International Federation of Library Associations and Institutions)
POB 95 312
2509 THE HAGUE
Netherlands

International Translations Centre
Schuttersveld 2
2611 W E DELFT
Netherlands

LADSIRLAC
Liverpool City Libraries
William Brown Street
LIVERPOOL L3 8EW

LASER
33/34 Alfred Place
LONDON WC1E 7DP

LIBER
Universitätfbibliothek Giessen
Otto-Behagel Strasse 8
D-6300 Giessen
Germany

Library Association
7 Ridgmount Street
LONDON WC1E 7AE

LINC
30 York Gardens
BRISTOL BS8 4LN

Select list of organisations

LIRG (Library and Information Research Group)
Library
Manchester Business School
Booth Street West
MANCHESTER M15 6PB

LISC (Library and Information Services Council)
Office Of Arts And Libraries
Horse Guards Road
LONDON SWlP 3AL

Library Technology Centre
Polytechnic Of Central London
235 High Holborn
LONDON WClV 7DN

National Acquisitions Group
Pilkington Library
Loughborough University
LOUGHBOROUGH LEll 3TU

Office of Arts and Libraries
Horse Guards Road
LONDON SW1P 3AL

Research Libraries Information Network
Research Libraries Group
1200 Villa Street
Mountain View
CALIFORNIA CA 04041-1100

SCONUL (Standing Conference of National and University Libraries)
102 Euston Road
LONDON NW1 2HA

Handbook of Library Cooperation

SINTO
Sheffield City Libraries
Surrey Street
SHEFFIELD S1 1XZ

Society of Archivists
Suffolk Record Office
County Hall
IPSWICH IP4 2JS

UK Office for Library Networking
University Of Bath
BATH BA2 7AY

UK Serials Group
114 Woodstock Road
WITNEY OX8 6DY

UNESCO
7 Place De Fontenoy
75700 PARIS
France

WANDPETLS
Battersea Reference Library
Altenburg Gardens
LONDON SW11 1JB

Index

1992 **42**, 52

A

AACR2   227–228
AAL *See* Association of Assistant Librarians
abstracting and indexing services   19, 22
academic libraries   **158–173**, 246, 284 *See also* compound cooperatives
access to catalogues   261, 284
access to collections   2–3, 164–165, 270–272 *See also* Universal Availability of Publications
  academic libraries   170
  audiovisual materials   202–203
  law libraries   175, 176
access to OPACs   **238–239**
acquisitions   4, 146, 162–163, **216–219**, 290 *See also* collection development
  law libraries   180, 184
ACURIL *See* Association of Caribbean University, Research and Institutional Libraries
ADONIS   31–32, 113, 194
Advisory Committee for the European Library Plan   59, 65, **89–91**, 115

AFNOR   228
African libraries   36–37
Agricultural Information Services   22
ALECSO *See* Arab League Educational, Cultural and Scientific Organisation
American National Standards Institute   38
Andrew W Mellon Foundation 104
Arab League Educational, Cultural and Scientific Organisation   35
archives
  audiovisual materials   202–203
Arts Plan for London   140
Asian librarians   36
Aslib   44, 121, 161
assessment *See* evaluation
Association of Assistant Librarians   126
Association of Caribbean University, Research and Institutional Libraries   34–35
Association of EDC Librarians   45, 47–48, 51, 53
Atomic Energy Commission   22
Atomindex   22
audiovisual materials   **197–205**
Audit Commission   142
authority control   229
automation   167–169, 247, 260

B

BABEL II 241
BCOP **265–280**
Bedfordshire 76
BEDIS 241–242
Berkshire 76
BIALL *See* British and Irish Association of Law Librarians
bibliographic cooperation **23–25**, 163–164, **225–244**, 257, 285
  See also standardisation
  British Library **105–109**
  databases **234–239**
bibliographic description 227–228
bibliographic records 105–109
  See also UNIMARC
  costs 236
  enhancement **240–242**
  exchange mechanisms 24, 38, 226, **230–233**
  licensing 108
BIN *See* Business Information Network
biomedical journals 31
biotechnology information 55
Birmingham Libraries in Cooperation *See* BCOP
Black Country 76
Blackwells 215
BLAISE-LINE 105, 106
BLCMP 12, 167, 231, 236, 257, 260, 271, 273
BLDSC *See* British Library Document Supply Centre
BLISS *See* Board for Library and Information Services in Sheffield; British Library Information Sciences Service

BNB *See* British National Bibliography
Board for Library and Information Services in Sheffield 279–280
Book Data 107, **238**, 241
Book Trade Electronic Data Interchange Standards Committee *See* BEDIS
Book Trade Electronics Communication Committee *See* BTECC
borrowing of material 271–272
Bradford 76
British and Irish Association of Law Librarians 45, 127, **177–179**, 180
British Council 113, 169, 193
British Library 44, **98–117**, 283
  Act 1972 98
  acquisition policy 99–100
  bibliographic services **106–109**
  document supply 110–113
  information services 109–110
  legal material 176
  medical information 192
  preservation policy **102–105**
  Research and Development **113–115**
  Science Reference and Information Service 109
  strategic plan 3, 84–85, 100, 115
British Library Act 1972 68
British Library Catalogue 106
British Library Document Supply Centre 13, 31, **110–113**, 163, 247, 290
  and law reports 176
British Library Information Sciences Service 119

Index

British Library Research and
Development Department
59, 68, 75, 76, 82, **113–115**, 254
British Museum catalogue 106
British National Bibliography
68, 106, 108, **234**
British National Bibliography
Research Fund 240
British Standards Institution 37,
124
British Union Catalogue of
Orchestral Sets 111
British Union Catalogue of
Periodicals 110
British Universities Film and
Video Council 200
BTECC 242
Buckinghamshire 76, 180
BUCOP *See* British Union
Catalogue of Periodicals
Business Information Network
109, 132, 145

C

Cambridgeshire 75
campaigns **137–140**
Caribbean areas 34–35
cataloguing codes **227–230**
CBI *See* Confederation of British
Industry
CCF *See* Common Communication Format
CD-ROM 31, 38, 38–39, 233–234
   BLDSC 113
   for national bibliographies 24–25, 108
CD-ROM (Biomedical) User
Network 189–190
Central Library for Students 286

Centre de Documentation
Scientifique et Technologie 31
Centre for Bibliographic Management 114, 240
Chemical Abstracts Service 19, 38
CICI *See* Confederation of Information Communication
Industries
City Information Group 45
City Law Librarians Group
177, 179
coalitions 11–12, **137–140**, 285
COCRIL *See* Council of City
Research and Information
Libraries
COFHE *See* Colleges of Further
and Higher Education Group
collection development 99–102, 111–112, 170, **272–273**
   academic libraries 162–163
   audiovisual materials **199–201**, 202–203, 204
   law libraries 180
   professional associations 119
Colleges of Further and Higher
Education Group 160
COMLA *See* Commonwealth
Library Association
Common Communication
Format 232–233
Commonwealth Library
Association 35–36
competition
   academic libraries 172–173
compound cooperatives **264–281**
conceptual framework **9–14**
Confederation of British
Industry 45, 50
Confederation of Information Communication Industries 128

305

Congress of Southeast Asian Librarians   36
CONSAL *See* Congress of Southeast Asian Librarians
conservation *See* preservation
Consortium of University Research Libraries 127, **160**, **237**
Conspectus   **100–102**, 162, 273
conversion utilities 24, 226, 231, 233
cooperative acquisition *See* acquisitions
cooperative cataloguing   168
COPOL   126, **160**, 164, 173, 217
copyright   124
  audiovisual materials 200, 203
Copyright, Designs and Patents Bill   125
Copyright Libraries Shared Cataloguing Project   107, 163
costs   289
  public library cooperation 147–148
Council of City Research and Information Libraries   149
Council of European Municipalities and Regions   45, 50
Council of Polytechnic Librarians *See* COPOL
CURL *See* Consortium of University Research Libraries
Currency with Coverage   107
Current British Journals   216
Current library cooperation and coordination: 133–134

D

data elements   241
data protection   124

Department of Education and Science   69
Depository Libraries   46–47
Detroit Public Library   137
Deutsches Institut für Normung e.V.   37
developing countries   34–36, 39
DIALOG   18, 32
Directorate-General X   64
Directorate-General XIII   54
Directory of Acquisitions Librarians   219
distribution libraries   199
document supply   31–32, 110–113, 163, 200–201, **245–263**, **269–272**
  See also Universal Availability of Publications
documentation   20

E

EAGLE *See* European Association for Grey Literature Exploitation
EAHIL *See* European Association of Health Information and Libraries
EC plan of action for libraries *See* Plan of action for libraries in the EC
EDCs *See* European Documentation Centres
electronic document delivery   55
electronic publishing   55, 72
enabling council   5
English Tourist Board   144
enterprise culture   79–84, 134–137, 141–143, 275–277
Entrepreneurial cooperation   12
Environment   13–14

ERASMUS 169
ESPRIT 60
Euronet-Diane 54
European Association for Grey Literature Exploitation 32
European Association of Health Information and Libraries 170, 187, 194
European Business Information Centres 52
European Commission 4
 CD-ROM project 108
 LASER grant 247
 links with BLDSC 113
 London Office 44, 45, 49, 51
European Communities **42–66, 87–91**, 293–294
 and academic libraries 169
 and Library Association 125
 bibliographic issues 233–234
 law libraries 175, 180, 183
 medical libraries 194
 publications 44–48 *See also* Library Association: Working Party on EC Publications
European Credit Transfer Scheme 169
European Documentation Centres 46–47, 52
European Information Market Observatory 55
European research libraries 37
European Space Agency 18
evaluation 144, 148
Exchange 11–12

F

FAO *See* Food and Agriculture Organisation
Farmington Plan 287

fax services 269, 271
FD3 *See* Future development of libraries and information services, 1986
Fédération Internationale d'Information et de Documentation *See* FID
Federation of Local Authority Chief Librarians 127
FID **20**
Fife 76
FIL *See* Forum for Interlending
Financing our public library service 83–84, 127, 134
 comments from Library Association 123
FOBID 228
FOLACL *See* Federation of Local Authority Chief Librarians
Food and Agriculture Organisation 22
Forum for Interlending 160
Friends of the Detroit Public Library 137
functional cooperation **214–224**
Future development of libraries and information services, 1982 2, 69, 72–73, 87, 249, 283, 290
Future development of libraries and information services, 1986 5, 73–74, 85, 133, 249, 283, 291

G

Gateway to knowledge 3, 84–85, 100, 107, 115, 284
Gift and Exchange programme 110
GLASS *See* Greater London Audio Specialisation Scheme
Glenerin Declaration 93–94

307

Gloucestershire 76
government role 4–5, **67–97**, 283
Greater London Arts 140
Greater London Audio Specialisation Scheme 199
Green Paper on public libraries 83–84, 127, 134
    comments from Library Association 123
grey literature 32–33, 112, 113

H

Hammersmith 180
health information **186–196**, 255, 258
Hereford and Worcester 76
HERTIS 167
history of cooperation 1–2, 286–288
HMSO 45
House of Commons Expenditure Committee **68–69**
House of Commons Library 45
House of Commons Select Committee on Education, Science and the Arts **70**

I

IAEA See International Atomic Energy Agency
IALS See Institute of Advanced Legal Studies
ICCSTI See Inter-Departmental Coordinating Committee for Scientific and Technical Information
IFLA **21**, 23, 194, 228, 232
    Office for International Lending 113

Universal Availability of Publications 113
IIS See Institute of Information Scientists
IMPACT 55, 56, 58, 60
incentive funding 79–82
income generation 167, 276–277
    public libraries 148
informal cooperation 78, 148–150, 183, 277, 290
information for industry 55
Information North 76–77, 78, 145, **254–256**, 262, 278, 293
information relay 52
information services 22–23, 109–110
Information Services Market **54–55**
information technology 6, 72, 184
    Plan of action for libraries in EC **54–65**
Information UK 2000 114
infrastructure 16–17, 19, 30, 37
INIS See International Nuclear Information Service
Institute of Advanced Legal Studies 179, 180
Institute of Information Scientists 44, 121
Institute of Local Government Studies 5
Integrated Services Digital Network 39
Inter-Departmental Coordinating Committee for Scientific and Technical Information 68, **88–89**
interlending See document supply
International Atomic Energy Agency 22

Index

international cooperation **15–41**
  academic libraries 169–170
  audiovisual materials 201, 202
  law libraries 179
  medical libraries 193–195
  sports information 208
International Federation of Library Associations and Institutions *See* IFLA
International Nuclear Information Service 19, 22
International Organisation for Standardisation 37–38
International Translations Centre 33, 113
International Union of Local Authorities 45, 50
ISBD 227–228, 232
ISDN *See* Integrated Services Digital Network
ISO *See* International Organisation for Standardisation
ITC *See* International Translations Centre

J

JANET 108, 160, 168, **237**, 249
  See also networks
Joint Consultative Committee 123, 125, 126, 161
Joint enterprise 4–5, 82–84, 134, 283
JWP *See* Newcastle upon Tyne Libraries Joint Working Party

K

Kenyon Report 68, 286

L

LA *See* Library Association
LA-Net 128
LADSIRLAC 76
LASER 111, 145, 147, **245–250**, 285
law libraries **175–185**
LCMARC 231
legal deposit 108, 111
Leicestershire 75, 76
LIB-2 62
LIBER *See* Ligue des Bibliothèques Européennes de Recherche
Librarians of London University Medical Schools 191–192
Library Advisory Council (England) **69**, 70
library and information advisory bodies: UK 87
Library and Information Cooperation Council 6, 78–79, **85–86**, 148, 255, 292–293
Library and Information Plans 5, 73, **74–79**, 110, 114, 133, 181, 253–256, 277–280, 291–292
  sectoral plans 78
Library and Information Research Group 126, **219–220**
Library and Information Services Committee (Scotland) 76
Library and Information Services Council 2, 65, 70, **71–75**, 82, 88, 124, 135, 147, 292
Library and Information Services Council (Northern Ireland) 76
Library Association 59, 62, 68, **118–129**, 219
  and enterprise 143
  and LISC 124
  and UNESCO General Information Programme 125

309

Library Association
    groups   160–161
  International Library and Bibliographic Committee   21
  LA-Net   128
  Medical Health and Welfare Libraries Group   **187–189**
  Special Interest Groups   120
  views on cooperation   120, 122–123
  Working Party on EC Publications   44–45, 48, 50–51
Library Association Library   119
Library Campaign   138–139
Library Resources Coordinating Committee   180, 191
library schools   266
Library Technology Centre   62
Ligue des Bibliothèques Européennes de Recherche   37, 102
LINC   *See* Library and Information Cooperation Council
LIPs   *See* Library and Information Plans
LIRG   *See* Library and Information Research Group
LISC   *See* Library and Information Services Council
Liverpool   76
Local Government and Housing Act 1989   248
local library cooperation   264–265
London and South Eastern Library Region (Limited)   *See* LASER
London Medical Librarians Group   192
London Union Catalogue   246

M

M5 Ltd   181

management information   166–167
management issues   **140–143**, 147, 265–269, 274–277
management plans   *See* Library and Information Plans
MARC 23–25, 38, 230–233, 247
  limitations   107
marketing   12–14   *See also* One-way marketing
materials databanks   55
McColvin Report   287
Media Resources Centre (ILEA)   201
medicine & health information   **186–196**
Mellon Foundation   104
Minister for the Arts   70, 71–72, 72, 79–81, 83–84, 135
modular cooperation   264
modular schemes   264
moral for documentation   19

N

NAG   *See* National Acquisitions Group
name authority control   229
National Acquisitions Group   160, **216–219**
national bibliographies   23, 233–234
National Campaign for the Arts   139–140
National Central Library   67, 110, 245, 246, 252
National Committee on Regional Library Cooperation   6, 85, 292
National Focus on European Library Collaboration   59, 90

National Forum on EC Information   45, 48, 50–51
national framework study   92–93
National Information System   22
National Lending Library for Science and Technology   68, 110, 287
National Libraries Committee   98
National Libraries Conspectus Group   101
National Preservation Office   103–104
National Sports Information Plan   **208–213**
NATIS *See* National Information System
NCA *See* National Campaign for the Arts
NEMROC   200
networks   128, 184, 247, 249
Newcastle Libraries Agreement   149, **153**, 273
Newcastle upon Tyne   253
Newcastle upon Tyne Libraries Joint Working Party   149, **265–280**
NEWSPLAN   105, 258
NHS Regional Librarians Group   190–191
NMCCL *See* Northern Metropolitan and County Chief Librarians
North West Thames Regional Information Technology Agency   190
Northern Arts   77
Northern Echo   255
Northern Metropolitan and County Chief Librarians   149

Northern Regional Library System   75, **252–256** *See also* Information North
Nuclear Science Abstracts   19, 22

O

OAL *See* Office of Arts and Libraries
objectives of cooperation   18–19
Office for Scientific and Technical Information   68
Office International de Bibliographie   20
Office of Arts and Libraries   59, 61, 69, 71, 73, 75, 82, 84, 85, 88, 134, 135, 147
online information services   19
online public access catalogues   229–230
OPACs *See* online public access catalogues
Open Systems Interconnection   6–7, 39, 234, 239, 247, 272
organisational structures   **265–269**
OSI *See* Open Systems Interconnection

P

partnership   73–74, 78, 79, 83, 93, 140, **142–143**, 279
patent information   55
Patent Office   109
Patents Information Network   109, 144
performance indicators   167
photocopying services   271
PIN *See* Patents Information Network

PIRATE   114
plain man's guide   18
Plan of action for libraries in the EC   4, **55–65, 89–91**, 115, 125, 232, 233–234, 282, 294
PLDIS   *See* Public Library Development Incentive Scheme
Polytechnic of Central London   62, 178
polytechnics   *See* academic libraries; COPOL
preservation   **102–105**
private sector collaboration in information provision 4–5, 82–84, 133–137, 141–143, 147
professional associations   **118–130**
   law libraries   177
   policy matters   **121–125**
Project Quartet   114
Public Information in Rural Areas: Technology Experiment   *See* PIRATE
public libraries   **131–157**, 246, 262, 284   *See also* compound cooperatives; Public Library Development Incentive Scheme
Green Paper   83–84
Public Libraries and Museums Act 1964   68, 70–71, 71, 74, 150, 246, 248
Public Library Development Incentive Scheme   5, 6, 76, 79–82, 83, **135–137**, 146, 247, 254

Q

Quartet   114

R

RAK   228
regional associations   **33–37**
Regional Library Bureaux   67
Regional Library Systems   **245–263**
Regional Tourist Boards   144
Register of Preservation Microforms   104
research   37, 219–220, 247, 255
Research Libraries Information Network   105
resource centres   201
resource issues
   bibliographic databases   235–236
resource management   288–293   *See also* Library and Information Services Council
resource sharing   2–4, 16, 274–277
retrospective conversion   233–234, 237
RICA   228
RITA   *See* North West Thames Regional Information Technology Agency
RLIN   *See* Research Libraries Information Network
Royal Society Scientific Information Conference   287

S

SALBIN   238
Saunders Report   129
SCECSAL   *See* Standing Conference of Eastern, Central and Southern African Libraries

SCONUL 59, 68, 126, **159**, 162, 169, 173
  and medical libraries 191–192
  Trainee Scheme 165
Scottish Law Librarians Group 177
Select Committee on Education, Science and the Arts *See* House of Commons Select Committee on Education, Science and the Arts
Selected Record Service 247
Selection for survival 4
serials **215–216**
SERLS *See* South Eastern Regional Library System
Sheffield 76, 180
Sheffield Libraries Coordinating Committee **265–280**
Sheffield Union List of Serials 273
SHEMROC 200
SIGLE *See* System for Information on Grey Literature in Europe
SINTO 266, 278, 279
SLLG *See* Scottish Law Librarians Group
SLS Ltd. 168
small and medium size enterprises 53
Society of Archivists 126
South Eastern Regional Library System 246
Southeast Asian librarians 36
Sport and Recreation Information Group **206–213**
sports information **206–213**
SPRIG *See* Sport and Recreation Information Group

staff training 146–147, 192, 255, 258, 270, 274
  academic libraries 165–166
  law libraries 178
Staffordshire 75
standardisation **37–38**, 39
Standing Conference of Eastern, Central and Southern African Libraries 36–37
Standing Conference of National and University Libraries *See* SCONUL
statistical data *See* management information
subject cooperation **174–213**
subject specialisation 246, 273
SULOS *See* Sheffield Union List of Serials
System for Information on Grey Literature in Europe 32–33, 113

T

Tourist Information Centres 144
Tradacoms 241
training *See* staff training
translation utilities *See* conversion utilities
translations 33
Treaty of Rome 52

U

UAP *See* Universal Availability of Publications
UBC *See* Universal Bibliographic Control
UC&R *See* University, College and Research Section
UK Office for Library Networking 114

UK Online User Group 121, 189–190
UK Serials Group   127
UKMARC   106, 231, 240, 241
UKSG *See* United Kingdom Serials Group
Unesco   21–22, 23, 201, 202, 232
Unesco General Information Programme   21–22, 125
UNIMARC   24, 232
Union Catalogue of Asian Publications   111
union catalogues   111, **145–146**, 246, 247, 251, 252–253, 256, 257, 260–262, 284
   legal material   179–180, 182, 183
   sports information   207
UNISIST   21–22
UNISIST Reference Manual   232
United Kingdom Serials Group **214–216**
Universal Availability of Publications   **25–30**
Universal Bibliographic Control   23–25
Universal Standard Bibliographic Code   32
University, College and Research Section   161

university libraries *See* academic libraries; SCONUL
University Medical School Librarians Group   191–192
University of London Library Resources Coordinating Committee *See* Library Resources Coordinating Committee
USBC *See* Universal Standard Bibliographic Code

V

viewing centres   201
VISCOUNT   111, 145, 247, 256, 257, 260, 261, 284
Vollans Report   287
voluntary cooperation *See* informal cooperation

W

WANDPETLS   76
Wandsworth   76
West Midlands Regional Library System   **256–258**
White House Conference on Library and Information   4
World Translation Index   33